C000182346

# TOMORROW BELONGS TO ME

# TOMORROW BELONGS TO ME

*Germany through*
*the Extraordinary Lives*
*of Ordinary People*

## PETER MILLAR

BLOOMSBURY

First published in Great Britain 1992
Bloomsbury Publishing Ltd, 2 Soho Square, London W1V 5DE

Copyright © 1992 by Peter Millar

The moral right of the author has been asserted

A CIP catalogue record for this book
is available from the British Library

ISBN 0 7475 1028 8

Typeset by Hewer Text Composition Services, Edinburgh
Printed by Clays Ltd, St Ives plc

TO PATRICK AND OSCAR, TIME BEFORE TIME

## ACKNOWLEDGEMENTS

I would like to thank all those Berliners who graciously, recklessly, generously lent me their lives, and in particular Alex Margan for his friendship over the years. Also Ronnie Payne and Celia Haddon, who lent me good advice and their idyllic cottage; their neighbour David for his companionship in the pub; and my wife, Jackie, who continues to lend me the invaluable commodities of understanding and common sense.

# CONTENTS

# Introduction
## Beer and Sympathy

This book has its genesis in a long beery conversation that took place in an East Berlin bar in late October 1989. It began about three o'clock in the morning; the stools were up-ended on the tables, the lights in the back room had been turned out and only the usual suspect characters were left around the *Stammtisch*, the regulars' table, with its wooden sign that read 'For anglers, sportsmen and other liars'. It was the one table where the truth was always told.

Horst, the handsome, dark-haired son of the landlady, was pulling glasses of frothy Berliner Pilsner on the other side of the bar. His mother, Bärbel, was chain-smoking cheap East German cigarettes and talking earnestly to Uschi, the gossipy musician's wife with her broad Saxon vowels who lived only a few doors away and was there later than usual that night. Wedged, slightly awkwardly, in the corner, the bulky figure of Manne Schulz was packing away the collection of cassettes of Western music that were the source of his black-market livelihood as a disco manager for private parties. Next to him, Hans Busch, a swarthy, bearded character with a sombre sense of humour, was trying to interrupt Bärbel's conversation and gesticulating to Horst to set up another round, including schnapps, and put it on his bill. The air of normality was deceptive. The bar was a microcosm of a world that was turning somersaults.

I sat across the table from Bärbel with Alex, her common-law husband, and talked, as one does with old friends after more than a few beers in the early hours of a cold morning, about the great universals: life, sex, drink and politics. We had known each other for more than eight years, but it seemed like several lifetimes. The wind of revolution had already blown away the stark certainties of life under communist rule and set us speculating about the force of the hurricane to come. Only a few weeks earlier I had been arrested by the People's Police as demonstrators took to the streets of East Berlin for the first time in thirty-six years. Bärbel's daughter Kerstin and her husband Andreas had fled the country, taking refuge in Poland, where they waited in hope of being allowed to move to West Berlin, just a few miles from where they had started; Erich Honecker, the former roofer from the Saarland in the far west of Germany, had just been deposed as dictator of the communist East German state. Nothing was certain any more; who knows, we joked, even the Berlin Wall might not last? It was a time for life stories. Alex told me his, and I began to understand why he was taking it all so calmly.

Alex came from real East Germany, from Danzig, the city I knew well as Gdansk, the home of Lech Walesa and Solidarity, a Polish shrine and one of the birthplaces of the anti-communist revolution that was now sweeping eastern Europe. His childhood had been determined by Hitler, his maturity by Stalin. Though he had met neither, their insanities had shaped and shattered his world. He had not been old enough to be a Nazi – though he had been headed for the Hitler Youth – nor convinced enough to be a communist – though he had once married one. He was an archetype of the grumbling majority, a hero in his own way of his own time.

As I looked around the table I realized Alex was not an exception. Almost everyone past middle age in modern Germany, particularly those who have lived through the aberration of the extended Russian occupation of the areas referred to since 1990 as the 'five new states', has lived a life that few foreigners can comprehend. Since long before it was given expression by the poet Ernst Moritz Arndt in the aftermath of the earlier, Napoleonic holocaust, the Germans have been dogged by the most basic of questions: *Was ist des Deutschen Vaterland?* What is a German's fatherland? The question is better in German than in English, for then it begs thought on issues of patriotism, allegiance, race and identity that can truly be understood only by a German-speaker. The language was, after all, often the only definition. Famous figures such as Beethoven, Mozart, Wagner, Kafka, Hitler, Catherine the Great, and even Charlemagne, had variously thought of themselves as Rhenish, Bavarian, Austrian, Russian,

Bohemian or Frankish but were all, one way or another, also Germans; as was my friend Alex.

The question of where Germany began and more crucially where it ended – geographically, ethnically and chronologically – has dominated the evolution of Europe for more than two thousand years. Depending on your definition and historical standpoint, Germany could have stretched from the edge of the Burgundy vineyards in the west, to the Gulf of Finland in the north-east, with outposts in Romania and the Russian steppes and ancient, established homesteads in the Italian Dolomites. On more than one occasion the great men of neighbouring powers have got together to debate the issue of whether or not there should be a Germany at all. Yet always behind the politics are the German people, the common people – artists, merchants, thinkers and soldiers – the same mixture as any other race. Only somehow more so.

The ordinary cluster of people I had got to know in East Germany over a decade had been buffeted by the great events of European postwar history. Their experiences, passed on to their children, are the underlying fabric on which tomorrow's historians will weave their own tapestry. Each of those sitting around the table with a glass of beer or schnapps that quiet night in the eye of a storm, had a story to tell that went beyond the personal, played out against the backcloth of events as reported in the newspapers and on television. They had been victims of the great delusion of the twentieth century: that of the common denominator. Their lives were testimony to the fact that the ideologies of the 'greatest possible good of the greatest possible number' resulted only in misery for individuals. They had been struck down by two plagues – 'brown and red', as Alex called them – two types of totalitarianism that had at least one thing in common: a belief in a collectivism, whether of race or class, that rode roughshod over common humanity.

As we sat around the *Stammtisch* in the grey early hours I understood the importance of the minor character on the world stage. There was Manne, overweight, in ill health and worried about the future of the black market; Hans, crippled by his conscience, his communism and three wives' alimony demands; Bärbel, battling with maternal worries and business problems; and Alex, the wit, raconteur and entrepreneur, plotting the future as he mapped out his past. Such people are the raw material for the

3

megalomaniacs, saints and statesmen whose deeds are the stuff of stereotyped history books. But their little lives tell us more about the reality of human experience. History can be read as soap opera. Politicians are the bit-players. It is the little man who is the star. This is his story.

# 1

## The Danziger's Tale

It was as if Danzig had a death wish. The fires that had gutted the Cathedral Church of Mary burned out along Holy Ghost Street. In the singed rubble small children played deadly games; out there, in an imagination still fermenting in that bitter winter of 1945, Günter Grass's midget hero Oskar Matzerath banged his tin drum in futile fury while in the white winter skies over the Baltic, Russian fighters wheeled. Germany was dying.

Alexander Margan did not have a tin drum. He had something better: a silver trumpet that reflected the sun. It even had a banner hanging from it, like that of a boy trumpeter announcing the arrival of the good knight Parsifal at some princely court; it was black and fringed with silver and bore like a talisman a single silver runic letter ⚡. But Alexander's mother lived in the real world. The trumpet had to go.

For the hard men coming from the East that runic letter was no magic talisman but a death warrant. For them it would have only one meaning: the one they knew from the shoulder-flash of the SS, the black-uniformed élite selected by the Führer in the same way Roman emperors had also once chosen the biggest Germans: like animals at a market, to be taught loyalty and brutality and how to kill. The fact that Alex was only fourteen would matter little, his mother rightly reckoned, to a conscript Russian peasant whose family might have died beneath the juggernaut of Operation Barbarossa. It was only three years since Barbarossa had begun. They had watched as the tanks rolled eastwards, leaving Danzig, only a short while earlier joyously reunited with the Fatherland, no longer an outpost but almost in the heart of the new and rapidly expanding greater German Reich. Now the shattered remnants of that seemingly invincible Teutonic crusade were in bloody retreat and Danzig was in its last days as a German city. The *Heimat* had all but had it.

For Alex it was hard to make sense of the elders' sudden decree that what was once duty was suddenly taboo. Surely they knew he planned to save them all, he and the other lads in the *Jungvolk*, that brave band of young teenagers who were just like the Catholic boy scouts, the *Pfadfinder*, they had been in the old days, when Danzig had been 'the Free City', whatever that meant and whenever that was. The *Jungvolk* was composed of those boys who were too old for the *Pimpfen*, the state and party organization for pre-teen children, but not quite old enough to join the *Hitlerjugend*, or HJ, who were considered the party's reserve and would soon be called on to make the final sacrifice in the impending Götterdämmerung.

Alex, because he could handle a trumpet, had been elected a member of the élite of the élite, the *Fanfarenzug*, the heralds who led the weekly parades on Sundays. He still remembered the pinnacle of their pride as his *Fanfarenzug* was chosen to accompany General Heinz Guderian, folk hero and warlord of the Panzer divisions, on his morale-boosting tour of East Prussia. Before the great soldier was due to arrive, the *Fanfarenzug* played to gather the crowds: small boys with bright eyes blinded by the swarming crowd and ears deafened by the roar of tank engines, blaring their fanfare for the conquering hero.

Now, even the boys knew, the matter was more than mere morale. The trumpet was part of the plan. When they heard the Russians were coming the lads from the *Fanfarenzug* would organize look-outs at the farthest edges of town and stand on the rooftops, each with his trumpet to blow a warning that would echo across the high Gothic gables of Danzig and up the coast to the stone and clapperboard houses of the suburban resort of Zoppot on the Baltic coast. That was where Alex lived. They would be safe.

Almost half a century later, as we sat in the ruins of another Germany, the half-hearted communist state created by Stalin almost by accident in the aftermath of that defeat, Alex, now fifty-nine and bemused to see another regime collapse around him, smiled ruefully at his 'youthful enthusiasm'. Back in Danzig, in the late winter of 1944–5, the trumpeters had been too late.

Alexander's mother had no doubts at all. The trumpet and its tell-tale banner must join the funeral pyre of Nazism she and her sister Martha had made in the backyard of the public house that her husband had run before he was called up: the Blokkusstuben in Franziusstrasse near the family home in Zoppot. There in the cellar the local SS had stored propaganda material, heaps of wordy paperwork in praise of the Aryan myth that had now evaporated. As the SS withdrew to the retreating front and the Russians advancing from nearby Danzig were only hours away, the two women hauled the papers, already tied into neat bundles, up from the cellar, and brought up the vast glass bottles of schnapps that were the last of the bar's stock and smashed them with hammers over the bundles, using the spirits to fuel the fire rather than the rude lust of the Russian soldiery. They then set light to the lot in a giant conflagration around which small boys stood for warmth in puzzled amazement. Alex kept his precious silver trumpet quietly out of sight: 'So I hid my trumpet in the rabbit hutch, in the hay, and the banner in the toilet. Our toilet was wooden, but at the back, near the bowl, was a lead pipe. I think it probably covered a rotten bit of wood, and I pulled it away, hid the banner behind it and nailed it back again.' And he thought nothing more of it, a relic left like an unexploded bomb.

As the last spring snow began to melt, the tramp of alien army boots was already sounding in the streets of Danzig. The Russian bombardment had already begun of the Westerplatte, once the Polish military harbour on the eastern edge of the free port. It was there the war had started on 1 September 1939 with a bombardment from the 'visiting' German cruiser *Schleswig-Holstein*; now it was the last gasp of German defence against the Russians' artillery and swooping planes. The Wehrmacht had already gone, fallen back towards Berlin, where the battle was beginning. They were never to return as an army, only as spurned stragglers in search of their families and in danger of their lives.

The soldiers now in the streets of suburban Zoppot wore different uniforms. For Alex and his family this was the beginning of a time of great uncertainty. Women, children and old men had gathered together for safety. The girls wore their grandmothers' baggy dresses and smeared dirt on their faces, in the hope of deterring rapacious Russians. It seldom worked; men who had marched from the depths of Siberia were not easily put off. The citizens of Zoppot hid and waited.

'It was a four-storey house,' Alex recalled. 'We rented a large flat on the mezzanine, but there was danger from shrapnel and random shells that had gone astray in the bombardment of the Westerplatte. We hid in the cellar. We said to ourselves, when the Russians come, we are safer together. In a way it worked; when the Russians eventually did arrive and grabbed the women, we all began to scream and they went away. It was shock tactics. It didn't work totally. There was a priest with us and one of the Russians panicked and fired off a round that hit him in the leg.'

The reality of occupation soon came more to resemble a surreal party: scenes from Tolstoy and Dostoevsky were imposed on German provincial life as the officers billeted themselves in the best apartments with the looted contents of bourgeois wine cellars and the prettiest girls – the age-old conqueror's insult to local patriotism. 'They were German girls – I don't know if they brought them with them or had picked them up in and around Danzig. But they were not girls I knew, not girls from Zoppot.'

It was an inauspicious meeting of the two races who had for most of recorded history battled over this part of Europe. Slav and Teuton looked at each other, Russian and German for the first time in this young generation, trapped in atavistic stereotypes. The Poles, who had always been caught in between, and suffered for it, were suddenly bit-players in the greater emotional drama. Those who, like Alex, were to spend most of the rest of their lives under the alien system that the Russian masters would impose on Pole and German alike, stored up the memories, not just of a cruelty that was endemic in war but of a mixture of inefficiency, incompetence and lack of elementary hygiene, laced with a seemingly mindless brutality: 'What really shocked us was that the Russians cooked their food in the rubbish bins. They'd emptied them at least and rinsed them out and thrown potatoes or meat of some sort in, lit a fire in the yard and boiled it up, and the officers got the best bits. The officers kicked their own men and hit them with their sticks.'

The Russian presence was a potent cocktail that would leave a lingering taste over the years, even among those Germans who had lived for years alongside Poles, as attributes of Slav race and communist system became fused and confused so that by the mid 1970s East Germans were not sure whether their government wanted to make them good communists or transform their souls into Russians.

But in the first chaotic days of Soviet overlordship in a city that was already being officially referred to as Gdansk, Alex had more immediate concerns: 'Me and my mate Herbert, Herbert Dobke, we had to go and paint the Russians' wagon.' It was an old, rickety cart, the sort of thing that horses pulled (though by now most of the horses had been slaughtered and eaten). The two boys were supposed to give it a lick of green paint, not so much for aesthetic reasons as to protect it against rot in the spring rains. But they also found it carried wheat flour for the troops and were able to scrape together enough to supplement their families' meagre diets.

In the afternoons Alex would earn a little by selling the new Polish communist newspaper *Gazeta Raboty* (*Workers' Gazette*). They found valuables left as litter: 'Stamp collections worth thousands, and once, on a tram, a copy of Hitler's *Mein Kampf* bound in gold amber with an inset swastika in rare black amber. We played football with it. We didn't know what the material was worth. And you can't get your teeth into amber.'

There were certainly worse experiences: 'When horses died they were cut up where they fell on the streets and people queued for hunks of meat.' Running water had been cut off and Alex had to fetch water in buckets from a stream. This meant passing a garage and, with the curiosity of youth, he took a look inside and nearly vomited what little food was in his stomach. 'There lay an SS man, a senior officer with two small children. They were green. They had taken poison.'

There were also insights into the Russian way of working: 'One morning the officers came and got together all of us who were relatively capable of manual work. We were gathered together in the yard, and then they led us through all the flats. And out of the flats we had to take knitting machines, mirrors, typewriters – anything that was of value or technical use to them. These things were all piled on the horse carts and the motorized trucks and taken in a ramshackle convoy to the station. At the station all this was piled together and eventually loaded in haphazard fashion on to a train' – even so long after it was this slapdash method that still rankled. 'All the furniture and everything we had brought was piled up there, and often for days on end left on the station platform, even in the rain, but they didn't care.'

For two days Alex and Herbert were part of the troop and made friends with one of the officers, who gave them a whole loaf of bread each for their work. His name was Nikolai; to them Niki. He had the great advantage of speaking German and realized that even in the role of victor among the vanquished, it was useful to have tame local help. Niki had installed himself with some style in a commandeered flat. But Alex was not impressed with Niki's fellow lodger: 'some Mongolian type'. If the clash of German and Slav was bitter, the scorn of the natives along the Baltic coast was more bitter still towards the slant-eyed men from central Asia who treated the Russians as masters. Unlike Britons, some of whom had spent time in India or at least learnt world geography if only to understand their empire, few working-class Germans had any concept of the far-flung corners of a globe where their nation had only belatedly bothered to spread its influence. The world was Europe and Russia was its edge.

Now these men had come from beyond the edge of the world to live in their houses, staring uncomprehendingly at their flushing toilets and even carrying them off as booty to tribal villages without running water. There was a certain truth to it. Many of them – Uzbeks, Kirghizians or Turkmenians – came from the depths of provinces welded to the Tsar's empire by the cossacks and still run as corrupt fiefdoms by satraps loyal to the new Tsar, Stalin. For them, Hitler's war had turned into the greatest adventure since the good old days under Genghis Khan. Alex summed it up from the other point of view: 'That character had no time at all for Germans; he was very hostile.' The contempt was mutual.

But Niki was a 'white man'. Besides, he loved cheese, a commodity as rare as gold in a time when cattle were today's meat rather than tomorrow's milk supply. The two boys had stolen a key to the store shed of the woman who kept the dairy shop. 'We could get into her cellar, and in the cellar, wrapped up under the heaps of coal, lay whole cheeses and tinned condensed milk.' Late in the afternoon, before the dusk fell and the streets became dangerous, Alex and Herbert would steal into the cellar of the dairy shop and shove tins of milk and lumps of dirty-rinded, but rich and creamy, Tilsit cheese into their pockets, making their way back through gardens and yards before pulling out proudly the extra rations they had purloined from the 'hoarder' to supplement their families' paltry rations. 'And we told Niki. For him cheese was such a great thing that we got everything in return: flour, bread, salt, oil, whatever there was.'

It was an early lesson, not only in barter but in the law of supply and demand, a lesson that, through an accident of history and geography, Alex would be forced to neglect for most of his adult life. In East Berlin it was to be restricted to bartering salami for light-bulbs, beer for biscuits. Like Rembrandt forced to paint houses in order to eat.

As spring edged towards summer and the Reich towards ruination in the ashes of Berlin, the situation on the Baltic coast seemed to have stabilized. The rape, the plunder, the random revenge, seemed to have ended as military order was imposed. A curfew came into force. No German could be seen on the streets after dusk. Valid identity papers again superseded the bullet.

The initial uncertainty gave way to a time of tension, and worse, a time of false security for a society of old men, women and children. One night, as Alex and his family sat at home, it seemed all their fears were about to come true. The door burst open and a group of heavily armed men burst in, attired not so much like Soviet officers as princes from Genghis Khan's hordes, in their capes, furs and white gloves. Alex, his mother, Aunt Martha and little sister Renate trembled as the first and largest of these 'Tartars' pointed to the white line on the wall, which Alex's father had drawn when putting in nails to help him get an embroidered wall-hanging straight. To the Tartars it was a foolish ploy.

'We knew what they were after. When the war was coming to an end, many people had hidden anything valuable, hiding it behind the walls or in their cellars. At one stage the Russians had even brought dogs through our gardens to see if they could find buried food supplies. That evening these Tartars began to bash at the wall with their rifle butts to see if it was hollow, and when it wasn't they were angry and demanded watches, and we thought they would grab the women.'

Alex and Herbert knew what to do: run for the white man. They legged it as fast as possible out of the back door, while the Asiatics were ripping open cupboards, and through the back gardens made their way to Niki, who, like a cavalry officer, with the two boys hanging on as his jeep bounced through the potholed, darkened streets of Zoppot, came to the rescue of this German family. But even that was a lesson for the boys in how they did things differently in the Soviet army: 'He fired his machine pistol in the air and laid into them with the handle of it, kicking them and thumping them, cursing them and beating them. It was frightening, but after that they left us in peace.' But this was only March; the war had two months still to run.

There was a new bond between the Russian and the Margan family. A few days later he came to the two boys and told them he wanted access to the cellar of the Blokkusstuben. It was a conspiratorial tone that implied he had something to hide. When they arranged to meet him there they discovered his secret: a live sheep. The animal was manhandled down the wooden staircase and the Russian smashed the bottom steps to prevent any possibility of it clattering back up and either escaping or attracting unwelcome attention. A few days later he came back and called on the boys' help. They were to hold the sheep while he slaughtered it with an axe. 'He probably didn't dare just shoot it in case someone heard and his precious secret would be out.' Even amid the horror of war, such first-hand butchery was too much for two young teenage boys. As Niki raised his axe to strike, they let the animal go. It hardly helped. The axe struck a glancing blow, leaving the creature half-dead, so the Russian finished it off with his bayonet. The deed done, the trio set about the less macabre task of skinning it. For the boys, in a time when the families of friends were still eating old horsemeat or even donkey, the rewards were worthwhile: 'We got the neck and the whole head.'

Alex and Herbert now became Niki's personal servants, doing his laundry, cleaning his boots. It was a relationship of mutual advantage that lasted until the early autumn, as the peace began to make its mark and one detachment of Russians was replaced by another. The closing act of the war, Hitler's suicide in the Berlin bunker on 30 April, was the non-event of their lives. Everything that would govern their future was decided elsewhere, by other men. After the Russians, independently but in their wake, came the Poles. These were not just soldiers from the rival exiled armies in England and Russia but the vast horde of ragged civilians, many themselves doubly dispossessed, first by the Germans driving west, for the lands lost by Poland to

Stalin's troops in 1939 were not to be returned. The great men of state sitting down at the conference table in Potsdam, near Berlin, were playing with the maps again. The Margan family did not know it then, but they had only a few months left in their home. They were pawns again in the Great Game of Europe.

After the Holocaust, it was a time of little brutalities. Alex noticed it most cruelly on Sundays, after mass, when the Poles would line up and kick or spit at the Germans coming out of the churches. Here, where even the Reformation had been milder than elsewhere and Pole and German, with a few bloody exceptions, had managed to achieve a curious symbiotic relationship over the centuries, there were new men. This was not just the old indigenous Polish population of Danzig, those who had always called it Gdansk, those who had always known neighbouring Pomerania – in German, Pommern – by its ancient Slav name of Pomorsze, the 'land beside the sea', and had never accepted its loss half a millennium before to the Teutonic knights. Those who were arriving now were refugees from Lwów – once Lemberg under the Austrians, now Lvov under the Russians, and one day in the distant 1990s to be officially rechristened Lviv by nationalist Ukrainians. They also came from the provinces known variously as Eastern Poland and Western Ukraine, the regions beyond the Curzon Line, drawn through ancient Europe in 1920 by an English lord as arbitrarily as through the jungles of Africa in a piece of scholastic ethnic differentiation that would give Stalin a foothold in central Europe.

The incomers were people who had been 'resettled' in the vocabulary of the politicians; in other words, told they had lost their own homes forever but could have those of the Germans instead. After all, the Germans had started it. It was an inheritance of bitterness that caused them to spit bile on the boys after church. But to Alex it was the hypocrisy of a Catholicism that was more a function of nationalism than devotion: 'This Polish Catholicism was foreign to us. They came on their knees behind their priests. But at the same time the collection boxes were broken open. And that had never happened under German rule. I was a Catholic; I was a ministrant, helping at the altar, but when we came out and spoke German we were hit with sticks. I remember it. It was summer and I had short trousers. There was some sort of company of uniformed Polish women there and they hit out at us with sticks. It put me off their sort of religion; for me that was not religion.'

It was not that the Margan family had not had long contact with Poles. Alex's father was born in Bromberg in West Prussia, a region that had profited from Frederick the Great's enlightened eighteenth-century attitude towards citizenship, which was fair to all – Protestant or Catholic or even Jew, German or Pole – so long as they paid their taxes and did their military service. Alex's father, like many Pomeranians, was a product of that adequate but imperfect fusion. His name was Bernhard Marganski. Only the lunacies of the Versailles settlement in 1919 had thrown his life out of joint. West Prussia became the 'Polish Corridor'. Bromberg became Bydgoszcz. But by and large Poles and Germans still lived together, each knowing what the other did best, as they had done since the Polish Duke of Masovia had summoned the Teutonic order to help him quell the unruly Baltic tribe who gave their name to Prussia in 1226. It was seven hundred years later that the peacemakers of Versailles justly recreated the annihilated Polish state, but by severing an arm of Germany and guaranteeing another war.

Bernhard Marganski spoke both German and Polish and did not mind living in Poland, but he had a Berlin wife and wanted his eldest son Norbert in particular to have a German education. The family decided to try for the best of both worlds and opt for the Free City of Danzig, to run a public house on the shore of the Baltic and finally drop the '-ski' from their name. Thus Alexander Margan, born in 1931 in Danzig-Langfuhr, was granted his 'Reichs-citizenship by virtue of the incorporation of the Eastern territories into the Greater German Reich', and subsequently a certificate of Aryan birth, and found himself head of the family, with his father and brother away at the war, when the Russians came calling.

Bernhard's best friend – the family called him uncle – was Johann Brosowski, who always remained for Alex the stereotypical Pole. In the pre-war days Brosowski was Bernhard's boss when he was a waiter at the Reichsadler hotel, before he got his own pub. Brosowski made money out of thin air. To be more accurate, he sawed ice out of the freshwater lake behind the hotel in Zoppot, built mountains out of it in the barn and insulated it with sawdust, for sale in summer. He made enough money to open a dairy shop and delivery service in Mariental.

Brosowski considered himself a Pole until 1939, then a German soldier until 1945, then a Pole again, becoming that rare thing: a rich capitalist under communism, a member of the party and a devout Catholic. He made his fortune as a mechanic importing from the West spare parts for the cars that communism might build but not maintain. In the 1960s Alex visited him and found him flourishing, even if the locals called him 'Hitler', and he ran a fur farm for muskrats on the side. 'Everyone liked him. He could hardly read but he could count. He was a business genius.'

But in the summer of 1945 the future was not so clear. The Margan family's first direct contact with the new masters of the territory that had been their home came in the form of an elegant, polite officer named Andrzei. He had been a member of the armed forces loyal to the Polish government-in-exile in London and had returned to take up a post in a ministry in the new administration being cobbled together in Warsaw, unaware as yet that it would founder on the rocks of Stalin's own communist fifth column.

For some reason Andrzei was convinced the Margan family should have a pistol to give him. They swore they had none. It was, after all, illegal on pain of death for a German to possess a pistol. 'He swore in return that he was not testing us, but that he wanted a pistol and was sure we knew where to find one.' Curiously, they did. 'We had no rubbish collection at that time, you see,' Alex would explain, as mystified as ever forty-five years later about where the gun could have come from, 'so we had to dig holes in the garden to bury the household waste. And it just so happened that we came across an oilskin bag containing a pistol in perfect condition, wrapped up with a magazine of ammunition. So we sat long and late and debated whether we should give it to him or not.' They did.

This odd little incident demonstrated with a brutal clarity to the Germans who was now in charge. It turned out that they had made a wise decision. A few days later Andrzei turned on the family, with whom he had now billeted himself, like an angry hound. Why had they not admitted that they were sheltering an SS cur? They protested that they knew nothing about any SS man, until Andrzei stormed from the room, to return, brandishing from the toilet the rune-inscribed banner of Alex's trumpet. Recognizing it, the boy for the first time came face to face with the danger it posed. The Pole was adamant. The boy would have to be handed over to the Russian commandant. They knew what happened in such cases: transportation to the labour camps of Siberia, if he was lucky. The women pleaded, with tears and beseeching and explanations that the *Jungvolk* was not the Hitler Youth and anyway these were only organizations for children and they had little choice but to join. In the end it was the intervention of the Catholic pastor that saved Alex's hide. He never saw his trumpet or banner again, but he learned to stay on the right side of the Polish officer who had so much control over their lives.

As Alex recalls, 'In the end we owe it to him that he brought us out of Poland. All the other Germans were evacuated. That is to say, they were dragged off at night, thrown out of their houses, allowed to take with them only what they could carry. They were loaded on to trucks and taken to camps. Most of them lost in these camps the few possessions they had been allowed to bring with them, and then they were carted off one way or another to what was left of Germany.'

The Margans were luckier. Andrzei had taken a liking to their house, and decided to have it for himself. But he wanted it with as much honour as was possible in the circumstances. He would help the Margans leave with dignity. They would travel by train, as if they were Poles, speaking no German until they reached Stettin, the port on the other side of the River Oder, which, it was thought at the time, would be the border. No one quite realized yet that Stalin had another joke planned: to give Stettin to Poland as Szczecin and create a fresh bone of contention between Poles and Germans. Andrzei went with them. Even so, they left at night, with as many belongings as they could manage, including suitcases. After one night's journey on a rail network still more attuned to military movements than civilian travel, they had to change to an ancient passenger train that snaked slowly along the coast towards Stettin. Alex stared out of the train hour after hour as it crawled west, his eyes aimlessly scanning the horizon, now flat and boring, now tree-lined. Here and there were a few villages, scarred and blackened, uncertain whether they were still German or already Polish, and most still uninhabitable anyway.

But this was the wild West. As the train went into a long slow curve the engine lurched to a violent halt, then started again. The jolted passengers hardly grumbled. Then they heard the sound of bullets smashing into the side of the coaches. As he peered out of the grubby window of the war-battered carriage, Alex witnessed a scene from one of the American Westerns he dimly remembered from his early childhood. It was an ambush. Across the flat Prussian plain, with the bright green of summer already camouflaging the desolation of war, rode a whooping posse of desperados – on horseback, in jeeps or driving stolen trucks and motorcycles – gangs of deserters, criminals and the general misfits of war who had followed the Russian advance like carrion crows. A train full of civilians was easy prey. 'They sprang on to the train, which was still moving but slowly because of the long curve. They were bandits, like wild men, except that some of them were women, swathed in weapons and ammunition belts, and wearing leather and torn jackets. It didn't matter to them if we were Polish or German.'

They plundered the coaches. Cases were hauled down from luggage racks, prised open with bayonets and their contents flung around the carriages in the search for valuables. Aunt Martha thought fast in her seat. As they heard along the corridor the screams and shouts as the bandits ripped open doors, plundered luggage and demanded their valuables and watches in pidgin German and vulgar Russian, Alex watched his aunt quietly drop the only real item of worth the family had – his father's pocket watch – into a deep ashtray and cover it with ash. Then it was their turn, but it was an anticlimax. The swarthy, Asiatic-looking and foul-smelling crew at the door merely grinned and grunted and flung clothes from suitcases, before lurching off down the corridor, swigging from bottles, and within minutes they were gone. From his window Alex watched awestruck as they sprang from the train as it began to accelerate again, taking the shell-shocked passengers on to a refuge that by now few believed in and least of all thought they would find amid the rubble of the *Reichshauptstadt*, Germany's devastated capital, Berlin.

★

I first went to Zoppot in the autumn of 1981, not long after meeting Alex for the first time. The clapperboard houses still stood along the coast, windswept and somewhat down at heel after forty years of communist rule. The shoreline was marked by boards advising against swimming because of pollution. I looked for the house the Margans had once lived in, but failed to find it. Too much had changed. Zoppot was called Sopot, but it was not this change that made the difference. This was no longer Germany. It had been claimed by fresh human sacrifice, the blood of Polish shipyard workers shot down by their own troops. Few locals remembered the brief conflict here between German and Pole; now it was Pole against Pole, but with one side symbolizing Russia. The hero of the hour was Lech Walesa. Alex could not come with me to see his old homeland; it was now the home of Solidarity and as such a dangerous threat to the new orthodoxy of communist East Germany. A few weeks later martial law was declared in Poland. But the torch of rebellion had been lit and it was there in Gdansk that the ashes would smoulder until 1989's great bonfire of communism's vanities.

Berlin in the autumn of 1945 was a city living on its wits. Women and children formed living chains, passing bricks from hand to hand to clear the streets and salvage what living space they could in the ruined buildings. Food was scarce. Prostitution was a way of life for many young women, though the Americans in particular frowned on 'fraternization'. The arrival of the 'Allies', a term the Western Allies were already beginning to use in a way that made it clear it excluded the Russians, had been relatively free of problems. The Control Commission that was to coordinate the running of all four occupation zones of Germany had been housed in the grandiose former Court of Appeal buildings in the American sector of a city that was divided, like the country, into four zones. The Russians had indicated that if the British and Americans wanted to be magnanimous to the French, whom they considered to have played no role in the fighting, then they could carve them a sector out of their two-thirds of the city. The Russians were keeping intact their third, which, as they alone had actually captured Berlin, was anyway slightly larger than the other two and included the central district of Mitte. The sector boundaries were laid down along the lines drawn by an older generation of

Prussian bureaucrats to demarcate the boroughs of the rapidly expanding city of Greater Berlin. They were never intended to be set in concrete . . .

But differences between the erstwhile allies were emerging fast as East met West for the first time on a daily basis and discovered the difficulties of doing business with each other. A secret report on the discussions about the amount of reparations to be paid by Germany, sent to the British cabinet on 29 November 1945, revealed deep differences over the kind of Germany that was intended to emerge from the ashes. The document contained more than one prescient remark:

> When the Russians were present, one always felt that it was more like a horse market than an intellectual discussion. The Russians seldom made a first proposal. This was as often as not left to us, after which the Americans and French would give their views. If there was much divergence of view between the three Western Powers, the Russians would normally agree with the proposal least favourable to Germany. If the three Western Powers were in substantial agreement, they would propose a figure for production in Germany perhaps 30–50 per cent lower. They seldom came along with much statistical material and one got the impression that many of their statements, e.g. about average European standards, were invented on the spot.
>
> The whole Russian approach was quite different from that of the Western Powers. We were concerned to work out a plan for a Germany that would be a workable and self-supporting economic unit; they were out to get as much out of Germany as they could, and had no conception whatsoever of a long-term general plan (one wondered sometimes whether the Russian five-year plans were so very carefully worked out). We tended to compare proposed German standards with our own; they, naturally, compared them with theirs, which are in many cases incomparably lower than the figures we were proposing for Germany. We usually insisted that Germany should not be reduced below the average European standard; they insisted, quite legitimately, that all that Potsdam said was that German standards must not rise above the average European level.

The difficulties extended even into protocol:

For example, hours were spent on one occasion trying to persuade the Russians that the purpose of Minutes is to record faithfully what had been said at meetings. They seemed to hold the view that, before Minutes were signed, it was permissible for each representative to add what he would like to have said. Whilst this is not uncommon practice in British Ministerial Committees, it is apt to lead to misunderstandings if carried into the international field.

The misunderstandings were slowly crystallizing into fact. The Russians insisted privately to the British that they found the French the most difficult to negotiate with. The British replied that France wanted a dismembered Germany, but Field Marshal Montgomery, British Commander-in-Chief, was sending memos suggesting that the French were scared of the Russians spreading communism to the Rhine. In October Montgomery wrote under the 'Top Secret' designation:

I suggest that one possible and simple way to banish fear in Western Europe is to extend the frontiers of Holland, Belgium and France eastwards to the Rhine. The Ruhr to be controlled internationally and supervised by an international corporation. The Rhine to be controlled by an international board with a French chairman. If the frontiers of the western powers are on the Rhine and the Allies hold and control Silesia and the Saar and the Ruhr then Germany could do no harm and fear will disappear.

But there was more than one type of fear growing in Europe. Winston Churchill's 'Iron Curtain' speech lay only months in the future, and already the Russian *kommandatura* had begun to apply to Berlin and its sector of Germany the sort of restrictions on movement that Russians knew at home, and was unwilling to allow the British, French and Americans to pass through its zone freely. Already there were corridors decreed as the only access for Western aircraft to the city of Berlin, lying as it did deep within the Soviet zone.

The British Foreign Secretary Ernest Bevin had wanted to write into the general agreement on principles of control in the occupied country a clause that provided 'free circulation of nationals of the

Powers represented on the Control Council in all zones by land and air'. In September he wrote to Vyacheslav Molotov, Stalin's Foreign Minister, reminding him of this and the objections of Marshal Georgi Zhukov, the hero of the battle for Berlin and now Soviet Commander-in-Chief in the occupied territory. Zhukov had said he thought the request was 'premature'. Indeed it was; it took forty-five years, five changes of power in the Kremlin and the official end of all occupation status before free movement for anyone throughout all of Germany became a reality.

But as they settled into their new home in Berlin the Margan family were unaware of any of the politics that unfolded above their heads and would soon sweep them along. Alex's family, at least on his mother's side, had lived in Berlin before, in the 1920s. His mother had been born in Berlin. His grandparents had had a baker's shop in the city centre at Dragonerstrasse. He had hidden under the bed there while visiting at age seven on 9 November 1938, on Reichskristallnacht, the beginning of the large-scale pogroms against the Jews, listening to the shattering glass of shop windows. He had had reason to fear. The Dragonerstrasse was on the edge of the Jewish quarter. The two flats above his grandmother's had been knocked into one and used as a synagogue. Stones crashed through the windows above his head.

In the months that followed, Alex's grandmother had secretly taken risks to flout a party dictum that she considered unjust and that was crippling her trade: not to sell bread to Jews. Instead, she would tack on to her old coat a yellow star and sell bread, as Jew to Jew, in the back streets. It was risky enough, not least because the family name was Remus, considered in the atmosphere of racial paranoia to be suspiciously un-Aryan.

But then being Aryan was a dubious business anyway. Alex did not get his own 'certificate of Aryan ethnicity' until he was a teenager in Danzig. Now all that was over. The Margan family was in Berlin to stay. But things were not what they might have been. Josef Remus, the baker, had died of diabetes in 1944. His wife had undertaken the long journey east by train to stay with her daughter in Zoppot, only to die of a heart attack an hour after arrival. When the Margan family arrived back in Berlin with their few suitcases in 1945, the baker's shop itself was only a bombed-out shell.

They found a billet at last in Mühlhauser Strasse in Prenzlauer Berg in the north-east of Berlin, an area of the city that had survived the bombardment and tank battles better than some. That is to say, the bulk of the tall tenement houses were only bullet- and shrapnel-scarred, the damage being reparable, given money. But the money only came when it was too late and Prenzlauer Berg became the cradle of the peaceful revolution of 1989.

The flat had belonged to a cousin, a man called Richard Krukk, who had 'stayed' in Russia, the euphemism for those who were captured at Stalingrad and died as prisoners. But Richard had had a girlfriend who lived near grandmother Remus's bakery in Dragonerstrasse. She was more than just a girlfriend – she was a liability. She was Jewish. When the witchhunts began, his grandparents looked after her and gave her the best cover they could: conversion to Catholicism. But she opted for even better security – exile – and escaped to England. In 1945 she came back, Jewish once more, and declared the flat that her boyfriend had once occupied was by right hers. It was a lack of charity that rankled with Alex all his life: 'Although she knew who we were, that my mother was Remus's daughter, and that she owed her life and freedom at least in part to my grandparents, she threw us out of the flat.' The family were lucky again and found room a few streets away in Stargarder Strasse, and when the girlfriend decided Germany had little left to offer and went abroad again, they moved back. It was a semblance of normality amid chaos.

In 1946 Bernhard came back. He had been in the navy and surrendered to British troops in Norway. It had not been a bad way to end the war. Because he not only spoke German and Polish but had learnt some English from his days as a seaport publican, he was used as an interpreter and was released early, having been told it was for good behaviour. He knew little at the time that the terms of the release of prisoners of war captured in Norway into what was now the Soviet zone had been the subject of strained negotiations between London and Moscow. There was pressure on the British to settle terms of release of their prisoners with Norwegian civilian authorities who were reluctant to take on such a task.

At first Bernhard Margan had returned to Zoppot, unaware of the upheaval caused by the political earthquakes he had glimpsed from afar. He had wandered the streets like a ghost, still in uniform, until a kindly soul warned him to change his clothes or face lynching. At last he had picked up the traces of his family and followed them to Berlin. At the same time they heard for the first time again from Norbert, the oldest son, twelve years older than Alex. He had been a soldier in Cyprus and on Rhodes, but was wounded in a sabotage bomb attack that left him shell-shocked. When he was released from a British prisoner of war camp he stayed in Celle, just north of Hanover, in the British zone, where he got a job as a barman. He was the only member of the family who was not then living under Soviet power. No one at the time thought it mattered very much.

Bernhard got a job as an odd-job man, then found his way back into the hotel business, as a waiter at the Hamburger Hof, an old establishment by the Sandkrugbrücke, almost on the edge of the Soviet sector. It was a fine, if rather dilapidated hotel, but by no means run-down in those days. Before the bombing raids the Hamburger Bahnhof had stood just across the road, and it had been a convenient place for travellers to have a quick drink before boarding the train or to find a bed for the night after arriving late in the capital. Now the station was rubble, but there was still a decent living to be made. Bernhard worked well and before long persuaded the authorities to let him take over the rental of the hotel. Alex decided to train as a hairdresser. Young Renate was at school. They could hardly believe it. The war was over. They were all alive, and had a roof over their heads and jobs. It seemed too good to last.

# 2

## The Innkeeper's Tale

Not everyone had it so good. Only a few streets away from the new home of the Margans in Prenzlauer Berg, the Klohs family were learning about despair.

They had been among the first in the half of Europe that was still in the process of becoming the Soviet Bloc to come to understand the dread knock on the door. Paul Klohs was an engineer. He had escaped military service because he was employed by Siemens on militarily important work at their giant plant in north-west Berlin. He was also deemed 'politically unreliable' because he had been an active trade unionist and a member from 1927 of the Social Democratic Party of Germany (SPD), when the National Socialist German Workers' Party (NSDAP), better known as the Nazis, came to power in January 1933. Since socialists who found themselves ill at ease with the 'nationalist' ethos ended up in the new concentration camp at Dachau, near a former artists' colony on the outskirts of Munich, Klohs soon realized that it might be better for himself and his family if he turned in his party card. But he had remained a socialist sympathizer and the bar run by his mother-in-law still had something of a reputation as a '*Roter Eck*', a 'red corner', where there was a certain difference of opinion to be heard around the *Stammtisch* when the company was trusted.

The bar was called Metzer Eck, standing as it did on the corner of Metzer Strasse and Strassburger Strasse in an area of Prenzlauer Berg amid the 'rental barracks', the tenement blocks housing the new workforce that was needed by Berlin's booming industry. These modest dwellings had been thrown up in the thriving capital of Bismarck's new Reich after Prussia had unified all the German lands but its vanquished rival Austria in 1871. The property barons thought their new residential district should bear the names of the cities of Alsace and Lorraine, the provinces that had been reincorporated into the new Germany with the defeat of France in 1870–71. It was, after all, this victory that had laid the foundations for the creation of the Reich.

Many of the tenement-dwellers came nightly to drink beer and schnapps in Metzer Eck. It was a typical Berlin corner bar, much loved by, among others, Heinrich Zille, the caricaturist and professional Berlin personality whose affectionate drawings of the lumpen proletariat around the turn of the century came to typify the city's view of its own working class.

Since 1913 the bar had been run by Klara Vahlenstein, Paul Klohs's mother-in-law. She came from Saxony-Anhalt, from the village of Jessen near Wittenberg, to whose church door Martin Luther had nailed his famed theses. Klara had been in domestic service in Berlin until the day she won a lottery and, with her husband Hermann, moved upmarket into barkeeping. In 1946 Hermann was dead and Klara lived in a back room behind the bar. Her daughter Charlotte and family lived above in a small, two-room flat on the first floor of the six-storey block. It was there, in the early hours of the morning of 20 April 1946 – coincidentally the first time in a dozen years that Adolf Hitler's birthday was not an official occasion in Germany – that the knock on the door came.

Bärbel Klohs was six years old when they took her big brother away. In the autumn of 1990, a lifetime later, sitting in the same room, she could visualize the scene in the grey hours of that distant dawn: 'Horst came in. I was asleep. My couch stood over there. And he came up to me and said goodbye. I remember it clearly. He leaned over and said, "Well, I think we won't see each other again, Bärbel." He was seventeen. And he was right. From that moment we never heard from him or saw him again.'

It was a Russian officer who had knocked at the door at six a.m., accompanied by a German interpreter. They gave no reason, but said Horst had to come with them and took him away in a small private car waiting in the street below. There was little room for argument. Berliners were in effect living under martial law. The word of a Russian officer was not to be challenged. The family were frightened. But, they thought, it was all a mistake; Horst had done nothing; that they knew. And anyway, the Nazi period was over. The liberators, so the new Socialist Unity Party told them daily, were restoring the rule of law. No one had any idea how they lived in Stalin's Russia.

Paul Klohs had rejoined the Social Democratic Party when it was legalized again at the end of the war. Now he decided to make use of this record. To have been 'unreliable' in the old regime was to be 'reliable' now. He became an enthusiastic supporter of the union of the Social Democrats with the communists (KPD) in the Soviet zone, quickly taking out a party card for the new Socialist Unity Party of Germany (SED) and simultaneously addressing a request to its chairman, Wilhelm Pieck, for help in finding out where his son had been taken and why. The women wrote to anyone and everyone who could or might have had influence, including Marshals Zhukov and Sokolovsky, demanding the right to know at least where the boy was being held so they could visit him. They paid large sums of money to translators so that their letters could be delivered in faultless Russian, to avoid any misunderstanding. But they had misunderstood the nature of the new regime. They received no answer.

'What is the reason why the parents of the youth Klohs have to date not received any news from him or been allowed to know where he is?' wrote Klara Vahlenstein to the Soviet commander. 'Why have his parents not been allowed to know the reasons for his arrest or to what punishment he has been sentenced? When will he be released?'

Horst's only known sin was that he had been a member of the Hitler Youth. He had had to join to continue his studies unmolested at the Grauer Mönch convent school. It was normal, they thought. The family was known to have no Nazi sympathies. In the autumn of 1945 Horst had gone to join his schoolmates in evacuation on farmland at the village of Sindlbach in Bavaria and had to spend Christmas there. He had written to his parents a long, touching letter on squared paper, full of boyish enthusiasm and hope for the future. It was decorated with two pencil-drawn bells, one marked in Latin, one in German: 'Pax in Terra – Frieden auf Erden' – Peace on Earth. He had also added the year, 1946, and the toast 'Prosit Neujahr, Sch . . . aufs alte Jahr' – 'Happy New Year, shit on the old year' – though with the mock reticence of an adolescent showing off his maturity to his parents, he had omitted to finish the mild obscenity.

It was a touching letter: 'I wish I could have been with you to celebrate Christmas 1945 and the festivities for the New Year, the first year of peace. What a difference between yesterday and today! Last Christmas we sat in oppressed mood around the table. An uncertain fate hung over us because of the Nazis' pointless prolongation of the war.' He called the armistice 'long overdue'. Paul sent the letter to the authorities to prove Horst's anti-Nazi sentiments. He went in person to see Pieck in his offices at Lothringenstrasse, named after Lorraine, which had now once again been lost back to France. It was an embarrassment that communist history assuaged by renaming it after Pieck. Paul was cordially treated and given an assurance that everything would be done to secure the imminent solution of this minor misunderstanding. But misunderstandings in Berlin cost lives.

Charlotte was now also writing to Russian colonels in the hope of eliciting at least some indication of where Horst was. She made trips to the Soviet armed forces headquarters at Karlshorst, to the east of Berlin, and to Sachsenhausen, the concentration camp set up by the Nazis at Oranienburg, north of the city, where gossip said many young men who had been rounded up by the Russians were interned. She handed in food parcels and was told they would get to her son by smiling, corpulent Russians who told her almost simultaneously that they had never heard of him. It was a tragedy of optimism in the face of hopelessness.

In December 1946 a letter in Russian arrived from Lothringen-strasse:

Dear Comrade Klohs,
I have received in response to my enquiries news confirming your son's detention and also the instruction that he should be released.
With Socialist greetings,
E. Winter (for Wilhelm Pieck)

Charlotte swept the bar clean for days and bought the biggest Christmas tree they could find, but he did not come home in time for that Christmas either. Fifteen months later they had heard no more. Then one dire day in March 1948 came a brief note from the same functionary:

Dear Frau Klohs,

On the instructions of Herr Wilhelm Pieck I am enclosing the notification of your son's death along with a German translation of same.
Respectfully,
E. Winter

No more 'socialist greetings'. It was a brief but brutal, if exaggerated, statement that Horst Klohs had been taken ill on 27 January and died on 12 March 1948 in the camp infirmary at Sachsenhausen of 'tuberculosis of the lungs and tubercular meningitis'. It was signed by a Dr Didenko, a Captain Lekomzev of the sanitation service and two token Germans, Drs Stumpf and Retzlauf.

For the women of the Klohs family it was the final proof of betrayal and callousness. In May, Charlotte's letter to Marshal Sokolovsky tugged at heartstrings she knew were not there, and made political points that fell on barren soil:

> We have not even been told where my son is buried. This is our one and only son, well brought-up and who did nothing wrong and nothing against the Soviet occupation forces. We anti-fascists fought against the sort of methods the Hitlerites used in Sachsenhausen, we were horrified that relatives of those who were murdered received only their cremation urns. We Germans are accused all of having blindly followed orders. We anti-fascists did not remain silent. Millions of our comrades were murdered on that account. Today we still do not want to remain silent and make ourselves accomplices in cowardice and fear, when it comes to defending human rights. We have been freed from the Nazi hell and have the right to hope for fairness and legality from Russian justice.

They had been told the stories about show trials in Moscow were Nazi propaganda lies. They dared not contemplate the truth. Charlotte wrote again and again, each fruitless epistle an outpouring of the most basic human despair and frustration in the face of the unimaginable brutality of a bureaucratic brick wall. Her letters were not even answered.

> No matter how awful the truth, I do not understand why I was not immediately informed. Even the most severe penal

authorities allow seriously ill patients to be cared for by their close relatives. The enclosed document promised us that my son would be released. But we have not even been allowed to have his corpse. I was with my private interpreter Herr Kuciani often in the headquarters of the NKVD [the People's Commissariat of Internal Affairs, the forerunner of the KGB] at Karlshorst and Potsdam, where the competent officer a year ago promised me that the child would be freed. But every time I got a different story. I asked in vain that he might be allowed to write so that we had a sign of life from him.

In Hitler's time millions of people were brought through this Sachsenhausen. I can only ask why now, after three years, this monument of shame still exists. . . .

If the excuse for this gruesome treatment is going to be that the Hitler criminals acted no differently, then I would like to repeat, as an anti-fascist, that we fought against these methods and were pleased that as the Red Army marched in, Stalin proclaimed that the Hitlerites were gone but the German people remained. We were pleased to see those who had committed crimes against humanity brought to the gallows. We did not fight only to see the new imposition of a system and methods that will create a new hell. We thought the concentration camps of Sachsenhausen, Buchenwald and Dachau had become superfluous. No more concentration camps, was our motto. And now, three years after the end of the war, my husband, a functionary of the communist party, must mourn his own son, dead in Sachsenhausen.

My husband, a completely broken man, who is your party comrade, cannot bring himself to ask you to fulfil the simple, obvious duty of informing us where the remains of my son are buried, therefore I do it. I am not interested in the many press reports about the numerous mysterious disappearances of people, I want only to know where my child is buried, and whether he lies in an unmarked grave in Sachsenhausen.

In the spring of 1990, that turned out to be the sad truth, as all over the territory of the East German puppet state, by then already all but dead, mass graves were discovered where the last victims of the war, the sacrifices of the peace, had been callously tossed to rot. But by then the new men in the Kremlin had already admitted responsibility for the massacre of four and a half thousand Polish officers in Katyn forest, and the bodies of tens of thousands of Ukrainians were also unearthed in the Bykovina forest. The murders had gone on much longer than anyone cared even to remember – except those who had lost their children.

Sitting in the same flat many years later, Bärbel, now a handsome, middle-aged woman who had prospered in the running of the same bar that her grandmother had taken over, pored, with the nostalgia of one who has seen too much humanity wasted, over pictures of her brother as a tousle-haired child, carefree small boy and serious youth looking stern but uncomfortable in his Hitler Youth uniform in the schoolyard.

Bärbel's mother did not give up easily the fight to learn at least where her son was buried and how he died. In September 1948, the year he died, she got in touch with a lad called Horst Schulz who had also been arrested and imprisoned in Sachsenhausen but had been one of the lucky ones who were released. He wrote to her: 'I can also hardly believe that your Horst is dead, particularly as from June 1946 until the end of February 1948, he and I lived together as closest friends in the camp. I have taxed my memory and recalled every detail I can.'

The Schulz boy revealed details the family were never told: that Horst had been detained in a local prison in Prenzlauer Berg for two months after his arrest and then transferred to a detention camp in Hohenschönhausen, in the northern suburbs of the Soviet sector of Berlin. They were moved together to Sachsenhausen in September, and lived together in barracks sixty-nine and then fifty-seven. He recalled that Horst had had a small lung infection but thought it had been totally harmless, certainly not life-endangering. He came to visit and touched the bereaved mother's heart, wolfing down the contents of her food cupboard with the enthusiasm of one who has learnt to take nothing more in life for granted, least of all food.

Horst Schulz gave her addresses of others who, if they had been freed, would certainly have more details of her son's end and 'maybe' could tell her more, but he hedged his optimism: 'But whether they are allowed to give any information I do not know, and if so, it will be only things that they know definitely from the camp, for it was a hard time . . . I will take what steps I can myself but God knows our hands are tied and it is not possible to act as one might wish. But you can believe me that the matter is one that touches me deeply.'

Neither Bärbel nor her mother nor grandmother ever believed the official death notice and saw Horst Schulz's comments as confirmation that their Horst had been simply executed, possibly just as a nuisance. 'Look, this boy was with our Horst until February, a month before he is supposed to have died and after he was allegedly taken into hospital. Something is simply not right. They murdered him. Who knows? Perhaps my mother made so much fuss they decided just to kill him and send us the piece of paper and then the matter was over for them,' said Bärbel with a bitterness that had mellowed but not lessened with the decades.

In 1951 Klara Vahlenstein died and her daughter Charlotte took over the running of Metzer Eck. Nothing was guaranteed. There were no rights under the new communist regime for anyone to take over the business of a parent. But somehow no one raised any objection to this little dynasty in a corner bar, even when Bärbel took it over sixteen years later. 'We were lucky, but we always wondered if it had something to do with Horst, with his death, that they perhaps had a bad conscience.' She meant the Germans, not the Russians, but added: 'No, I know they had no conscience, but we persuaded ourselves that there might have been some connection.'

Bärbel married a local man called Falkner in the 60s and her first child, a boy, born in 1966, was called Horst. 'Everyone thought it was a stupid, old-fashioned name, but my mother, she was pleased.' Charlotte died in 1968, her heart still broken. Her husband Paul lived until 1971, still a party member but only because he could never see the point of leaving. Anyway, so much else had happened by then.

# 3

## False Resurrection

*Auferstanden aus Ruinen und der Zukunft zugewandt, lass
uns dir zum Guten dienen, Deutschland, einig Vaterland.*

*Resurrected from the ruins, and turned to face the future, let
us serve you for the good, Germany, united Fatherland.*

Johannes R. Becher
(National Anthem of the German Democratic Republic)

At the Hamburger Hof, just across the as yet invisible frontier in
the Soviet sector, the Margan family had noticed a few changes
in the political rhetoric as the occupation forces began to entrench
themselves. But they had not really felt them as yet. Germany had
been defeated, but at least the bloody war was over. Berlin was
occupied. The fact that the enemy were now squabbling among
themselves was a matter of secondary concern to ordinary people
amid the general chaos of a city that was largely rubble.

Alex would make a short journey to a kiosk a few streets away
to buy cigarettes rather than purchase them in the one on the
corner, because his father preferred the American blends. He and
his mother and father still lived in the flat in Mühlhauser Strasse, a
short tram ride away in Prenzlauer Berg. Alex had got a job as an
apprentice hairdresser with a small shop in Moabit, which was in
the American sector; he travelled to work by tram and came back
to the hotel in the evening to help his father. His sister Renate had
decided she wanted to become a nursery nurse and was studying
at a convent school on the other side of town. Still too young
to make a daily return journey across a city filled with soldiers,
tramps and homeless vagabonds, she had left the family home to

become a boarder. The school happened to be in the American sector; no one thought anything much of it at the time.

The communist state that came into existence in October 1949, encompassing that part of the city of Berlin where both Alex Margan and Bärbel Klohs lived their still separate lives, was an accident of history. Even today there are many rumours about its gestation and parentage. Both the Russians and the Western Allies claimed they wanted a new, united, democratic Germany, but each wanted to control it.

On the face of it, when the communists in the Russian zone of occupation gathered in the eastern sector of Berlin on 7 October 1949 to proclaim the existence of the independent German Democratic Republic, complete with constitution, it was not so much an independent action as a 'sour grapes' reaction to the free elections that had just taken place in the western part of Germany. From being a king on the world chessboard, Germany had been reduced, not merely to a pawn but to the board itself. The whole pattern of events in Germany was mirroring the clash between the world forces that Hitler's war had brought into contact. East now met West along a line through the dismembered Reich, and only the heart, Berlin, remained to be dissected.

It seemed a sudden shock, but the surgeons had been sharpening their knives for the best part of a decade. Already in the early months following the war, the relations between Stalin's Soviet Union and the Western powers had become increasingly uncomfortable. It soon became clear – particularly to Churchill – that the Russians were intent on setting up a puppet empire in all of the countries from which they had expelled the Germans: Poland, Bulgaria, Romania, Hungary and Czechoslovakia. Only Germany itself, the focus of the old *Mitteleuropa* that Hitler had tried to smelt into a vast nation-state, now remained to be apportioned. Hitler's warriors had torn down the continent's internal frontiers in their blitzkrieg war; not since the defeat of Napoleon had the plans of one man, even in destruction, so required a redrawing of national boundaries, a rethinking of the whole concept of Europe.

Alex and his family, preoccupied with the day-to-day business of personal survival and earning a living, had little idea of the genesis of the events that were about to shake their lives. Ever since an alliance between Britain and the Soviet Union had been mooted, with the Nazi launch of Operation Barbarossa in June 1941, the politicians had been taking their cartographers to meetings. It was abundantly clear that there would be hard negotiations over the redrawing of the map of Europe, now that Adolf Hitler had ripped to shreds the one drawn up in 1919 at Versailles. Everyone readily recognized that the Versailles agreement had been a disaster. Here was a chance to correct it, if only they could agree how. The German people, insofar as they were considered at all, were an abstraction.

The British Foreign Office thought that Versailles had been a vengeful French solution that was unfair to Germany and wrong-headed over Poland. Poland had been obliterated over the previous one hundred and fifty years by the encroachments of the three sur-rounding empires, Austria, Russia and Prussia. It was obvious in 1919 that, if it was to be restored to the map, then the new country would need a seaport to guarantee it a degree of autonomy from its still powerful neighbours. But the solution – a 'Polish Corridor' separating East Prussia from the rest of Germany – had made future conflict between Germany and Poland a foregone con-clusion, even without Hitler. When war broke out, the Allies soon recognized that it would need to end with a new definition of Poland, and therefore of Germany. Even as Bernhard Margan had sailed to Norway and Alex and his comrades in the *Jungvolk* band in Danzig saluted General Guderian on his eastward march, cartographers in dusty offices in London and Moscow were redrawing the continent.

Already, back in 1920, Lord Curzon had put forward the argument on an ethnic basis for a Polish frontier much further to the west, that would leave the city of Lwów and much of eastern Poland, which had a large proportion of ethnic Byelorussians and Ukrainians, in the Soviet Union. His line of demarcation went unheeded until 1939, when it was adopted by the enemies of both England and Poland in the Nazi–Soviet non-aggression pact that paved the way for a fresh partition of Poland. It was scarcely surprising that, when the British Foreign Secretary, Anthony Eden, flew to Moscow in December 1941 to negotiate terms for an anti-Hitler alliance, he found himself in turn presented with a new secret protocol that guaranteed the maintenance of that frontier, and would promise the Poles compensation by ceding them East Prussia. The Russians had other whimsical suggestions too: they suggested the detachment from the rest of Germany of the Rhineland, Austria and possibly Bavaria, all to be constituted as small, independent states, in effect returning Germany to the patchwork it had been in the Middle Ages. With German artillery pounding Leningrad, a vast army marching through the Caucasus and tanks nearing the outskirts of Moscow, it must have seemed a fantasy world.

When America entered the war she sent her own mapmen to join the game. The Americans suggested restoring Austrian independence and making five separate states out of the rest of Germany: Prussia, Saxony, Bavaria, Hesse and Hanover, while the industrially important Saar and Ruhr regions would be internationally managed. The British briefly considered a plan that would make one small, industrially viable state out of the Ruhr and Saar along with the Rhineland, while splitting the rest into a North German state and a South German state that would unite Austria and Bavaria.

And it was not just Germany lying there to be played with. Roosevelt was for a time keen on giving the Francophone Belgians their own state of Wallonia. Churchill, with more of an eye to his own affection for monarchy than historical common sense, proposed recreating a version of the Habsburg monarchy in a central European state that would unite Austria, Hungary and Czechoslovakia, with Bavaria thrown in – for no obvious reason other than that they spoke the same sort of German as the Austrians and had similar customs. The Foreign Office thought he was mad and told him so. It did not, however, stop him from putting it forward at the Tehran conference in 1943. Nor, indeed, did the East German communists – thirty years later – hesitate to publish Churchill's solution in a historical atlas as part of the propaganda campaign to prove that it had all along been the West rather than Moscow that was intent on the division of Germany. Understandably the secret protocol proposed by the Russians in 1941 was, like that signed with Hitler in 1939, discreetly omitted from the communists' history books.

The redrafting stages continued every time the representatives of the new allies met; the maps were unrolled and serious diplomats marked the lines where the backroom boys suggested frontiers should run. The Great Game of Europe was literally being played on the table. The Margan family, with their little lives, loves and losses, were somewhere beneath notice, on the human scale that the statesmen could not bear to see: cannon fodder recast as cartographers' commodities. By the time of the

Tehran conference, the fantasy was beginning to be in need of flesh. An Allied victory, which once seemed a remote possibility, had begun to look not only probable but inevitable. The British, Americans and Russians all now agreed on one point: that the 'Polish Corridor' problem should be solved by giving Poland East Prussia and a large chunk of the Baltic coastline.

Alex Margan and his family, waiting for news of his father and brother away on the far-flung fronts of the seemingly indomitable Reich, had no idea that in the minds of Germany's enemies Danzig was already Gdansk. But it was also already becoming clear to the British and Americans that, if the Red Army managed to get its cumbersome but monolithic steamroller into gear, it would probably roll right into the heart of Germany and be exceedingly difficult to dislodge. The British had been debating their position at Cabinet level since the middle of 1943 at a Committee on Armistice Terms and Civil Administration, presided over by Clement Attlee, the man who – to the surprise and amusement of Stalin – would oust Churchill in the 1945 election and take his place at the crucial Potsdam conference. Attlee was more concerned with breaking down the empires of those industrialists who had contributed to the Nazis' success than with redrawing frontiers. But the Foreign Office men had come to believe – as the Americans eventually agreed – that a Germany divided into tiny parts was a reversal of history that would not help postwar economic reconstruction. A reduced Germany – minus East Prussia, Danzig, Austria, Czechoslovakia, Alsace and Lorraine – considerably smaller than in 1937, let alone in 1914, should be left as a unitary state that might at last become a normal European nation.

These lofty political deliberations were little noticed by the people on the ground. When Alex's friendship with the Russian officer Nikolai had been succeeded by the family's more complicated relationship with the Pole, Andrzei, they did not perceive the reality it indicated: that Stalin had pre-empted the West again by withdrawing his troops, westwards, to pose as the Poles' protector. For by the time of the Potsdam conference in the summer of 1945, with Germany lying in rubble at their feet, the Allies' views were determined more by circumstance than theory. The Americans had already agreed to concede the northern half of East Prussia, including the ancient city of Königsberg, to the Soviet Union rather than Poland, as had been the general understanding. It seemed an academic affair, as the city, fishing port and trading centre, once home to Immanuel Kant and site of the coronation of the first kings of Prussia, was now little more than a heap of rubble, destined to be rebuilt in unrecognizable concrete as Kaliningrad (named after the stooge who gratified Stalin by posing as president of the Soviet Union, even to the extent of signing the execution order for his own wife).

By the time Andrzei had shepherded the Margans out of the territory that he knew was to form part of the new Poland, the 'temporary solution' reached at Potsdam had already come to look suspiciously permanent. Stalin had never intended it to be anything else; the Soviet dictator had been amused, nothing more, that the vagaries of human frailty and 'imbecilic' democracy had removed Roosevelt and Churchill from the negotiating table and furnished instead Truman and Attlee. He had already made up his mind and nothing short of war with his erstwhile allies would alter it. Western amendments were shelved 'pending the peace conference'. That conference never took place. The nearest equivalent was the final meeting of the 'two plus four' talks in Moscow in September 1990, which restored full sovereignty to the reunited Germany.

While Alex and his family tried to make a new home in the ruins of Berlin in those difficult years of 1945 and 1946, the country they had known as Germany was an ill-defined entity awash with refugees. Most, like the Margans, had come from the east, from Silesia, now overrun by Poland, from East Prussia, divided between Poland and Russia, and from the Czech Sudetenland, where the new regime was brutally determined not to leave any substantial German minority that could be an excuse for future aggression. The expulsions became revenge; thousands died, many of them young children and women whose men were still prisoners or tramping among the thousands of demobilized troops back to a home that was no longer theirs. In 1946 the ruined rump of the German Reich had at least ten million displaced and homeless. Not all found it as easy as the Margans, but most settled somewhere, nursing their wounded pride and their resentments.

The actual division of Germany happened, like its reunification, apparently by accident, at the end of a long series of events, each tipping into the next like dominoes. Soviet Foreign Minister Molotov had let it be known on 19 September 1946 that he considered the political decision about the eastern border of Germany to have already been taken, despite Western objections that too much territory had been given to Poland. At the same time Moscow was, in fact, insisting on a politically united Germany, but it envisaged the economy, if not the politics, being run on a Soviet-style centralized model. The Americans, through Secretary of State James F. Byrnes and his successor, George Marshall, were meanwhile carrying out plans to rebuild a functioning capitalist economy in the three western zones. Much of the argument came down to a Russian demand for a say in the running of the Ruhr and a stake in its industry, against a British and American demand for the return to Germany of the almost equally important industrial region of Upper Silesia, in the hope that they would thereby gain a say in its future. But Moscow had deliberately handed the region to its new Polish vassals. The Russians wanted the new German state to have a strong central government. But the British and Americans, fearing this could facilitate a communist takeover, wanted a devolved federal system.

The result of the stalemate was that each side went ahead with its own plans in the area it controlled. In the western zones a strengthening of local government went hand in hand with economic integration. A currency reform was essential. After careful planning and preparation of the population, it was carried out like a blitzkrieg overnight on 20–21 June 1948. Throughout western Germany queues formed at banks in the drizzly dawn of that day to exchange the old Reichsmarks for the new Deutschmark. (It was a scene not to be repeated until 1 July 1990, when East Germans would queue up to exchange their money for the currency of West Germany, which had beyond all expectations transformed itself in forty years to the most stable currency in Europe and a global rival to the mighty dollar itself.)

On the following day negotiations broke down in Berlin over the Allies' plan to introduce the currency. The Russians insisted that Berlin should not have a different currency from that of the Soviet occupation zone around it, but Moscow would not accept a currency 'made in America'. It was, in effect, a battle for the economic soul of Germany. As the eventual demise of East Germany showed, whichever side shaped the economy to its own fashion would also control the politics. The result was an arbitrary

Russian decision to introduce a separate currency in its zone on 23 June. Simultaneously the Western Allies introduced the D-mark, as it was already becoming known, into their sectors of Berlin. By now the dominoes were falling faster. Only a day later the Soviet Union announced the closure of all roads and waterways linking Berlin to the western occupation zones.

It was the beginning of the blockade, designed to force the western part of Berlin to accept that it was under Soviet control. For eleven months the Western Allies called the Russians' bluff, flying food and essential goods into the city. The American military governor, Lucius D. Clay, laid down the gospel of the Cold War: 'If Berlin falls, then West Germany falls next. If we intend to hold Europe against communism then we must not move from this spot.' In November the communist-controlled council in the Soviet sector of Berlin elected its own governing body, a '*Magistrat*' and banished the freely elected members of the city parliament from the western sectors from the 'Red Town Hall', the traditional seat of Berlin government.

It was in effect a division of the city, although Berliners them-selves – in whatever part of the city they lived – did their best to ignore it. While the world went into a Cold War sweat over the Berlin blockade, apart from the sleepless nights occasioned by the roar of aircraft landing at Tempelhof with supplies, the chief impression made on the population of the East was that there were fewer luxury goods freely available in the other half of the city. They were used to hardship and, although living conditions did not improve, even when other provisions were short there was always beer and schnapps. The bar of the Hamburger Hof was rarely empty, especially as beer could be bought for the less valuable eastern mark.

Alex bicycled readily about town as a trainee hairdresser, earning West marks here and East marks there. There were money-changing stalls in the street and they changed back and forwards, depending on what they needed. They coped quite happily with the D-marks from the West and marks of the German Notebank in the East, carrying out exchanges with a competence in currency handling that had, after all, already handled not only Reichsmarks but Danzig guilders, Polish zlotys, Lucky Strike cigarettes and nylon stockings.

The real business of dividing Germany was happening far

away, it seemed, some of it on the Rhine, in the insignificant university town of Bonn. In May 1949 a constitutional committee headed by Konrad Adenauer, an ageing conservative Rhineland politician, finished work on a constitution for the western zones. It included a little-heeded article, number twenty-three, which defined the territories for which the constitution had validity, and ended with the line: 'This is to have validity in other parts of Germany following their accession.' It was a deliberate open door that would allow the return to West Germany of the Saarland from international jurisdiction in 1955 and then go unheeded and unregarded for thirty-five years. The acceptance of the constitution by the governments of the provinces (*Länder*) effectively created the Federal Republic. The elections held in August gave the largest number of seats to the Christian Democrats under Adenauer, who formed a coalition government on 20 September.

To Berliners, the mirror creation in October 1949 of the 'first Workers' and Peasants' state on German soil' seemed little more than a reinforcement of the occupation status; the really important matter was the presence of the troops: British, French and Americans in their limited garrison in the West, Russians in tens of thousands in the East. The resurrection of the monolithic Soviet Embassy on the main thoroughfare of Unter den Linden was declared a top-level construction priority in a city of bombed-out ruins. No one had any doubt that this was the real seat of power in the 'Zone'.

Alex's father and mother continued to make a modest but acceptable living from the hotel and its bar. He had moved to another hairdressing shop in Bersarinstrasse, which was in the Soviet sector. He had made the change, however, not because of which zone the shop was in but simply because it was closer to home and offered a better training. He took his qualifications in cosmetics with the firm of Alcina. But Alex's mind was filled with more immediate matters: for one thing, he was tired of cutting hair. It was time for a young man to see the world, or what was left of it.

In May 1951, at the age of nineteen, Alex decided the time had come to take a break from what he had quickly come to consider settled family life, to spread his wings for a little and see something of the world. He set off by road with three friends, Heine, Gerhard and Alfred, to see the West. As Germans and

Catholics they had two wishes: to see their two grails: the Rhine and Rome. This was difficult in an occupied state that was becoming increasingly jealous of its reluctant citizens. But it was not impossible, provided one had obtained the necessary travel documents. Unfortunately Alex had not. When they reached the border crossing point at Marienborn the others went ahead by train to Hanover, leaving 'dimwit Margan' to sort himself out and meet them if and when he could. There were, of course, preset routines for such occasions. Alex, after a few discreet enquiries, met up with a group that regularly crossed the border by night along a forest path. They were small-time smugglers who regarded the frontier arbitrarily thrown up between two ancient German towns as an alien nonsense. Alex was to get a more accurate picture of the future.

There were not yet electric fences, nor yet scatter guns or mines or even deep ditches, but there was a frontier and there were armed men to guard it, even in the depths of the forest. 'As luck would have it, I was the last and was just about to cross when a patrol came along. I threw myself on the earth beneath a bush. But the bush was in the middle of the path and as the pair came by they looked down, flashed their torch straight on me and said calmly, "Just what do you think you're doing?"'

It could have been worse. These were still early days, after all, and not even the guards really believed in the permanency of the border. Alex said he wanted to visit his brother who had settled in Celle, in the British zone – both he and the guards still talked of zones rather than states, though the division of Germany into two countries was two years old – and pleaded that he had lost his transit papers. They were not interested. He was taken back to Marienborn and thrown in the cells for a night. They were chaotic days; the cells were full of people who had been apprehended laden with geese or margarine – anything that could be sold for a higher price on one side of the border than the other. Usually they were fined and released back on their own side of the frontier to get on with negotiating their next deal.

During the night the cellmates swapped anecdotes. One, a bright, intense-looking lad of twenty, promised Alex he would get across that day. He was one of a coming breed of '*Flüchthelfer*', the men who made it their business to know how to move people between one Germany and the other. Already he normally charged about a week's wages for his pathfinding services. It was the early days of an underground boom trade in humanity. By the time the Wall was built across Berlin a decade later, it would be an industry, run on the edge of the criminal world. Its organizers had prices on their heads in the East and those who were caught faced jail sentences of up to fifteen years. In the West too they kept a low profile, paid and used with a lack of conscience by the secret services that played their adventure games across the Iron Curtain, but regarded less as unsung heroes than as parasites living off others' misfortune. In 1951 it was still a lucrative sideline.

The court sat first thing in the morning. As his overnight companion had predicted, Alex, at nineteen then still legally considered a minor, was set free and told to report to the police station in Berlin and behave himself. His boastful new friend was also dismissed with a fine. But he made good his promise. 'Come on, I'll show you the right way this time,' he said to Alex as they left the courtroom and headed not for the station to catch the bus back to Berlin but through the centre of the small town and out on to a country road. Some little way beyond the last red-brick farm labourers' houses, Alex's companion led him off the path and into a forest plantation marked with signs that read 'Newly planted trees. Keep out'. Several hundred yards through the plantation, Alex's new friend grabbed him by the sleeve and thrust him to the ground. As they lay together conspiratorially in grass still damp with early summer dew, he pointed to a burnt-out bus that stood on a track about half a mile away. 'That,' he said, 'is already in the West.'

They lay low for hours, waiting for the border guards who strolled almost casually along the edge of the plantation and occasionally chatted to the handful of forest workers, to disappear from view. At one stage they feared they would be lying there until night fell. Then it began to pour with rain. Pressed into the long grass, they were soon soaked. But it was the break they needed. The border guards followed the foresters into the woods to take cover. For the few minutes the boys needed, no one was paying the least attention to the strip of open countryside between them and the shell of a bus that seemed so near but which they already sensed was on a road in another world. They saw the chance and took it, and within minutes were slapping each other on the back and striding out like any two young men on a Sunday afternoon stroll into the woods beyond, which were in the other half of Germany.

Near the city of Helmstedt, the first stop in the West, was a large reception camp for refugees from the East. Alex had already said goodbye to his helper and made for the camp, which had turned into a hitchhikers' clearing house as the restrictions on the silently growing frontier intensified. Long-distance lorry drivers would stop to take anyone from the East on to wherever they had friends or relatives. Alex's first intention was indeed, as he had told the border guards who had captured him outside Marienborn, to go and visit Norbert in Celle.

The first driver took him. It was a short but bumpy journey in the back of an open truck, and when he jumped out and made his way to the bar where his brother worked, Alex was greeted as if he were a ghost; he was covered almost from head to toe in white plaster dust. It was an emotional reunion, but not for long. Alex was still too young for much sentimentality and as yet the frontier that would soon divide his family and his country seemed more the stuff of adventure stories than international political realities. Norbert had been to visit the rest of the family in Berlin on several occasions. So, greetings and gossip exchanged, rucksack on his back once more, Alex set off to meet his friends, as they had arranged, in a youth hostel in Hanover, to tell them the tale of his exciting crossing, like a boy's magazine brought to life.

In the few brief months that followed they travelled the length and breadth of what was left of the Fatherland, whose glories they had been taught in school in Berlin or now distant Danzig. They hitchhiked to the Rhine, separating into pairs to get lifts more easily, meeting at prearranged rendezvous in Cologne and Karlsruhe. Even bombed and shell-torn, these were cities redolent of Roman Germania and the medieval German empire of Karl der Grosse, whom the French wooden-headedly still called Charlemagne. The magic these names and places evoked was increased, though the boys would have been loath to admit it, by a Nazi education system that had instilled a deep respect for the grandeur of history, even if it reworked that history for its own ends.

Hitchhiking was easy in those days when Germans still felt the camaraderie of a nation struggling to rebuild life together, and they found much to talk about with the drivers who gave them lifts, especially when they said they were Berliners: 'Absolutely every one of them had been to Berlin at some stage and they all wanted to know something: Is that street still there? Is this building still standing? How does it work with the four sectors? We made ourselves specialists; one talked about the economy, one about culture; we each had our long-playing record to put on so the others could sleep.' They camped in fields and on campsites. Each had carried twenty East marks and twenty West marks. Alex earned a few pfennigs here and there by cutting hair, wrapping their old triangular tent, ex-Wehrmacht, around the customer's neck, and in the picturesque little Bavarian town of Oberammergau, famed for its passion plays, an English priest gave them ten pounds, a fortune that sustained them for weeks.

For four boys who had seen war as children and were now on the brink of manhood in an uncertain world, it was an epic voyage of discovery: down to the Rhine Waterfall at Schaffhausen, through the Black Forest with its lakes, dark woods and medieval villages where cuckoo clocks were the main industry, down to the pastures of Bavaria, where they drank beer for the first time in the southerners' giant litre-pots (so alien in Berlin), then across the border to the snow-capped majesty of the Tyrolean Alps and back to Mozart's magical city of Salzburg to join a train of pilgrims bound for Rome. And that was their mistake. They had no passports. The crossing into Austria was itself illegal. They knew it, of course, but it had so recently been part of the Reich that the frontier seemed as artificial as that between the Democratic Republic and the Federal Republic. These were times when frontiers meant life or death but still seemed artificial abstractions to a generation who had seen states destroyed several times over and knew the borders between them were no more real than lines on a map, except for the armed men who guarded them.

On the Austrian–Italian frontier they encountered their first Western equivalent of border troops. They were taken back to Innsbruck and held for ten days, ten to a cell, pending deportation. 'That's when I learnt the important things in life,' Alex recalled, 'how to make fire without matches and how to make chessmen out of cigarette packets. We were treated well by the Austrians. They wanted to know what we would tell people back in Germany; they were anxious that we should have a good impression. We had nothing to complain about. We were from the East, the "Zone"; here we were pleased to get sausage for breakfast, meat at lunch, and a half-hour's walk in the afternoons.' For the Austrians it was more a collection point than a prison. When there was a large enough group, about a dozen, they were taken in a van back across the border to Garmisch-Partenkirchen, where they were brought before a Bavarian magistrate who decided he had no time to waste on such trivial cases: 'He asked us what had we done. We told him we had crossed the border illegally. He said, "You're a pack of idiots. Have you had supper?" "No," we said. "Well clear off down to the jail kitchen. Give them my regards and tell them you're to eat your fill and clear off out of my sight."'

It was all well that ended well, but for a slight bureaucratic hiccup that turned out to be unimportant but could have been a catastrophe. Four weeks later, back in the Hamburger Hof, across that tell-tale line into the eastern half of Berlin, Alex received a letter that almost caused him early heart failure. 'It was from the Bavarian court, confirming that the case against me for illegal crossing of the border had been dismissed.' A relief, one might have thought, as the Bavarians no doubt had, so tenuous was the grasp still on the new postwar realities. But 'Those idiots had sent it to me by open mail, to an address in the Soviet zone! It was proof that I had crossed the only frontier that mattered to our authorities, the one between *us* and *them*. I could have been locked up on its evidence.' It was a stroke of luck that even later the state security apparatus then being constructed in the Soviet zone under the tuition of men from the Moscow Lubyanka could not manage to read every letter. The Stasi, the security police, would be brutal, almost omnipotent in a state where the will of the Community Party was the only law that counted; but it never quite managed to be omniscient.

It had never occurred to Alex or any of his friends on that adventurous journey that they should remain in the West. They still hardly perceived it as abroad, and home was still home. Yet the division that had seemed so illusory was quietly setting in cement. When he stood up in the new parliament in Bonn to make his first policy declaration, Konrad Adenauer had made a point of referring to what, if anything, the concept of a united Germany now meant: 'We must still remember that Germany and the German people are not yet free, that we do not yet have equal rights alongside other nations, that – and this is particularly painful for us – our nation is ripped in two parts. But . . . no one here can lose his liberty or his life through secret police or other similar institutions, as was the case in the National Socialist Reich and is now, to our sorrow, the case in wide areas of Germany in the eastern zone.' When the communists in the East retaliated with the formation of their own state, Adenauer parodied the old pun on the first Reich – which was condemned as neither Holy, nor Roman, nor an Empire – by declaring the new state neither German nor Democratic nor a Republic.

But despite having been, by implication, branded a Russian Dictatorial Fiefdom, the new state was deemed by its German communist masters to be in need of a national anthem. It was duly written by the poet Johannes Becher to a tune by Hanns Eisler, a secular hymn to reconciliation and resurrection, a hopeful embodiment of humanist ideals. Becher became minister for culture. The first verse included a reference to '*Deutschland, einig Vaterland*' ('Germany, unified Fatherland'). As Moscow's policy changed down the years and the communist puppets in East Berlin danced to the changing tune, it would become an embarrassment. The order went out from the party that it was not to be sung. As they climbed the Olympic rostrum the athletes who became the flag-bearers of this unregarded half-nation kept their lips tightly pursed. Suffer no one to sing of Germany, for they knew not what it was.

Only on the street of Leipzig in the autumn of 1989 was Becher's refrain to be heard again.

# 4

# Death and Stagnation

When it happened, it was like an earthquake: the death of Stalin in 1953 shook the foundations of the communist world. Lenin had long receded into mythology; communism, as the world knew it, was Stalin's creation. The creed and the man were identical; now the man was dead. In Moscow Nikita Khrushchev began to formulate the secret speech that three years later would strike the first blow against the totalitarian edifice. Mikhail Gorbachev, the man who would one day pull it down, was a politically obedient law student, still afraid to talk openly about his grandfather who had been sent to the gulags.

In the schools and colleges of the Soviet sector of Berlin the students formed discussion groups and watched each other to know how to react. The pupils in Alex's teacher-training college were advised to join the German–Soviet Friendship Society. But the workers on the streets knew otherwise. They had had enough.

Throughout 1952 the economy of the 'Zone' had deteriorated while that of West Germany improved. As a result tens of thousands, denied access to a secret ballot at home, had begun to vote with their feet. They came from Dresden, Rostock, Leipzig, but almost always through Berlin; in the months that followed Alex's travels any possibility of a repeat performance had been eradicated. The frontier between East and West Germany was increasingly well guarded by armed troops. The patrols became regular; the dogs were trained to seize and savage if necessary; the guards to shoot, if need be to kill; the fences were erected and would soon be electrified.

But in the government in East Berlin the communists quarrelled. The winning faction moved the emphasis from light to heavy industry, preposterously following the Soviet decision that had

47

been made in time of war and would, there also, prove inappropriate for the peace. They penalized the small businessmen, who were now deemed politically inappropriate to the new times. In April 1953 the government withdrew ration cards from those who lived by private enterprise. The intention was to force small shopkeepers, private publicans, restaurant owners and those who lived on the rent from property to change their lifestyle and become part of the new collective society; to abolish the middle class and strengthen the proletariat. In Berlin the chief effect was to encourage everyone to become more dependent on the western half of the city. Or to leave.

Alex found life becoming every day just a little bit greyer. In Prenzlauer Berg, the old 'N.O.' postal district – standing for North East – that Marlene Dietrich had sung about, the bars began to close. Before the war it had been the vibrant centre of working-class night-life in Greater Berlin; even if it occasionally came down to brawls between Nazis and communists on street corners, these were only the backdrop to a bustling scene of quickfire repartee over foaming beer and tots of *Korn*, the rough schnapps from Nordhausen. It had suffered, of course, during the war. But there was a 'blackout and Blitz' mentality beneath the incessant British and American bombing raids; if Berliners had lacked the British stiff upper lip, their *Schnauze*, a rebellious, cock-a-snook sense of humour – often black – had seen them through. Even at the height of the Gestapo terror there were still jokes about Hitler in the bars of Prenzlauer Berg, where Berliners in their own impenetrable dialect would exaggeratedly mimic the comic rolling vowels of their Austrian leader. Towards the end there had even been a barely repressed *Schadenfreude* at the ruins of a Reich that had struck many down-to-earth Berliners as preposterously pompous. But the unceasing dull austerity that had followed the occupation had shown its effect in a steady attrition of morale.

Alex's father's bar was state-owned and therefore under no threat, but it was a cavernous hotel bar and could never aspire to the cosy *Gemütlichkeit* of the street-corner pub. Now, when he went out in the evening, wandering around the shabby streets, Alex was dismayed to find one after another of his old haunts closed and boarded up; sometimes there was just a sign that said 'Closed for repairs' or 'Temporary closure', but the result was the same: there was no longer anywhere to swap anecdotes, to sink a beer and share troubles. In their zeal to recreate a new society the communists had torn apart the crucial fabric of working-class Berlin life. Alex sighed despondently at the blind stupidity of it. He had never subscribed to socialism but he loved the working-class culture of Prenzlauer Berg that he now saw being eroded by those who posed as its champions. One day, he thought, the inarticulate workers would find a way to tell them what they thought. It was to be sooner than he thought, and the response more brutal.

On 20 April 1953 the government raised the price of meat, sausage, bread and jam. On 28 May it announced a ten-per-cent rise in the 'norms', the regular work quotas on which wages were based. It was the opposite of a productivity bonus; it meant that, unless workers raised their output by ten per cent, they would suffer a cut in wages. It was a sacrifice that the workers would understand they had to make, the party said, for the sake of the communist future. The measure was due to be put into effect by the end of June, and – by way of compensation – ration cards would be restored to all citizens, even the little businessmen, and the food price rises would be rescinded. It was a confused reaction to a deteriorating situation.

By 16 June the workers had had enough. The builders on the new Stalinallee, a monolithic reproduction of the Lenin Allee in Moscow, put down their tools and marched to the government offices, now located in what had been Goering's Air Ministry, a few hundred yards from the site of Hitler's bunker, hard by Potsdamer Platz, once the busiest traffic point in Europe and now, amid the ruins, still a main road crossing point between the Soviet and Western sectors. They demanded that the increase in norms be cancelled and declared a general strike for the next day. In the end the ministers panicked and gave in, but such was the lack of communications that they were unable to get their decision to the strike leaders in time.

In the dawn hours of 17 June there began the biggest protest East Germany was to see for the next forty-five years. The construction labourers from Stalinallee led the marches to the government building, joined by thousands of workers from all over the Soviet sector and hundreds of enthusiastic supporters from other Berlin enterprises that happened to be in the West. It was workers' power challenging the self-appointed representatives of the Workers' State. That things were serious was immediately clear. By nine a.m., right across the city centre, on every main square – the Alexanderplatz, Potsdamer Platz, along Unter den Linden and the parallel, wide thoroughfare of Leipziger Strasse, which led to the government offices – Soviet tanks, the same T-34 battle tanks that had eight years earlier blasted their way into the rubble of the city, stood poised again for action.

The fiction of German communist rule was threadbare; whatever the quislings in grey suits with little red books might declare, beneath the tense surface it was Russian against German again. Workers pushed over the signs that were still all that marked sector boundaries, hurled stones and petrol bombs at party offices and set fire to kiosks that sold only communist newspapers. By eleven a.m. the first workers had climbed the Brandenburg Gate and dragged down the red flag, which they ripped to shreds. For the men on the streets, many of whom had been soldiers in the army of a state that had called itself National Socialist, and who therefore felt doubly duped, the red banner was no symbol of workers' power but a token of Russian oppression.

Across the country the scene was the same, with mass protests in Leipzig, Dresden and other major cities involving some three hundred thousand workers. Their demands were concrete and comprehensive. The strike committee in the industrial centre of Bitterfeld north of Leipzig sent a telegram to the government in Berlin putting forward a list of demands that they knew in their hearts to be impossible. Political prisoners were to be freed immediately, the army was to be disbanded, the police withdrawn to barracks and the government was to resign in a tacit admission that it had rigged the elections. In its place the workers would set up a provisional administration that would hold free elections by secret ballot within four months, allowing the major West German political parties to organize.

But the reality of their situation filtered through in the almost pathetic final demand: no recriminations against the strikers. It was, in effect, an acknowledgement that their cause was doomed to defeat and a prayer for mercy. It was a waste of breath. Soviet troops, in whose ranks nationalist, atavistic hatred easily won over ideological illusions, opened fire. On the Potsdamer Platz the strikers scattered before a hail of bullets that left bodies lying in the roads and on the steps of the U-Bahn station entrances. By one p.m. the Soviet commandant had declared a state of emergency in East Berlin and banned demonstrations and meetings of any kind. Once – in 1917 – Trotsky had placed his hope in the German workers allying with their Russian brothers to lead a world revolution; in 1949 the myth had been resuscitated, with minor character changes, of course, such as the deletion of Trotsky, for the sake of contemporary politics. But now the truth could be shown: Stalin's Red Army had no time for revolution, least of all carried out by Germans.

Alex first realized what was happening when he looked out of the windows of the Hamburger Hof and saw tanks on the Sangkrugbrücke, pointing towards West Berlin. His first instinct was to dash out to see what was happening; if there was a demonstration he wanted to join it. But the bar was full and his father kept calling on him to serve drinks. There was a hubbub of gossip in the bar: excited, uninformed rumours of large-scale revolution, of bloodshed, of clashes with police and Russians on the sector boundary. It was only eight years since these people had been mortal enemies. Then a large Russian officer came in and asked for water for the men; after a while others improved on his idea and came in for beer or schnapps in hip flasks. 'They did it all secretly, of course; no one was supposed to know.' And Alex served them; after all, business was business, particularly when the customers carried machine-guns.

The armoured repression was swift and merciless. Thousands were arrested, hundreds jailed and dozens – although no one knew it at the time – secretly executed. The politicians in Bonn declared the date, 17 June, a national holiday: German Unity Day. It was a deliberate provocation, in tune with the Cold War, but also in sympathy with the sentiment so vividly expressed in the other part of Germany. The events in the East helped Adenauer's party to their greatest electoral victory three months later. The hard line was set; the first major skirmish in the Cold War had been fought and lost. It was time to retrench and prepare for a long siege. The East German Communist Party newspaper *Neues Deutschland* had its own version of events ready to hand: the disturbances were blamed on 'paid criminal elements from West Berlin', 'rowdies' and 'bandits', who 'did not shrink even from directing their attacks against a police hospital, where they smashed the windows of the women's ward.' 'The population distanced itself,' the newspaper summed up.

Indeed it did. Under the Nazis the opposition had gone into 'internal emigration'; now there was an acceptable, even patriotic, alternative: escape from Germany to Germany. In 1953 alone, a total of 331,390 East Germans left for the West. Among those who remained protest went underground. In his studies Alex and his friends noticed with scorn how every teacher now avoided any discussion at all of politics. One who had stood up in the school hall on 17 June and told the students that the workers outside were right was dismissed within days. The students prepared their own token protest for the next month's examinations: in the German literature section each one in his or her own little way chose their form of rebellion in the *viva voce* examination by the teacher. It was a simple business: a recital of a piece of classical literature. Each chose a text to make a point. When it came to his turn Alex recited a piece of Schiller's *Egmont*, dedicated to freedom, the irrepressible human spirit and opposition to tyranny. The weary examiners nodded resignedly, understandingly, and marked him, and the others, only on their memory, not on their choice.

It was the tiniest of protests, a curious opportunity offered by the breadth of an education system that had grafted, still loosely, half-baked socialist principles on to German educational thoroughness; a system that demanded that would-be teachers of plumbing and hairdressing apprentices alike had a mastery of history and literature. When I expressed my amazement that the general level of education was so good, Alex smiled and explained proudly: 'It was a sort of general leaving examination, an *Abitur*. To be a hairdresser you have to have a good general education. If I speak about rococo, then I have to know something of Frederick the Great, Voltaire, Diderot. I have to have at least some idea of who those people were. I can hardly separate the style of a hairdo from the style of a dress or a building. I can hardly teach people without telling them about the philosophy of the period, the thinkers and the writers. That's part of being a hairdresser too, you know, like chemistry so you know about fair colouring, and biology so you know about texture and ageing and which chemicals produce which effect. That's what we did. The shops taught you how to cut hair.'

Life after 17 June 1953 was suppressed, quiet, suffused with a sense of hopelessness – an entire society waiting for Godot. The following year Walter Ulbricht, a Saxon with a strong accent and a pointy beard who had spent much of the war in Moscow studying Stalinism, took over the leadership of the party. There was much talk, by Ulbricht and others, of a new type of party, a new type of socialism for a new type of Germany, the *Neues Deutschland* of the party newspaper. The southern Saxon industrial city of Chemnitz was renamed Karl-Marx-Stadt. East Germany was recognized as a proper country, but only by the Soviet Union and its other satellite allies. The steady drain of the population through Berlin to the West fell back to the still unacceptable level of 184,198 in 1954 but began to rise again in 1955. Within two years the annual human exodus had reached a quarter of a million.

But the Margan family were involved in their own affairs. Early in 1954 old Bernhard took seriously ill, and Alex had to give up his training to look after the business. He was granted permission by the state authorities to run the Hamburger Hof until his father recovered. It was quite a challenge: 'I was just twenty-two and I had to administer this huge, rambling hotel, with its bar and kitchen and some twenty rooms, alone.' But Bernhard did not get better. He had lung cancer and died. Unlike the Klohs family in Metzer Eck, the Margans did not get permission to carry on the business; Alex was considered too young and inexperienced for such a large concern. The family sold what they owned of the contents. The hotel was taken over by the state and promptly began to lose money. Three years later the Hamburger Hof was closed and pulled down. Another landmark on the road to despondency.

Alex went back to his studies, which he finished successfully in 1956, and started to run a school for hairdressing apprentices. To the already exhaustive list of cultural subjects that these sixteen- and seventeen-year-old boys and girls were to study, he added music, training them as choristers for the district championships. It fitted in theory with the communist state's conception of 'Culture', not as an expression of the life of a society but as 'Art for the People', something harmless that would keep the masses' minds off politics. At the championships they won second prize. He trained them to sing a four-voice canon, remembered from his Catholic youth. Even many years later his eyes would burn with enthusiasm as he hummed the arrangement: 'Slow at first, rising in tone, then the second voice, then the third, then at last the three simple words *"dona nobis pacem"*, ever greater, swelling ever more powerfully to an explosion of sound. We brought the house down.'

But in the new climate of ideological orthodoxy, even an overly successful choir performance could be suspected of allowing religion, the opium of the non-party people, to rear its head: 'The next day the party secretary came to me and said, "What are you doing? That was a church song."' Church songs were definitely 'off' at communist-party song competitions. 'I told him it was an international song and he stomped off. But I heard only later he had gone to the librarian and asked him, "What does *'dona nobis pacem'* mean?" Of course, I had the last laugh, because "give us peace" was part of the party programme and he could hardly object. But he knew what direction I came from, what my philosophy was, and he gave me no peace.'

In keeping with the public-spiritedness that had by then become obligatory, Alex registered in the summer of 1957 as a volunteer helper in a camp for the children of Berlin transport workers at Wernigerode. It was a depressing experience. The parents were instructed to send the children with proper clothes but often the youngsters arrived carrying only a shoebox with a lump of soap, one change of underwear and a couple of vests. It was partly an indictment of the general state of postwar poverty, from which the bulk of the population in the East were never to escape. But the camp's answer was clear and hard: 'We dressed them properly and bought them what they needed for three weeks' holiday and the money was directly debited from their parents' wages.' It was also a holiday for a young man. One incident at the camp brought home further to him the nature of the society he had become part of.

It was supposed to be a happy holiday home for deprived children from the big-city slums, who would exchange for a few weeks their everyday atmosphere of high, concrete courtyard walls and waste bins for mountain air and deep, dark pine forests. For Alex it was curiously familiar: 'It reminded me of my own youth and the camps we went to in the countryside around Danzig, when early in the morning some boy would stand up and read a poem "For Germany" or "In praise of Adolf Hitler". We were greeted with "Heil Hitler". Here it was not so very different. We heard a poem "To Stalin", or "To Lenin", or a socialist song or something, and we had to use the "friendship greeting". We had a roll-call before the flag first thing in the morning, just like in the Nazi times. The children were supposed to have a good time, and, to make sure, the camp had a watch-tower that gave a lovely view, enabled us to watch for forest fires and by chance to spot any child strolling without supervision.

There was one particular boy in the camp, a timid character who refused to join in the games and made a point of being an outsider. His was an attitude frowned upon by the organizers. Alex realized the trouble that this would cause: 'It was a basic rule that all the letters the children wrote home were "controlled" – that is to say, they were read and checked by one of the camp officials.' The anger of the authorities erupted when they read this particular child's letter to his parents, for in it he complained that he was shut in, beaten, locked up, very unhappy and wanted to go home.

This was not the way the camp liked to be seen. The boy had broken the rules. In the best communist fashion the camp leaders, fresh from the party school lessons in public criticism and self-criticism, gathered together in their own common room one evening and discussed the child's letter. For Alex it was a first object-lesson in the hypocrisy and repressed hysteria that were the ground rules of the Stalinist system of control. One apparently sane young woman from a Berlin party group stood up and took it upon herself – 'in the interests of collective discipline' – to take a clear line on the issue. She said the boy's letter was not just a catalogue of complaints but a deliberate calumny on the socialist system. It was, she said, the product of the class enemy's insidious propaganda campaign; in all but the detail the child's letter had been effectively dictated by RIAS (West Berlin's Radio In the American Sector) in order to discredit the Young Pioneer camp system. Alex thought she was mad: 'Then she waited to see what the reaction was, but the reaction was zero. So she demanded that the next morning the boy should be called out before the whole three hundred in the camp and made to admit that his letter was a shameful lie that had been dictated to him by the agents of the class enemy. Can you imagine? The boy was only ten years old.'

It did not happen. Alex grabbed hold of the boy himself, an undersized, red-haired, well-brought-up lad – 'by which I mean he knew how to use a knife and fork and a napkin' – for which his peers had accused him of putting on airs – 'as I said, the children of Berlin Transport workers were not the last word in refinement' – and made fun of him. The boy felt himself truly tortured. Everything he had written in his letter was true, only his presentation of the facts was politically naïve, 'but how can you expect a ten-year-old to know what to write to please the party?' For Alex 'it was an indication for me that as far as certain people in this state of ours were concerned, anything that went wrong could never be their own fault but had to be that of the enemy.'

Nonetheless, Alex enjoyed the camp and went again the next year as a group leader. But now he found the parents causing a new problem. Some of them had sent notes requesting that their children attend church on Sunday and the strict communist camp leader was opposed, refused to organize the expedition and expressed the hope that none of the camp helpers would do so. But Alex, still Christian and Catholic somewhere beneath the philosophical baggage he had gathered over the years, volunteered. The problem remained that there were thirty children who had notes saying they should attend church and rules stipulated that at least two adults had to accompany such a large group. Just when it seemed hopeless, a young woman he had met once or twice in Berlin said she would go with him.

Her name was Helga Baumgart and she was a communist. And worse: her father worked for the Ministry for State Security, the hated Stasi. 'We got to talking about one thing and another, about our philosophy, our *Weltanschauung*. I talked to her about the Christian point of view when we were in church and was helped by the priest, who gave some sort of sermon that moved her deeply. I can't remember now what it was, but I like to think it was the story of Saul on the road to Damascus converted to the apostle Paul. It might not have been, but that was the effect.'

It was an affair that quickly turned to lust but shied from love and the concomitant difficulties of a mixed marriage in the German Democratic Republic. 'How could we have children if we did not agree on how they would be brought up?' But back in Berlin Alex's unconventional style worked its effect. They saw each other regularly and in 1960 she began to take lessons in the Catholic faith in Saint Joseph's convent in Pappelallee and converted. It was the basis for marriage, although her parents came only to the state ceremony in what was now Wilhelm-Pieck-Strasse, not to the religious wedding in the Herz Jesu church in the Fehrbelliner Strasse. But conversion was not the end of their philosophical differences. Helga wanted to work, but Alex was against it. He believed that a wife should stay at home if there were small children – and Helga was soon pregnant – 'to nurture a bit of nest warmth for the little ones'.

Luckily Alex now had an opportunity to earn more money and make Helga's working unnecessary. He was offered the job of heading a centralized school for craftsmen set up to create a forum for apprentices to learn their trade from masters who were brought together to teach them, rather than learn on a daily basis in their workplace. It seemed a good idea at the time. That it was only another arm of the creeping process of bringing everything under state control was not evident, nor important. For Alex the main thing was that his salary would soar from seven hundred to eleven hundred marks a month. It was much-needed money, for in the next three years Helga bore him two sons, Winfried and Thomas. But it was a cruel world they were born into.

On 13 August 1961 they started to build the Berlin Wall. The Cold War entered a new ice age. The rhetoric had been going on for months. But the reality still came as a shock. It was perceived by most Berliners dully, uncomprehendingly, like the first impact of bereavement. It was not to be believed; it was a temporary situation, they felt. There was anger, outrage, resentment, but above all a bloody-minded refusal to believe that fate could deal them such a blow.

The troops had begun to pull the barbed wire across the city at dawn. As Berliners woke up to a new day, they found armed men from the border troops, the army and most of all from the communist paramilitary groups organized in the factories, standing with their automatic weapons at the ready in a human wall through the heart of Berlin. Behind them other paramilitary troops were already laying concrete blocks. Most Berliners thought it was a bad dream, at worst a return to the crisis of the blockade. Somehow it seemed at first to be directed against the West Berliners, though it was immediately clear that if they could not come east, then East Berliners could not go west. The hole in East Germany's hermetic seal was being plugged to stop the westward trickle of its own population becoming a flood.

When the first news broke – euphemistically – that drastic new restrictions were being introduced along the sector boundary, Alex rushed the few hundred yards from the flat in Prenzlauer Berg towards the neighbouring district of Wedding, which history had accidentally left to the French rather than the Russians among Germany's conquerors. He stood with his best friend, Heinz Herzberg, dumbstruck as the morning light revealed how Bernauer Strasse, a nondescript street of six-storey tenements, had become the front line in the ideological conflict that split the world.

The Prussian civil servants who, more than fifty years earlier, had drawn the lines dividing the Berlin boroughs had marked the border between Prenzlauer Berg and Wedding along the pavement of Bernauer Strasse. These bureaucrats had not seen it as a particular problem that the houses were in one borough, while the street in front of them was in another; but they had not reckoned on the world being divided along their line. This particular border between the French and Soviet sectors of Berlin became a symbol to the world of the failure of a system that had to use force to keep its citizens from fleeing.

That August morning, having taken possession of the ground-floor flats in Bernauer Strasse, troops soon began bricking up the doors and windows and evacuating the inhabitants. Some of these, however, had already decided to make a leap into the unknown, literally, by throwing themselves from upper windows into blankets held by West Berliners in the street below. Alex and Heinz, in disbelief, watched with their hearts in their mouths. 'We wondered, should we follow their example? Was this the last chance for freedom? But both of us had elderly mothers living in the East.' Alex was also by no means certain that his new wife would join him; he suspected her father stood somewhere on the frontier that day with a weapon in his hand. 'Anyway, we thought it was some sort of temporary game, like the blockade had been. We could hardly imagine how they could even think of totally dividing a city of millions, not just the streets and houses, but the underground, the trains and the sewers, the electricity, and rip families apart. It all seemed too preposterous. I watched them jump from windows, saw them spring over barbed wire. But we thought it was all too fantastic and in any case surely the Western Allies would never tolerate this.'

That was what the West Berliners believed too. They did not know that the secret services of the Allies had for months been compiling data on a project known by the code name Operation Chinese Wall. They were taken by surprise not by what happened but by when it happened, although the West German secret service had pointed out an accumulation in the Soviet sector of building materials and barbed wire. The flood of refugees from East to West through Berlin had reached colossal proportions and both sides knew something would have to be done if East Germany was not to collapse from within.

The question was: to what extent would each side play 'chicken' before risking war? Moscow wanted West Berlin's separate status from the Federal Republic to be internationally agreed. It should be a Free City, as Danzig had been between the wars. But the West would hear nothing of it. The *status quo* of West Berlin was an anomaly, but it was also a gaping wound in the side of the communist world, and they saw no reason to cure it. The decision to build a wall had been taken in Moscow two weeks earlier as Walter Ulbricht persuaded his fellow communist leaders from the Warsaw Pact that nothing else would save the situation. But Berliners failed to understand – and still do – why the West failed to react, why it took four days to send a formal protest to the Russians.

Willy Brandt, the man who later as Chancellor would begin a process of reconciliation with both East Germany and Moscow, to be known as Ostpolitik, was then Mayor of West Berlin. He shared Berliners' bitterness but was obliged to express it diplomatically. Nonetheless, he put forward his points forcefully in a letter to US President John F. Kennedy:

Whereas previously the commanders of the Allied forces in Berlin readily protested against the parades of the so-called People's Army [forbidden under the Potsdam accord banning any German military activity in the occupied capital], now, following the military occupation of the Eastern sector by the People's Army, they have had to make do with a belated and not very forceful démarche . . .

The Soviet Union has already achieved half of its Free City

proposal by use of the Volksarmee. The second act is only a question of time. After that second act there will be a Berlin that will not only have lost its function as a refuge of freedom and symbol of the hope for reunification, but will also be cut off from the free part of Germany. Then we may see a change from refugees pouring into Berlin to refugees pouring out of Berlin . . .

I cannot think without bitterness about the declaration that we should not negotiate with the Soviet Union because it was wrong to negotiate under pressure. Now we are in the position of total blackmail and already I am hearing talk that says it will be impossible to refuse negotiation.

Brandt was right, though it took ten long years for the negotiations to come about, and he would reach a conclusion only when he himself was Chancellor, that in effect accepted the *status quo*, leaving West Berlin as an anomalous, walled-in democratic enclave in the communist world.

On the eastern side of the new Wall there were also unpredictable human consequences. The 'anti-fascist protection barrier', as it would come to be known in the jargon of the party, divided not only East and West Berlin but the hearts and minds of those it trapped within communism. It polarized society and broke up families. Alex Margan's family was one of them. His brother and sister were now in another world; for his wife they were simply relegated to the status of 'class enemy'. As soon as the children reached kindergarten age Helga found a job at a refrigerator factory, where she too taught German and history to the apprentices, boys and girls of fourteen to sixteen. It was a combined general education with vocational training. The working class had to be educated, but it also had to work.

The return to the workplace reintroduced Helga to the party. The comrades worked on her. She kept quiet about her conversion to Catholicism. But like Christians themselves, the comrades hated to lose a sheep simply because she had fallen by the wayside. Helga rejoined the party and sowed the seeds of the destruction of her marriage. Her parents added to the pressure. Alex had close relatives in the West; by then not only was Renate working as a nurse in West Berlin but his mother had become a pensioner, and as such an irrelevance to the construction of socialism and allowed to leave; she had gone to join her elder son Norbert in Bad Pyrmont, a spa town in the south-west. Alex regularly received post and parcels from them. It was not the right sort of connection for a good communist girl whose father had the honour to serve in the State Security department. He told her to send the parcels back, for they were superfluous, a calculated insult to their self-sufficient socialist state.

Helga at first tried to convert Alex, to get him into some sort of acceptable political involvement; he had a state medal after all, she argued, an award for 'outstanding achievement in the field of education'. If he would not join the SED, perhaps he would join the Christian Democratic Union? He was repulsed by the idea. Unlike some of the other Soviet Bloc states, East Germany's communists had never banned other political parties; it was considered too controversial a step, particularly in a country where the Red Army had, initially, ostensibly marched in to restore democracy and end a one-party system. The communist leadership had to adopt a more pragmatic approach to other political groups: they castrated them.

The other parties were allowed to continue to exist – Christian Democrats, Liberal Democrats and several other puppet groups set up to absorb, sponge-like, political activity in certain sectors of the population: the Farmers' Party and the National Democratic Party. This latter was created specifically to sop up soldiers returning from prisoner-of-war camps and others who had not yet been fully purged of the nationalist element of Nazi philosophy, and harness them to building socialism in their own country. Each party was allowed to exist, but only within the umbrella of the National Front, the communist-controlled body that decided on the composition of the single-list ballot slips. The parties therefore got guaranteed seats in the People's Chamber, the Volkskammer, but always the same number and the communists had the majority. Alex had no doubts about the hypocrisy of those who masqueraded as Christian Democrats but had sold their souls to the communists.

There was no way out but divorce. In 1967 Helga employed a lawyer to put her case. The separation was agreed on terms of incompatibility, but the legal document made clear to anyone who read between the lines that it was a political case: the difficulties cited included arguments over how to bring up the children:

in the Church or in the party. She was awarded custody of the children. Alex moved out of the flat. But wheels within wheels were turning. Within weeks he lost his job as head of the crafts school. 'I cannot prove this, but colleagues told me that my dismissal was based at least in part on the fact that I had been divorced on political grounds. But I have no piece of paper to prove this. The reason they gave for sacking me was the fact that I had not taken my master craftsman's qualifications as a hairdresser. I had in fact been obliged to do so, but with the trouble in the family I never got round to it.'

It was a curious decision by the state; eight days later he was offered the job again after intervention from the education ministry, but he suspected his colleagues' analysis was correct: 'I turned it down. I said, "No. Never again will I take a job with a state enterprise. I have had it with this state."' In 1968 he packed up all his state awards, from the 'Outstanding achievement' medal to the sports certificate 'For readiness to defend the homeland', and sent them to Walter Ulbricht, the General Secretary of the party. It brought him some little satisfaction and a summons to the Mayor of Prenzlauer Berg. 'But I saw no point in turning up. I rang his secretary and said, "What does he want? If he wants to convince me of the righteousness of socialism, then it's a waste of both our times. I have made my point of view known. There is only one thing we could talk about: will he discuss conditions for giving me my children back?"' He received no further summons.

The problem was to find a new job. It required a certain flexibility. The best position open was in a small privately owned firm called Bremer Vivaristik, in Bötzowstrasse, mixing animal feeds. It was, on the face of it, a social come-down from teaching to mixing and selling pet food. But as a private business it did well, and Herr Bremer could afford to pay decent money. Alex mucked in with an enthusiasm and found his feet again.

The shake-out of property as a result of the collapse of the Reich was still going on, however. In fact it lasted half a century as the reclamation of confiscated houses after the unification of Germany in 1990 was the final stage. Alex's involvement began in 1970. He received a letter from his Aunt Martha, who had ended up in West Berlin – coincidentally married to the father of the man who married his sister Renate – and had inherited a property on the Baltic coast. It was a small stone house standing on a not inconsiderable six thousand square metres of woodland at Kölpinsee, a seaside holiday resort. It had been bought before the war by a Herr Goebel, an insurance company executive from Stettin, as a weekend retreat. As the result of an ancient friendship, the details of which Alex was never certain of, he had left this to Martha; but she was in the West and the land was in the East. The simplest thing was to send Alex to inspect the property and complete the legal formalities, which were considerable as the communist state preferred private property to be left to 'the community' but could not enforce its rules and so just made it difficult. It would take several months, he was advised.

The solution was simple. He gave up his job and set off, footloose again, to the Baltic, where he got a job as a waiter. It was a blissful interlude. He bought a bicycle and supplemented his income by renting it out while he was at work, and in his spare time developed a love of fishing that would last a lifetime. Evenings were spent gathering anecdotes in the bars and perusing with a rueful fascination Herr Goebel's secret treasures: a vast collection of mint-condition postage stamps and first-day covers that were a history of Germany in the run up to Armageddon. They were, for example, postmarked Linz, 'The Führer speaks', Hitler back in his old school town only days after the Anschluss; Vienna, 'The Führer's birthday'; Nuremberg, 'The Reich party congress of peace', adorned with pictures of goose-stepping storm-troopers. Somewhere, out there, he knew, it would be a historian's treasure-trove worth a small fortune; at that moment, in his hands, it was worse than junk, a collection of fascist mementoes that could not be sold, could not be taken out of the country and could not even be shown to friends for fear of attracting the dead eye of the Stasi, confiscation and political suspicion.

The legal paperwork in connection with Aunt Martha's inheritance took the best part of six months and at least a dozen trips to the local administrative centre at Wolgast on the island of Usedom. A year later Aunt Martha was confirmed as owner of the property, but to reward Alex she gave him exclusive use of it. In the meantime he had returned to Berlin, at first without work, but the job as a waiter had rekindled his enthusiasm for the restaurant and bar work he had first experienced at the Hamburger Hof during his father's illness. He now looked for a job in the bars of Berlin. Soon he became acquainted with a woman who was recently divorced and had only a few years earlier taken over the running of a moderately successful *Eckkneipe*, or corner bar, after her mother's death. Her name was Bärbel Falkner and she ran a bar called Metzer Eck. The little girl who had seen her brother plucked from the family home by Russian troops at dawn, never to return, had grown into a handsome woman, vivacious, full of street-wise common sense and a love for Berlin. Now in her mid thirties, she had two children by her first, failed marriage: Kerstin, a striking, dark-haired girl and a fine, athletic boy named – inevitably – Horst.

Alex took to her immediately and moved into the bar as head waiter. A few months later he moved into her bed.

# 5

## 'Somewhere a future awaits, unseen . . .'

Over the following decade of his stewardship of Metzer Eck, Alex made Bärbel's bar the toast of the East Berlin cognoscenti. The key, he discovered, was nostalgia.

Behind all the fine abstractions, behind the bold invention of a brave new world, the party had failed to understand that the people still had a deep-rooted love for the city that they had created according to instinct rather than ideology. As Alex became involved full time with barkeeping, which he had tasted working for his father at the Hamburger Hof, he realized he had found his true *métier*.

But it was with a heavy heart that he watched the competition evaporate, despite the commercial advantage. It became one of his catch-phrases that the communists had sucked the soul from Berlin. He would detail the process: the party had realized there was no real point in pretending there had been a popular revolution. Land reform in the German Democratic Republic started with the redistribution of the properties of those who had fled the Russian advance and opted to stay in the West; with the principle established, the process accelerated. Private housing was not taken over, nor was it maintained; and in a state where raw materials were scarce and labour controlled by the government, it became hard work to keep a big house in order.

It was not illegal to own and rent out property, but those who owned tenanted property found the rents paid them were fixed at the same minimal rate as for the state flats, and they themselves were held legally responsible for repairs, which could only be done by paying extortionate black-market rates for labour and material. It was simpler to 'make a gift' of the property to the state. However, because most owners only gave in when the property was in a disastrous state, the list of repairs was endless and growing, so that by the time the real, anti-communist revolution came in 1989, over eighty per cent of homes in the once prosperous bourgeois city of Leipzig could be classed as slums.

The same had happened to private enterprise in the service sector. During his years behind the counter in Metzer Eck, Alex kept a mental graph of the declining number of bars in Prenzlauer Berg. Some had been casualties of the war, but more were casualties of the peace. The hard work required to run a pub was little rewarded by a state salary. Only Bärbel's determination to keep a family business going had allowed Metzer Eck to survive until the authorities realized there would soon be no watering-holes in East Berlin other than sterile cafeterias, and changed the rules enough to allow tenants to make a proper profit. By the end of the 1970s decades of socio-economic mismanagement had almost totally deprived East Berlin of the city's most famed working-class institution: the corner bar.

Ironically, in their hearts the communists knew it and regretted it; they just seemed not to know what to do about it. The complete collapse of East Berlin night-life, such as it was, was prevented only by a last-minute relaxation of the drive against private enterprise. The pressure on those who, like Bärbel, were tenants rather than salaried employees of the state, was let up; she and Alex were of course still restricted to taking all their supplies from the state-owned brewery and distillers, and to charging state-regulated prices; they had to keep the hours dictated by the local city council and pay their sub-contracted staff less than the state-run bars, but they could keep their profits. For Alex, an entrepreneur at heart, it was the restoration of incentive. He set about making sure that not only was Metzer Eck always full but that the customers spent more than they would anywhere else.

He found in the pile of papers that were the bar's records a letter from Heinrich Zille, the turn-of-the-century artist and raconteur who was to Berlin what Dickens was to London, a paternalistic archetype. It was just a scrawl, a note to the *Sparverein*, the working-men's savings club to which the regulars in the bar contributed to subsidize outings to the coast for their children or picnics *en masse*. From the assorted backroom rubbish Alex rescued the original box with its numbered slots, into which each member put his weekly contribution. It was cleaned, polished and varnished and hung back on the wall alongside the framed Zille letter. It was a master-stroke of public relations, using genuine artefacts to tell a tale of local history that pandered equally to popular nostalgia and to the ideologically correct concept of the dictatorship of the proletariat.

From a rubbish tip he had acquired an old Berlin market cart with great cast-iron wheels. He cleaned it and painted it and made it the centrepiece for special occasions in the bar. For these, he would ruthlessly exploit his network of catering contacts. He knew how to make the most out of the promise of a regular place at the counter on a cold night when the other bars had filled their quota of customers. He got hold of an excellent salami here, a ham there, the best bread from the bakery boys who fetched buckets of beer for their night shift; he and Bärbel cooked Berlin *Bouletten*, traditional meatballs made from mince, onions and spices, that tasted better than any bought in the state butcher's; they made *Schmalz*, old-style meat dripping, and served it with *Schusterjungen*, the little brown rolls known as 'cobbler's boys'; he brought freshly soused herrings back from occasional weekend trips to the house inherited from his aunt's old friend at Kölpinsee on the Baltic. Fishing had become his love; he went there whenever he could, even in winter, when he would haul fish, Russian-style, through holes drilled on the ice of the inshore bays that were more freshwater than salt.

The bar thrived. Alex and Bärbel could provide nothing that was particularly unusual, but they made sure they had the best quality and the best selection of the finest traditional Berlin food; they made a virtue of plenty out of the vice of East Germany's gastronomic desert, and arrayed it on the market cart to order for special parties. Alex had realized that the official organizations of East Germany were awash with cash but lacked the imagination or the skill to enjoy it. Bärbel and he provided the means. The word spread, helped by the artistic and intellectual clientele that Alex cultivated with his banter at the *Stammtisch*. One after another, the official and semi-official organizations queued to arrange the office party at Metzer Eck: the composers' union, the German–Soviet friendship society, the union of customs and excise officers. And each one was the source of a potential favour in future. A tolerable existence in East Germany necessitated a large amount of reciprocal back-scratching.

For anyone who was anyone in the world of the East Berlin

intelligentsia – that is, those who thought twice at least about following the party line – Metzer Eck became a home from home, a freethinking haven where hedonism and philosophy were mixed with the freely flowing beer and schnapps. Bärbel was delighted. The bar, which under his father had been a centre of open argument even under Nazism, was again a place where anyone said what he or she thought, and informers were unwelcome. Even those whose jobs required at least a tacit collaboration with the new autocracy knew better than to risk the right of admission to one of the most convivial bars in town for the spurious and short-lived cachet of telling tales on a drinking partner.

It was into this subtly stratified, suspicious society that I arrived in June 1981 as correspondent for Reuters news agency, a young man running his own office for the first time, ill prepared for the complexities of life under communism. I moved into the flat that had been occupied by Reuters men since the agency controversially – against the advice of the British and American sector commanders in West Berlin – opened an office in the Soviet sector, having decided that, whatever politics might wish, for news purposes Berlin was divided.

That was in 1959. The Cold War was approaching its peak. Reuters had just got over their own embarrassment when John Peet, one of their reporters in West Berlin, a quiet Marxist and convinced pacifist, defected to the East. He had done so in the most professional manner, leaving a telex tape containing, in best Reuters house style, the news story of his own defection, with instructions to the office clerk to send it to London after he left for the night. This was duly done, but the newsdesk in London panicked to such an extent that it failed to release the story until Peet had turned up in East Berlin at a press conference organized by the communist authorities. As a result Reuters were scooped on their own story – a double embarrassment.

When I arrived in Berlin Peet was still alive. A tall, angular, shambling, bearded figure reminiscent of Hemingway's Old Man of the Sea, he had been editor of a defunct English-language propaganda magazine. He was gently disillusioned with communism but, although he had kept his British passport, never really considered returning to England or going back to live in the West. I do not know if he felt there might have been some form of retribution, though his only known sin was political naïvety. He lived on a small pension from the East German government and a little freelance journalism, and would go out to lunch occasionally with spy writers to provide them with background. Len Deighton in particular was a friend and would glean colour for his novels from Peet's reminiscences over lunch.

It was in the nature of Berlin that spy writers would pop in to the Reuter's office from time to time. All the files of copy sent to London from the year 1959 on had been kept, neatly arranged in chronological order on yellowing telex paper in box-files stacked like ministerial archives around the walls by the office secretary, a jolly, portly woman with a shock of dyed red hair and the improbable name of Erdmute (a corruption of Earth Mother, even to a German a preposterous curse of a name, which she said owed to the historical accident of having been born under Hitler, much as Russian boys under Stalin were named Traktor). This orderly filing system had the curious result that such journalistic gold dust as the first reported reaction of Berliners to the building of the Berlin Wall and the eyewitness account of the Reuters man who was the first to pass through it, were buried among basketball results from Dresden and reports of a soccer match between Lokomotiv Leipzig and Ballymena, of Northern Ireland.

As the one fixed element in an apparently transient world of young men who came and went over the years, Erdmute had a naturally possessive attitude to the Reuters office. As this was situated in one room of the flat that went with the job, it was difficult for any of the incumbents to feel as much at home as she did. She doted on Frederick Forsyth, who had briefly been an occupant of both the Reuters Berlin job and the flat, although his main claim to fame while there had been almost launching a world war by sending an urgent report that Russian tanks were on the move towards the centre of Berlin. In fact, he had merely stumbled on to preparations for the annual 7 October national day parade. My amusement at this 'amateurism' was tempered within two weeks, however, when I was so shocked by the rumble of armoured vehicles passing my bedroom window that I came within an ace of making the same mistake.

The flat and office were situated on the first floor of a solid nineteenth-century Berlin tenement block, one of those that had been thrown up during the city's rapid industrialization and expansion. The flats at the front, like ours, had been reserved for the 'gentry'. The long corridor that gave off into the various rooms was dark, gloomy and echoing. There was a long-standing request from Reuters to the magnificently named *Dienstleistungsamt für ausländische Vertretungen*, the body responsible for servicing the foreign community, that it be painted. Eventually, about a year later, it was. There was also a cupboard off to the right that contained a flush toilet and a pile of yellowing newspapers: *Neues Deutschland*, the official organ of the central committee of the Communist Party, dating back to the opening of the office in 1959. Erdmute liked to portray this pile of decaying newsprint as a secret treasure trove, it being theoretically illegal to hoard old newspapers, for two reasons: firstly, it was considered wasteful in a society where recycling was done for economic rather than ecological reasons, but also the authorities did not want the public to perceive their *post factum* rewriting of even their own version of history.

We received Western newspapers delivered by a special postwoman who toured foreigners' flats, a middle-aged paper-girl who considered herself the carrier of a diplomatic bag. At least once a week there would be a knock on the back door and I would find myself facing the swaying, rat-like, beer-belching form of 'Müllerchen', the little drunk who was, in communist jargon, our *Kommunalwohnungsverwaltungleiter* (communal accommodation administration leader), which meant he was the tenants' representative, supposed to contact the authorities when there was a building problem. To his mild annoyance he was universally known as the *Hausmeister*, the old word for the same functionary under the Nazis. All he wanted was the Western newspapers. At first I suspected him, thinking he wanted to trap me into breaking the regulations; later I learnt that all he wanted was to note the times of the Western television programmes in case he missed the football. It was a first lesson in the double-double think required by life in a totalitarian society: sometimes things *were* simply what they seemed.

Our flat had another luxury denied ordinary East Berliners: gas central heating, though this was rickety and often failed to work properly. Most of the other flats in the block were heated in the time-honoured way, by brown coal (lignite) delivered to the damp cellars and fetched up the dark staircases when needed to be burnt in the free-standing tile ovens in each room. Some of these were magnificent creations with ornately decorated enamel tiles; others were plain white or brown. The one in our spare bedroom, off the living room, still bore shrapnel scars etched across its brown tiles by a wartime British bomb. But the brown coal itself was a leitmotif of the city: great unruly piles of it dumped by the walls of the tenement blocks, the distinctive smell of the smoke leaving an ochre tinge even in the crisp, blue winter skies.

We were situated on Schönhauser Allee, a wide avenue with linden trees in the central reservation. It was the main artery of Prenzlauer Berg, the working-class district that lay slightly north-east of the city centre. Once, its upper section had been one of the most prestigious shopping streets in the German capital. Now it was little more than a cobbled racetrack for the Volvo limousines of the politburo on their way to and from their homes in the exclusive suburb of Pankow. Its shops were dingy and grey, the shelves filled with the same dull commodities in their uninspired packaging. The West German service of Reuters was particularly keen that I should write horror stories about the shortages in East Berlin; but the truth was that the situation was poor but not desperate. True, it was a far cry from the magnificent food hall in KaDeWe, the Harrods of West Berlin, but in many shops the limited displays and choice were little worse than I had seen in the west of Ireland in the early 1960s. My wife went regularly to the butcher in Dimitroffstrasse and returned without meat only if we were tired of the same selection of pork: knuckles, sausage, fatty bacon and chops. For drinks, the staples were Bulgarian tomato juice, Romanian red wine and thankfully plentiful supplies of the excellent Berliner Pilsner.

We could, of course, always shop in the West. Travelling on a regular basis those few miles across the heart of a once-great city was an arduous, time-consuming and cathartic experience. When I first arrived in East Berlin I had no driving licence and bought a bicycle. But although cars could be taken freely from East to West and back again by those entitled to travel, bicycles, for some obscure reason, could not. I was reduced to cycling to Checkpoint Charlie or to Friedrichstrasse, where the overground S-Bahn railway from West Berlin ended in a station that had become a landmark for the lines of old people who, as pensioners deemed unimportant to the state economy, were allowed to travel to the West and queued outside for their documents to be inspected. The scene on the platform itself, from which the increasingly dilapidated trains of the old Reichsbahn ran their Cold War shuttle service, was cinematic: the silhouette of the jodhpur-clad guard with automatic weapon slung over his shoulder marching along the gantry against the glass wall below the arch of the railway station. It was like a journey through Dante's inferno to board here and emerge amid the Turkish dossers and teenage heroin addicts of West Berlin's Zoo station.

By the early 1980s some of West Berlin's affluent glitter, poured over the city to make it shine out as a beacon of capitalist success amid communist poverty, had begun to flake off. The military-occupation status, by which the city nominally remained under the jurisdiction of the British, French and American garrison commanders, meant its inhabitants were not fully regarded as West German citizens; they travelled to Eastern Bloc countries not on West German passports, but on West Berlin identity cards. But the side-effect was that they were not subject to military call-up, and as a result West Berlin was a magnet for left-wing extremists, radicals and anarchists. The run-down houses near the Wall, particularly in Kreuzberg, were occupied by squatters; drug addiction was rife. Even the Free University – set up because the old Humboldt University buildings were on Unter den Linden, the wrong side of the Wall – was oversubscribed by draft-dodgers.

The city's accommodation problem was heightened by an influx of asylum-seekers from Asia and Turkey who arrived via East Berlin. It was a cynical business operation in which the communists, resentful of the West's non-recognition of their frontiers, exploited it to erode West Berlin's economy and make money at the same time; they ran a cheap charter service on the state airline Interflug's flights from Third World destinations, and offered the passengers instant transit into West Berlin. At its meanest the Cold War had come down to a petty racket in humanity.

In that summer of 1981, newly married and journalistically still wet behind the ears. I was primarily concerned with settling in and coming to terms with the 'story'. There was one basic problem: there was not a lot happening. German unity seemed a nonsense; the GDR was as real as Austria or Hungary. Indeed, for office-political reasons of preserving autonomy in my own little fiefdom, I was keen to fight off the influence of the much bigger Reuters office in Bonn and put my budget under the more distant and less threatening bureaucrats in Vienna, the traditional centre for those who were deemed to be Eastern Europe-watchers. And that was the Berlin office's purpose. The matter of Germany, the world believed, was gathering dust in a thousand Foreign Office pending trays from Smolensk Square to Foggy Bottom via Whitehall and the Quai d'Orsay.

Poland, only a stone's throw away, was the real story. Up in Gdansk, Alex's Danzig, the stocky, bumptious shipyard electrician who would one day become President of Poland was making the running. Lech Walesa's name was banned from the East German press, as were almost all reports of the wave of strikes and the eventual legalization that August of the first independent trade union organization in the communist bloc. The events were scarcely mentioned on East German television but no one was watching anyway; everyone sat glued to the news reports on the West German channels. There was a morbid fascination with the news. What would be the result, it was wondered in bars and private homes, but never in the newspapers, if – or when, as most people thought – the Warsaw Pact intervened, and German troops again were sent to invade Poland? That seemed the only answer, as it had been in Hungary in 1956 and Czechoslovakia in 1968, though the East German National People's Army had been deliberately kept to the rear by the Russian commander for fear of awakening stiffer resistance through recent memory.

But the events in Poland had already had a cruel impact on East German life. The 'friendship frontier' had been closed; families who for decades had been used to driving from Berlin to the Baltic coast in summer, and had continued to do so even when it became part of Poland, were suddenly cut off from their traditional holiday spots. Despite the distance, Alex's childhood Zoppot had been to Berliners like Margate or Clacton to Londoners. Now, anyone wanting to go there, even for a weekend on the beach, was suddenly required to produce a written invitation from a Polish host. It was a panicky move by Erich Honecker's worried communist leadership to seal East Germany hermetically from the contagion of dangerous Polish democratic daydreams.

With Leonid Brezhnev senile but seemingly still secure in the Kremlin and the Brezhnev doctrine of the right to intervene in

Moscow's sphere of influence still undisputed, East Germany was the flagship of the Soviet empire in Eastern Europe, ideologically as hard-line as Romania but more efficient. The cliché was that the Germans could make anything work – even communism. It was a slur the communists could live with; unfortunately, as history would show, it was not true. But in 1981 my mission was to watch as the Poles threw stones, and report on the ripples, if any, in this supposedly rigidly run society. The best place to start to gauge public opinion, it seemed to me as an Irishman, would be to visit a few pubs.

My first stop was the one built into the corner of our block. It was called Wörther Eck, being on the corner of Wörther Strasse, and was a dingy place lit by neon strip lights that cast into garish relief the plastic-topped tables and rickety metal chairs at which the old soaks slurped beer. The barman was called Jup, a misplaced Polish *émigré* who I thought at first would be an invaluable barometer of public awareness of Solidarity until I discovered he was semi-literate and had no memory. His one comment, 'Good old Poles!', although endlessly repeated, was not really enough to hand to the newsdesk as an analysis of popular sentiment. More interesting was Volker Schernewski, a long-haired would-be hippy who lived in a miserable single room in the basement of our *Hinterhof*, the bin-cluttered backyard where rats rifled our rubbish despite the clear signs that it was to be recycled by feeding to pigs.

Volker was a peacenik. His jeans were adorned with the famous 'swords to ploughshares' sticker that with church sponsorship had turned a Biblical saying into a motto of dissent. His friends were all thinking about refusing to do military service and weighing up the opposing disadvantages of eighteen arduous months in the army defending a system they despised or eighteen months in jail in a token protest that would leave them consigned for life to being underpaid and insecure. They were impressed by Walesa and shocked by the apparent recklessness of the workers who followed him.

It was the nadir of the corner bar in East Berlin; many were still closing. On most street corners was the mark of an old bar sign: often the 'Schultheiss' trademark of a magistrate (*ein Schultheiss*) holding a frothing mug. It was a familiar sign in West Berlin, where the brewery of that name had survived. But there it had amended its trademark, painting out the Red Town Hall, symbol of old Berlin but now in the East, with its landmark clocktower that had peered over the magistrate's shoulder. In the East a few bars still kept the sign. One such was Hackepeter next to the old brewery buildings. Before the war the street had been named after Danzig; now it was named after a more politically acceptable Bulgarian communist, on the sole grounds, according to locals, that his name – Dimitroff – also began with 'd'. Across the road was another bar – Schusterjunge. They were twins. *Schusterjunge* – 'cobbler's boy' – was the name for a Berlin brown-bread roll, while *Hackepeter* was a mixture of raw mince and onions, like steak tartare, spread on the rolls as a favourite bar snack.

In the 1930s the two bars had been frequented by rival Nazi and communist gangs and the street crossing between them had been the scene of bloody fights. We would drink an occasional beer in Hackepeter, where there was music of a sort at nights – a geriatric duo who played a succession of almost identical tunes on a small organ and skiffle drum – and a fat waiter who would be accommodating in finding a table for a secretively slipped West-mark tip. The brown walls and smoky atmosphere had changed little over the years, and at the back hung a pastoral picture, forgotten over the decades and no more than part of an unnoticed décor to regulars and staff alike, but enough to strike a chill into the perceptive foreigner; it depicted a forest glade in the Harz mountains, as the caption explained in harmless words tainted with evil: 'Buchen Wald im Harz'. It took some time for me to understand that its continued presence was not a sign of covert, lingering Nazi sympathies, merely an example that in Germany even geography can be traumatic.

There was a Jewish cemetery down the road from where we lived. It had survived the ravages of the Nazi era largely intact. It was a pleasant enough place for an afternoon stroll when the rain dripped from the linden trees on to the old stone gravestones of the Mendelssohn family. The only sinister aspect was that it abutted the high walls of the police station with its forbidding iron bars across the windows. But even there the lamentable state of the Soviet Bloc car industry let it down. Passing it on a rainy November night after an evening in a local bar, I once fell into hopeless laughter at this symbol of a brutal totalitarianism in which the tough servants of the dictatorship of the proletariat were reduced to driving cars that most of Britain's striking Ford workers would have been ashamed to sit in.

The nearest U-Bahn station was here, at Senefelder Plaza, and occasionally at night, after returning from a day in West Berlin, I would wander slowly home and maybe stop at a corner bar for a beer and a taste of local colour. That was how I discovered Metzer Eck.

It was one damp, early-summer evening, returning from a day covering yet another Polish hijack to West Berlin and a routine clash between squatters and police near the bar named after Bobby Sands, the IRA hunger striker, that I first ventured up a side street and stumbled into the secret heart of Berlin. As I creaked open the door and glanced into the warm, smoky atmosphere, the bar appeared as welcoming as any I had yet encountered in East Berlin: not very. There was the immediate sharp sense of mistrust, the unspoken question: Who is he? What does he want here? In the western half of the same city the answer would have been simple and obvious: A passing stranger, in search of a quick beer. In the East there were always second thoughts. There were many more would-be customers than places in bars. In addition, everyone knew everyone – at least everyone they wanted to know. Anyone else was by and large not worth knowing or a risk to the comfortable security of your everyday life. A large number of East Germans had as far as possible created for themselves and their families a cocoon of friendship and routine.

In Metzer Eck after hours the locals could gather and tell jokes against the Russians or damn Erich Honecker's eyes in political arguments of breathtaking honesty, for the simple reason that they knew everyone who was present. Even convinced communists knew the rules. Those whose jobs required them to have a working relationship with the Stasi knew that to maintain any sort of humanity they had only two choices: either to laugh with the better-humoured jokes and add a few of their own – and there were some good ones at the expense of the Russians (that was only racism, not ideology) – or leave when the conversation became uncomfortable. In a society where almost everyone was compromised by collaboration with the authorities, even the representatives of the authorities had to compromise to live a life worth living outside their party functions.

I was an unknown outsider. The few West Germans who found

their way into East Berlin bars were treated politely but slightly shunned with an unspoken resentment, much as Englishmen after the war felt about richer Americans: they had more money, more freedom to move about the world and took it all for granted with little awareness of how their high-handed patronage might offend those who blamed their lesser lot primarily on geography. Barmen treated Westerners well, while harbouring a sullen resentment against themselves that they did so in the hope of a hard-currency tip. It was a situation that soured relations and even the brutal medicine of the overnight currency union in 1990 would not quickly heal it.

I stood at the bar, having ordered a small beer, and soaked up the atmosphere, nodding as pleasantly as I could without seeming cretinous at the burly, grumpy barman. After an hour of sipping at a couple of beers plonked down unceremoniously on my beer mat, on which the tally was religiously noted, I abandoned thoughts of striking up a conversation at random and took out an English newspaper, partly out of boredom, partly to observe the reaction of introducing such an obviously foreign article which, even had they been able to read it, most East Germans would have been wary about producing in public.

It did the trick. Within a few minutes a bearded, bespectacled character leaning on the other side of the tiled stove came over and asked in polite but strongly accented English if he might borrow it for a few seconds. He looked at me curiously and repeated the question in German. I answered in German and his wary attitude returned. I did not know it then, but pretending to be a foreigner was for some young East Germans a game, as elsewhere in the Soviet Empire, a way of assuming temporarily another identity, perceived as granting immunity from ordinary conversations. He tried me in English again, testing whether my command of the language matched his. I could see him grudgingly, wonderingly, admitting that I might be the genuine article, an adventurous tourist perhaps strayed way off course. His name was Jochen, he ventured. We bought each other beers.

We met again, by arrangement, a few days later, again each leaning on the stove by the bar. He insisted on speaking English, which irritated me as it drew attention to us and I wanted so much to fit unnoticed into this society in order better to understand it. But I understood that for Jochen one of the main reasons for talking to me was to practise his English. He was, he explained, a stage designer. When I admitted to being a foreign correspondent he was initially sceptical; there were, after all, no other English-speaking media in East Berlin. But he soon came to accept it and found it gave our conversations the spice of political danger, though Jochen's politics were as perversely complex as his personality. He cultivated an artistic persona, wearing a battered leather jacket over a black polo-neck sweater, with a tooth – presumably his own – on a chain around his neck. He wore a wide-brimmed black hat over his close-cropped hair.

Jochen's sexual preferences were, I quickly decided, at best ambivalent. He doted on his mother, a plump, giggly and self-consciously learned academic woman in her fifties, with jet-black hair and the ear of the party. She was a specialist in Latin America and travelled to Cuba; years later they would write a book together on the history of the Sandinista movement in Nicaragua. It was Jochen's one overt gripe against the party that they never allowed him to travel with her. Jochen had little memory of his father and less time for him. His father had been a soldier in the war and had abandoned his wife when she opted to stay in the communist East. Jochen's personal and political life, I felt, had become fused, his hatred for capitalism mixed with his scorn for the father who abandoned him for it, all set against his devotion to his mother and her ideology. He was a textbook case of Cold War psychology.

He was not a party member; perhaps, I speculated, because he did not want too much prying into his private life. He was an amateur intellectual of the type that flourished on the fringes of cultural society in a state where the arts were subsized as long as they toed the political line. He lived in a small flat with no amenities. It was a Bohemian lifestyle enforced by the poverty of the state. He had little money and did little work. He lived on beer and basics. He taught me how to make Prussian potato soup, the sort of delicacy, he said, that gave you 'stamina in the winter months'.

My conversations with Jochen at the bar had had the advantage of making me an accepted fixture in Metzer Eck, if still considered an outsider. Gradually I came to know the regulars: Hans Busch, the communist who ran the neighbourhood printing apprentices' home; the giant, ailing Manne Schulz, who sat in the corner nursing his hundred grams of schnapps; Axel, the television producer; Ulla, the gap-toothed waitress from the bar down the road; Bernd, the musician from the East Berlin philharmonic, and Uschi, his uproarious wife from Leipzig with her broad Saxon vowels; the Schwill family, an actor and his shop-assistant wife; Erwin the bus driver; Lothar the stocky landlord of the pub across the road who came in on his nights off; Udo the overweight clarinettist and the lads from the bakery down the road, who came in to fetch draught beer in buckets for the night shift. Like the best of well-run pubs, it was a microcosm of local society, much as it might have been a century earlier. And behind the bar: Bärbel Falkner and her man, Alex Margan.

At first, to them as to the other regulars, my wife and I were harmless oddities, foreigners who were most likely trustworthy and in any case probably unable to penetrate the thick Berlin dialect in which most risqué political anecdotes were told. Soon, however, I was able to match the language and join in the banter. But by that stage we were accepted, had passed the intangible acid test of trust; I knew it the night Alex offered me a seat at the *Stammtisch*. In a Berlin bar, that is as good as it gets. In the months that followed we became family friends, getting to know their daughter Alexandra, then still a little girl, and Bärbel's two children from her failed marriage: daughter Kerstin and son Horst, named after her unfortunate brother. At that time Horst was a soldier counting off the days still to serve in the National People's Army with notches on a tape measure, as did West German boys across the border and all their fathers before them in Hitler's Wehrmacht and their grandfathers in the Kaiser's legions.

It was a rare breakthrough into a world that most correspondents only visited. At Christmas that year we held a party and served English roast turkey to a group of twenty that included Alex, Bärbel, Jochen, Udo, Günther, an actor from the People's Theatre, the Volksbühne, and Manne, an overweight, unemployed regular who was applying for a pension that would enable him to travel to the West. We found ourselves tottering on the edge of social schizophrenia. For us, practically alone among all our acquaintances, from Berlin East or West, this great city was still one. To be more precise it was two, linked by the umbilical cord of Checkpoint Charlie, like Siamese twins, joined but separate and looking in opposite directions.

We could enjoy the bustling luxury of West Berlin but also retreat from it, behind the Wall. After a night watching squatters hurl petrol bombs on the streets of Kreuzberg, it almost seemed a relief to escape into the ordered calm of a police state. The night Ronald Reagan came to town, when for five hours I cowered in and around the streets of Charlottenburg and Kreuzberg dodging tear-gas and cobblestones, there was a palpable feeling of involuntary relaxation in crossing the Wall and passing the dead-eyed, sober policeman on guard outside the sedate, silent monolith of the Soviet trade mission.

For it was easy to forget. There was an old-world charm about the dilapidation of the GDR, with its fewer, less threatening cars, evocative clanking trams, its stalls where we bought sausage and beer under the overhead railway or in Friedrichshain park at the annual 'Neues Deutschland' press festival, sitting on the grass amid the unregarded red banners, clanking sturdy mugs of frothing beer. Even at Checkpoint Charlie, the one border crossing between East and West Berlin where non-Germans could bring a car across, there was a semblance of normality after a while. I came to know the border guards; these minor demons of Western spy fiction became to me human beings, though I never knew their names until the end. One though, one of the few women, was nicknamed Rita; when, contrary to the letter of the law, I tried to bring a hired truck through, she relented only on hearing that it contained a new living-room suite. She peeked in the back appreciatively and on every subsequent occasion would ask with a twinkle: 'How's the sofa?'

The party, it seemed, was part of life and if you followed the rules and did not get in its way your life could go on its own way without too much effort. While wealthy West Berliners – walled into their enclave – packed the Tiergarten park on the other side of the Brandenburg Gate with cars, tables, chairs, tents and radios on summer afternoons and irritated each other with their proximity, we would drive out on empty roads to swim in the Brandenburg lakes. With Alex and Bärbel we would go to their little *Laube* or summer house – Alex called it his dacha – at Karolinenhof outside Berlin and sit in the little garden plot around the building, which was little more than an overgrown shed with a couple of beds in it, drinking beer, talking fishing and politics and telling anti-Russian jokes. It was like living on a set for *Cabaret*. This realization struck me explosively one summer afternoon in 1981 as I cycled in the warm sunshine through the golden cornfields near the village of

Buchholz outside East Berlin, and inspired to song, found myself
singing the old Nazi song from the beer-garden scene in the film:
'The sun in the meadow is summery warm, the blossom embraces
the bee . . . but somewhere a future awaits unseen; tomorrow
belongs to me.' But it did not. Nor did it belong to Alex and
his friends. For they were hostage to a lie. And they knew it.

# 6

# *The Communist's Tale*

If East Germany was a prison camp for most of its population, there were others who were not unhappy with their lot. There were even volunteers.

The big man with the thick, jet-black hair and the neat beard would roll into Metzer Eck late most evenings, take his place at the regulars' table and accept the brunt of most of the jokes for the next several hours. Alex Margan was his chief tormentor, and great friend. The big man's name was Hans Busch. And he was an exception at Bärbel's *Stammtisch*: a communist. He worked across the road at a home for apprentices in the print trade, who came from all over East Germany and lived there five days a week during training for jobs in the state-run press. It was a responsible job. There were sixty-eight apprentices aged between sixteen and nineteen, who lived in dormitories on four floors, two for the boys and two for the girls.

The home was owned and operated by *Neues Deutschland*, the main newspaper of the Communist Party. It was a secure life. The trades unions were run by the government, which was also the employer, so if conditions were bad and wages low, at least there was job security – at least for those who toed the party line – and no risk of one side forcing the other to accept new technology, which would bring the return obligation to find jobs for those made redundant. It would have been too complicated, had it not anyway challenged basic principles, such as the dignity of labour and the much-vaunted right to work. This latter had the result that everyone had a job, no matter how useless or demeaning, while the managers were content to draw their own salary and not think about improvements that could create unemployment. Anyway, why bother? The practice of the right to work had ensured that human labour was the cheapest component in any production line. Efficiency was measured purely in political terms.

Hans Busch did not see it that way at all. East Germany had its faults but it was a society on a human scale, restricted in some ways, as he would concede to the gleefully nodding Alex, but free from the pressures of the capitalist rat race. He was happy with his life. He had to be; unlike everyone else around the table, he had chosen it. Busch was that rare thing: a defector from the West.

It was a long story, he always said. In reality it was quite a short one, but hard to drag out of him. It began, and you had to begin with real roots, he said, with a certain Polish nobleman, a Count Wranitzky, who had a passion for gambling and adopted a German 'von' to his name when he came to visit the casinos and elegant hotels of the Rhine resorts in the 1920s. Unfortunately the count's enthusiasm for the fast life and ladies of Weimar Germany was not matched by his skill at gambling. He quickly fell into debt. Luckily he hit on a solution: an auction. In a brief afternoon's work, with some smart bidding, he raised ten thousand marks – by selling his title.

But even that did not last forever. The Wranitzky family's existence was chaotic, very much hand-to-mouth. The ex-count's daughter, Liselotte, learnt her lesson. When she grew up she became a committed communist. It was not a hard decision anyway for a girl of obviously Polish extraction in the increasingly polarized society of Germany in the 1930s. Slavs were more welcome among the communists than among the Nazis. And she could model herself on the most famous woman of the German Left, Rosa Luxemburg, also of Polish origins, who had been murdered in 1919 by the Freikorps, the right-wing paramilitary organization, only two weeks after she had been a founder member of the German Communist Party.

When Hitler came to power Liselotte, like the rest of her comrades, went underground. But with the outbreak of the civil war in Spain she enlisted in a secret force of couriers involved in smuggling funds and information across the border to the International Brigade. It was an occupation that inevitably brought her to the attention of the Gestapo. But she was warned in time and demonstrated her resourcefulness; she got married. Her choice was perfect: a staid, conservative, nationalist tradesman called Hinnerk Busch, twenty years older than her, not a Nazi but safe enough for the Gestapo to decide her past might be excused as girlish folly and leave her to get on with producing sons for the Führer. This she did, though she was damned if she would let him have them.

The Busch family lived outside the small town of Leer in East Friesland, close to the Dutch border. It was not an easy childhood for young Hans. His mother was bored by the small-town atmosphere and despised the bourgeois life and the Nazi rule that had carried them into war and made them hated by their Dutch neighbours. There was also a double set of prejudices to conquer; the East Frisians are the Irish of Germany, which is to say that other Germans brand them stupid. 'Leer' is also German for empty; and for Liselotte Busch the town was empty by both name and nature.

Hans was born at the beginning of the war and stuck out like a sore thumb in the village. While almost all the other children were blond, he was more Polish-looking than his grandfather had been: large, black-haired and with high, Slavonic cheekbones that argued an ancestry from even further east than Warsaw. Even after the war, when it was no longer wise to boast about who was and who was not pure Aryan, Hans's striking dark good looks made him the brunt of playground bullying. With the Nazis defeated, the strains on his parents' marriage of convenience began to tell more clearly. Even in middle age Liselotte Busch had lost none of her communist idealism and she looked with fascination to the new socialist state being created on German soil. It was, Hans later reflected, quite clearly only a matter of time before her curiosity won out.

At the beginning of August 1956 Liselotte took the sixteen-year-old Hans, already a hulking youth, and his sister, both of whom had embraced her enthusiasms, leaving a more cynical elder brother behind with their father, and set out on a hitchhiking tour to the new world. They took lifts from Leer to the next town of Emden, then to Bremen and finally to the big city of Hamburg, where Liselotte had contact addresses from her old days, of communist cells that had revived since the end of the war. They welcomed her with open arms as an old comrade and agreed enthusiastically with her plans.

On 9 August Liselotte and Hans took bicycles supplied by the comrades and set out to the town of Lauenburg on the south-eastern border of the *Land* of Schleswig-Holstein. From there they left the road and began cycling by the side of the main Hamburg–Berlin railway line. Before they knew it they were halfway to Boizenburg in what had been the province of Mecklenburg but was then Schwerin administrative district of the German Democratic Republic. 'I remember when we came across the first border guards. They were all smaller than me,' recalled Hans later.

'Escapers' from West to East were a rarity but not completely unknown in those days when shifting populations were still a comparatively recent memory. Partly as a retaliatory boast, the East German government had set up its own, albeit little used, reception camps. Liselotte left Hans in one and went back – they had only two bicycles – to Hamburg to fetch his sister. They embraced the new, communal, collectivist life wholeheartedly. They first went to a reception centre in the village of Warin near one of the many small Mecklenburg lakes. From there Hans separated from his mother and sister and was sent off by train to a training home, such as those he was later to run, in the woods of Thuringia. The craft taught there was forestry. It appealed to Hans enormously, as did the life in the home. It was a classic romantic setting, deep in dark pine woods amid the rolling foothills of the Harz mountains, which rose to the west.

To a boy raised in the drab lowlands of the north-west, the Thuringian forest was fairy-tale Germany and the leaders of the home told the trainees that they were on a magical mission to create the first truly fair, egalitarian society in German history. 'It was like a bug,' Hans later recalled, 'if you caught it, it was irresistible.' It was a passionate political enthusiasm that incorporated a spirit of adventure, of adolescent togetherness, creating a new sort of society. Being a communist and a teenager in a new state had the same sort of attraction as being in the scouts or volunteering for work on an Israeli kibbutz. There was also the added zest that although political indoctrination was strict, it was the only morality that counted. The leaders had a *laissez-faire* attitude to sex between comrades. 'We thought we invented free love,' boasted the older Hans, 'but look how much it's cost me,' he laughed at fifty, detailing the expense of maintaining six children by four women.

For the adolescent Busch the argument that communism was being enforced by the Russian army of occupation was hollow.

All of Germany was under occupation and each side had merely imposed its own system on the territories it ruled; the fact that the British, American and French systems were all compatible did not mean that they were necessarily any better. They too had not exactly been invited into the country. Whatever the scale of the internal resistance, left alone the German people had chosen Nazism. It was also only natural that the Russian communists should help their German comrades, by force of arms if need be. The links went back a long way. The Germans had, after all, been the first to try to follow the example of the 1917 Russian Revolution to the extent that Berlin had been on the brink of civil war. The new East German state was keen to portray itself as the republic that might have been formed had the 1918 revolution in Germany been successful.

Rosa Luxemburg's friend and ally Karl Liebknecht, who was murdered with her in 1919, had been in close touch with Lenin and throughout the interwar period Stalin had supported the struggle against the Nazis. Moscow had been actively supporting plans for a revolution in Germany in the early 1920s at much the same time as Hitler was involved in the failed Munich beer-hall putsch of 1923. Wilhelm Pieck, who had been named president of the new German communist state, had spent long years in the Soviet Union, even before the war. Pieck's son had joined the Soviet army but he himself was able to construe Soviet involvement in German affairs as aid to the communist state rather than the *de facto* annexation it would become. It may be wondered if the truth dawned on Pieck when he received letters such as those from the father of Horst Klohs, who found the cause demanded too much blindness to too much pain.

But for young Hans Busch the new East Germany was excitement. As a communist from the West he found himself in a position where he could be a self-professed revolutionary and still join the establishment. On his eighteenth birthday he left the apprentices' home and went to the administrative district capital, Gera, to volunteer for the *Bereitschaftspolizei*, the wing of the police that dealt with public order. It was an alternative form of military service. It also gave him the chance to see a bit more of his new, limited Fatherland. Within eighteen months he had been posted to the industrial city of Leipzig, Erfurt, the pretty medieval capital of old Thuringia, and the stately city of Schwerin in the north.

But Hans had retained his enthusiasm for the more relaxed form of camaraderie; he had fallen in love with a girl from the West. To his own astonishment, his superiors had a quick answer: early discharge from duty. 'Why?' he asked, with the wounded pride of the volunteer who is told he is not good enough. 'Your liaison is a security risk,' was the blunt reply. It caused his first moment of doubt.

Prematurely forced to think about what he would do with the rest of his life, the young Hans toyed with alternatives to the career in forestry that had seemed so predetermined. He considered being a butcher or a bricklayer, or even working on one of the new collective farms. In the end it occurred to him that what he had enjoyed most about communism was the communal life in the apprentices' home. He would study and become a teacher in one of the homes that were being set up across the country to provide vocational training for the new generation of skilled workers who would build the new, socialist Germany out of the ashes. It was indeed a brave new world.

He spent three years studying the vast range of subjects required for anyone who was to be in charge of young people, even though he would only be supervising their free time: German, history, chemistry, woodwork, Russian. He was no linguist, but worked hard to master the language that to him was not the alien tongue of the conqueror but the vehicle for a new ideology, the language in which Lenin had written works that were building blocks for a new world order. He had to choose a special topic: either 'Art in the USSR' – 'Iskusstvo v SSSR', he proudly recalled more than thirty years later – or 'Lenin in October'. He studied both but got a lower than average mark.

But Hans had other successes. His sultry looks, sturdy physique and lively humour won him a string of girlfriends. In Germany, as never in Russia, sex was considered ideologically safe. Some accused the communists of building on the *Kraft durch Freude* (Strength through Joy) philosophy of the Nazis, which had encouraged Aryans to breed; some said only that they corrupted an ancient Germanic hedonism. Hans left the analysis to others, and devoted himself to the practice. In double-quick succession he married and had a son, then divorced, fell in love again and got engaged, his girlfriend producing another son before they split up. He went through the same routine again: another girl

and another son. It was what he called later, likening himself to
the young Goethe, 'my *Sturm und Drang* period'. It was also time
he got a regular job to pay the eighty marks a month maintenance
to each mother.

His first full-time job was in a home for girls studying agri-
cultural science; then he moved to a home for problem teenagers
near Berlin. At short notice the head of the home left and Hans was
offered the opportunity to take over. He was delighted. When it
was pointed out to him that, although it was not strictly necessary,
it might be a good idea if he formally joined the party, he readily
agreed. He had hardly realized he had not done so already. In
1967 he married his second wife, Petra, who began to correct
the imbalance of his earlier life by bearing him three daughters.
He cut an unorthodox figure in the staid world of communist
functionaries; he affected cowboy boots and a jacket with fringes.
But he was popular for that very reason among the young people
in his care.

Hans's second moment of doubt about the communist society
he had opted to join came in 1970, when he had word from his
brother in Leer that their father had died. He applied for an exit
visa to go to the funeral, but was turned down. Several years
later he applied again for permission to visit his brother and was
surprised to be allowed to go. He stoically refused to take the
cynical view that the state was calculating on him repatriating
some of his hard-currency legacy.

But the biggest test of his allegiance to the cause was yet to
come. He had chief responsibility for the teenagers' recreation,
but there were problems in getting equipment. In particular he
wanted to organize weekend excursions, to take these city-bound
youths camping and sailing, yet there were more requests than
facilities. Hans hit on a solution. When the kids went for their
work experience at a textile plant they would put in extra hours
and in return the factory would make them tents. It was a great
success, and soon supervisors from other homes heard about it
and asked to borrow the tents. At first he agreed. But the tents
were treated with the same regard as all 'socialist property': scant.
They came back torn and dirty. After that, he refused. The tents
were not listed on the inventory of the home. He hid them in the
attic and used them only for his charges. All was well until they
decided to grandify the home by naming it after Rudi Arndt, a

hero of the anti-Nazi resistance, and party functionaries carried out their own inventory of the premises.

It was as if they had discovered espionage equipment. Comrade Busch was accused of concealing for particular use property owned in common. Arndt's widow made a fuss. There was a party inquiry at which Busch had to appear, answer for himself and receive the black mark on his party record that would hinder promotion. He told himself he did not care. He did not want to be promoted anyway. But he was wounded by the stupidity of it all. Shortly afterwards he had a mild heart attack and was moved to a 'less taxing' position as a subordinate in the Neues Deutschland home in Metzer Strasse.

It was one of those incidents that he and Alex could agree on, though it rarely cropped up in conversation. Alex, the occasional Catholic, and Busch, the off-duty communist, would compare the process of self-criticism and 'voluntary' confession in the party to the medieval church. 'You're right,' Hans acknowledged, 'communism is a form of lapsed Christianity. That, of course, is why I believe in it.' We laughed appreciatively; the advantage of living in a dictatorship was that it improved the calibre of pub repartee.

That was the sort of comment Hans would make in defence of their society. For him, communism provided a simple, secure existence within recognized bounds and with largely laudable aims, even if the means occasionally fell short. For an essentially wise, good-humoured, sensual man, it was a difficult dichotomy: on the one hand his own experience and common sense told him the system was inefficient and the party rotten from the core out; on the other, the weakened idealist, still inspired by the vision of a better world that had been held out by a mother-figure who seemed a distant, romantic heroine, still wanted to believe he had moral superiority even in saloon-bar arguments. His eyes twinkled, his tongue darted in and out of his cheek, as his heart tried to advocate the faith his mind had rejected.

Mostly he played his part as the butt of Alex's anti-communist jokes, but every now and then they would lapse into serious political discussion that ritually ended with Alex giving the table a disgusted slap and leaving it with a shrug and an apocryphal 'Na, Freunde . . . Well, friends.' This, to those who knew the well-rehearsed format of these arguments, signified: There you have it then. What can we do with a country run by blockheads who won't even listen to the force of rational argument? He would then go back behind the bar, to the relief of waiting, thirsty customers. Pouring the beer was a form of therapy. So was drinking it. Life had become a waiting game; except that no one was expecting anything to happen.

# 7

## The Smuggler's Tale

Manfred Schulz was perfectly happy that nothing should happen. He had always distrusted events; they had a nasty habit of taking a turn for the worse. Manfred, or Manne as most of the regulars in Metzer Eck knew the lugubrious, obese character wedged in the corner with a tumbler of schnapps, was the improbable disc jockey at Alex's special parties.

He was a formidable collector, of just about anything: stamps, postcards, foreign coins in small denominations (large ones were too valuable not to realize on the black market), beer mats, china cups and, most importantly of all, records. It was the passion of an overgrown schoolboy, for whom material objects had taken the place of affection. Life had not been good to Manne Schulz. His obesity, a largely genetic problem, had made girlfriends a rarity; his one permanent relationship had produced children but ended in divorce. He lived an essentially lonely existence, in a semi-permanent state of familial hostility with his elderly grandmother, who had been more than a parent to him all his life. He was a Berlin character, a quintessential figure from one of the turn-of-the-century caricatures by Zille, the artist so beloved by Alex.

Alex had hit on the ingenious idea of making use of Manne's dedication to Western pop music by employing him as an added attraction. Particularly whenever there was a wedding party, but also when some state functionaries wanted to let their hair down behind closed doors – even if it involved dancing to music illegally taped from the American Forces Network – Manne was the man. He would come to the bar early, install himself in his regular seat before a formidable array of more or less antiquated valve amplifiers, tape decks and turntables, have Bärbel's son Horst, who worked behind the bar on his leave from military service,

91

hoist speakers on to shelves, and set to work. His special delight was to insert into the programme, without introduction, the latest piece of Western provocation, such as West German pop star Udo Lindenberg's ode to Erich Honecker – sung to the tune of 'Chattanooga Choo-choo' – and watch the dancers falter. There were rarely complaints. Alex's mix of banter, rhetoric and freely flowing beer and sausages was one that even the most die-hard *apparatchik* was reluctant to jeopardize.

Manne lived only a short staggering distance from Metzer Eck. Just as Bärbel's family had always lived above the pub, so his family had always lived in Strassburger Strasse; at least, as long as he could remember, his grandmother had, and that had made it the family home. Of course, she had not always lived there. She was a real 'Eastie' – '*ein Ossie oos Russland*', as he put it, from Russia – a Volga German.

Even Manne, the archetypal Berliner, had a story that was rooted in Germany's troubled history. His family album, had it still existed, would have offered a geography lesson for students of Eurasia, a witness to the political consequences of a continent that, instead of ending, evaporates into Siberia. His grandmother knew all about it once; she had been there. Sitting in the front sitting room of their ground-floor flat in the autumn of 1990, gazing through the curtains at the shuttered windows of the house opposite – only days earlier unmasked as the luxuriously equipped headquarters of a firm acting as a cover for the defunct Stasi's attempts to import illegally high technology from the West – she tried hard to penetrate the veil cast by more than seven decades that separated her from her childhood in Tsarist Russia.

'I don't remember now where I was born.'

'Oh yes, you do, grandma,' interrupted Manne. 'You were born in Zielona, in Russia.'

'Ah, yes, that's right,' she smiled vaguely, her vowels rounded, her consonants clear, each 'g' a proper 'g', not the sloppy 'j' ('y' sound) of Berlin dialect, but the deliberately schooled German of those who had lived far beyond the Fatherland's fringes. The old lady creased her wrinkled face and drew, as if from the depths of her soul, with a smile of tired self-satisfaction, the phrase '*Dobry vyecher*', and asserted: 'That means "good day" in Russian.' It actually means 'good evening' but it would have been an unnecessary act of cruelty to correct her.

Emma Wiese was born in 1909. Her father was a coffin-maker and general carpenter in the tiny village of Zielona in the Russian-ruled Ukraine. They lived as Germans among Germans, speaking their own language and dealing with the natives only when they came to order a table, or a box for their loved one. That was what the Germans had always done in the Russian Empire: made the bits that worked. It was the First World War that spelt disaster for their quiet world.

'When the war broke out, they suspected us, the Russians did. We were a security risk. We were sent away, east, far to the east,' she recalled, gazing as if through a dark glass. 'On trains, I recall, always on trains. Too many trains, too many trains in my life.' The trains took her and her family into internal exile, Russia's time-honoured way of dealing with potential enemies by absorbing them deep within her empty vastness, losing them in the frozen bowels of the state: Siberia. For two long, hard years the Wiese family found themselves isolated from humanity in the crowded European sense that Germans understood. They were not quite compatriots, not quite enemies, in a landscape of exiles and descendants of exiles, the bits of society that Russia found hard to swallow. It took Lenin to liberate them.

In 1917, as the revolution spread from Petrograd, the city the Wiese family and the other two million German inhabitants of Russia still baulked at calling anything but Sankt Petersburg, the restrictions of war evaporated overnight. Russia had other things to think about than the future of its scattered German minorities. The situation was too uncertain as Red and White armies manoeuvred across the steppes. The family headed west again, and this time kept going, through Russia proper and a Ukraine in ferment, back across the undefined line that separated real Europe from the part that petered out into Asia, back into Germany. But it was an alien fatherland, a country they only half understood, a Prussian empire preening itself on having implanted the disease of revolution in the heart of its enemy, only to find that it had contracted the contagion itself.

Wilhelm Wiese settled his family in the tiny village of Koprieben in Prussian Pomerania, safe within the boundaries of even the emasculated Reich that Germany had become. They felt safe at last, incontestably within Germany and much better than those left stranded in East Prussia by the corridor cut through the territory of the Reich to give the recreated state of Poland access to the Baltic Sea. 'I remember it well. The church was next to a pond and we went in up rickety steps. We went to school there, me and my sisters Sophie, Marie, Anna and my brothers August and Wilhelm, the oldest, named after our father. There was another boy, Fritz, but he died as a baby.'

But in such a small village carpentry could not long support a large family. The bright lights beckoned. By the time the girls were teenagers, Emma and one of her sisters had been found places in domestic service in Berlin. For some of the family, however, enough was enough and agriculture and village life were preferable to the uncertainty of the big city. They remained in Pomerania, even when the winds of a new war buffeted their lives. One branch of the Wiese family had put down roots. It resulted, after 1945, in their becoming Polish.

Emma became a housemaid to the Nikolaus family in Berlin's Kniprodestrasse in Friedrichshain, the district immediately east of Prenzlauer Berg. They seemed rich to her, but in reality were only comfortably-off tradesmen, running a fruit and vegetable store in the great, noisy, smelly, bustling market hall on Alexanderplatz, the vast square where the trams turned, named after a Russian Tsar; to Berliners, it was just the 'Alex'. To make a few extra pfennigs Emma worked in the evenings behind the bar at a little beer stand in Schöneweide, out in the eastern suburbs.

This was a period of rapid expansion for Berlin as industry continued to concentrate on the Imperial German capital. Schöneweide was a *Gartenkolonie*, a little area of allotments and elaborately fixed-up sheds called *Lauben* where the better-off workers and some of the middle classes spent their weekends (a custom that persists in Berlin today) pottering among the vegetables and pretending they were on their country estates. 'When they all came out of the nearby dancehall, they would come and buy a few beers at the stall I worked at. It was a few pfennigs cheaper, you see. There was also custom from the steamers that ploughed up and down the river, packed with sightseers. But I suppose it's all gone now?'

'Oh, yes, all long gone,' nodded Manne with the overweening wisdom of the younger generation.

# THE SMUGGLER'S TALE

It was there one spring evening in the late 1920s that Emma
Weise met the man who would become her husband: Alfred
Pflaum, a strapping lad who took a fancy to the pretty girl behind
the counter and helped round up the glasses for a free beer or small
schnapps and an excuse to make conversation. They married on
New Year's Eve 1930 in Belforter Strasse, in Prenzlauer Berg,
under the shadow of the great nineteenth-century water-tower
that dominated the 'Schlachtviertel' (a district full of street names
commemorating the Franco–Prussian War of 1870–71) from
Strassburger Strasse to Kolmarer Strasse. They moved into a small
flat in Metzer Strasse and then, in 1935, round the corner into
a four-room flat in Strassburger Strasse, where Emma would
spend at least the next fifty-five years and bring up a family and
a half.

Alfred was a cobbler. It was a good trade and enabled Emma
to leave service with the Nikolaus family and work fulltime with
him in the shop, at first in a semi-basement in Metzer Strasse, then
in the front room of the new flat. 'The door was here, opening on
to the street,' said Manne, showing the corner of his bedsitting
room in 1990. 'And here, roughly, was the tile stove, and here
were grandad's machines.' Emma and Alfred did not then have
the whole flat; accommodation was short in Berlin even in the
1930s. One of the rooms was let out. They had four children,
one of whom died in infancy. The three survivors were Fredi,
Pauline and Brigitta, Manne's mother.

The war was slow in coming to Berlin. But when it came, it
was with a bloody vengeance. The first British bombing raids
on Berlin took place in the spring of 1942, and soon gathered
momentum. It was a merciless game of tit-for-tat, but no one
pretended it was fair. It was war. The Germans had got in the
first blows at London in the Blitz of 1941, but now, as the
British began to wreak nightly revenge on Berlin, Goering's
Luftwaffe was too occupied with the crumbling attack on Russia
and the faltering siege of Leningrad to offer any real retaliation.
The battle over Berlin each night was almost the reverse of
that fought over the skies of southern England a year earlier:
now it was small squadrons of fighters battling merciless air
armadas.

Kurt Wyberneit, who grew up to be an accordion player,
composer and regular in Metzer Eck, could recall the horror of

those days. 'We sat together, me and my mother, listening to the dire formal words on the radio: "Warning: raiders approaching. Direction Hanover, Brunswick, Magdeburg." It was sinister, the direction like a clear, straight arrow pointing at Berlin. Then we began to hear the bombs fall and feel the house shake. It was especially hard for my mother because we had just heard that my father had gone "missing" at Stalingrad.'

Emma Pflaum and the children were evacuated to the country-side near Bitterfeld, outside Leipzig. Alfred was at the war. He considered himself lucky; he was in the SS: 'Leibstandart Adolf Hitler, no less,' mused Manne with that mix of pride and shame that only Germans can feel about their forefathers' war record. Alfred's record was harmless. Not all SS men had either the gruesome task of guarding concentration camps or the bloody glory of the élite guards regiments. Alfred was in France, plying his trade as a cobbler. 'After all,' as Manne put it, 'someone had to mend the jackboots.' He had what his wife would call 'a good war'. He came home in 1946, safe and sound, his only injury a slight, by then long-healed, shoulder wound.

Emma and the children also came back unharmed from evacu-ation to the ruins of Berlin, only too glad to see their home still standing. 'My God, we'd had enough,' the old lady recalled, her lined face drooping like a sad cocker spaniel's at the welter of memories, 'fleeing here, fleeing there. Trains again, always more trains. They were the worst times, and I've known bad times.' For her, in 1990 aged eighty-one, it was already clearly difficult to tell the difference between the evacuations of 1915 and 1942. There was only the memory of packed trains grinding slowly over war-scarred countryside, squalling children, old men and tired mothers.

They reopened the cobbler's shop, too happy that they still had accommodation and the basis of a decent living to worry about which of the former enemies' occupation zones they lived in. In 1948 their daughter Brigitta, just sixteen, met a young man, scarcely older than herself, an apprentice painter named Günter Schulz who worked with a private firm painting bridges. Within three years their first child was born: Manne. The following year they got married but lived with Brigitta's mother until Manne was two and the next child was on the way. At that stage the KWV (*Kommunale Wohnungsverwaltung*), the communal accommodation administration, in its bureaucratic wisdom granted them a one-room flat in the north of Prenzlauer Berg, in Senefelderstrasse, a small street that led off the main thoroughfare, its name already changed from Danzigerstrasse to Dimitroffstrasse – the ancient Hansa port swopped overnight for a Bulgarian communist as a sign of the brave new world. But Emma's flat was still home.

The shock of the events of 1953 had been a brutal demonstration of a reality that they had not fully understood, so that Günter's firm began to look more and more for jobs in the West. Living conditions at home were tough enough already. In 1956 a second boy was born, Rainer. Brigitta lived in one small room with the two children and soon was pregnant with a third. There were inevitable rough arguments. When he was old enough – five or six – Manne would take himself off early in the day back to grandma's. She put up a bed for him and, often enough, he would stay the night. To let his mother know where he was – neither she nor grandma had a telephone – he would pop in to 'register' with 'Uncle Paul' Unterbäumer, who ran a *Kneipe* across the road. His mother would call from a public telephone box for reassurance when she noticed he was missing again. It was Uncle Paul's bar that became the Stasi cover firm when the state in its wisdom began to put pressure on private enterprise.

Grandfather Alfred also eventually – though only in 1958 when he was fifty-eight – gave up the unequal struggle to maintain a private business in a society where the government was trying not to encourage small traders but to squeeze them out of existence. He gave up the shop and moved to the new cooperative, named with exquisite bad taste Production Comradeship 'Hans Sachs' after the cobbler in Richard Wagner's *Meistersinger von Nürnberg*. It was the sort of toytown obeisance to traditionalism that the communist authorities thought would inspire the proletariat. At first 'Hans Sachs' had a branch in Prenzlauer Berg. Then it was centralized further into a large, factory-style shoe-repair operation in the northern suburb of Pankow. The idea was 'progressive', Soviet-style; the logic, simple: why have lots of small independent shops wasting equipment all over Berlin when there could be one central repair point? The result was a bureaucratic log-jam, with shoes entering a repair production line only to come back weeks later, if at all, haphazardly repaired by anonymous workers for anonymous clients whose only recourse to complaint was to write a letter to 'Hans Sachs', where it was filed with the others by the newly necessary complaints department.

That same year Manne's father followed his boss to West Berlin, where they had found regular jobs that paid a multiple of what they received in the East. His mother stayed in Prenzlauer Berg for another year until he had found them all somewhere to live. By that stage, however, Manne was living more or less constantly with his grandmother and well settled at the old redbrick, nineteenth-century school by the water-tower. He stayed where he was. No one insisted he should do otherwise. They were wild, unrestricted years for an eight-year-old boy. With his dog Lumpi he wandered through the backstreets all over Berlin, knew every piece of waste ground, every underground and overground station. He went at least twice a week to his parents, now living near the old Tempelhof aerodrome in the south of the city. The biggest blow to his world was not his parents' moving but the death of his dog. The animal had been sickening and his grandparents could scarcely afford to feed it well, let alone pay for medical treatment. Alfred took it quietly one day to be put down. When he came home he told Manne the animal had run in front of a tram; at least that way they could share the tears.

Manne continued his after-school explorations of the backstreets of his city, now with the added excuse of visiting his parents down in Tempelhof. Just before Christmas 1960 he was stopped by an East German customs official at the sector boundary because he was carrying a great cast-iron cooking pot.

'Who are you? Where do you think you're going with that?'

They were stupid questions, for which the small boy standing in the bitter December wind had a ready answer: 'I'm Manne. This is a cooking pot. I'm taking it from my mummy to my grandma.' Only the insanity of a city divided by alien powers could have provoked the situation. The guard inspected the interior of the cooking pot for contraband, lifting the heavy lid to discover: 'Christmas biscuits'. For no good reason the boy was held for half an hour, until one said: 'Oh, for God's sake, let the little fellow go.' There were rules about moving foodstuffs across the sector boundary, but only from East to West.

But there were other things to be moved. Manne's parents had been forced to leave most of their few valued bits and pieces in the East. There were no restrictions on people crossing but they could not have taken their radio, their kitchen equipment, their few bits of furniture. The answer was deceptively simple. They had friends living in Sebastianstrasse in the south of Mitte district, right on the sector boundary. Here, as in Bernauer Strasse in the north, the dividing line ran along the front doorsteps of the houses. The houses were in the Soviet sector, the street outside the door in the American sector. So Manne helped his parents go visiting. They moved their possessions one at a time to the back door of their friends' house, then, perhaps half an hour later, out through the front door. As soon as they stepped on to the street they were in the West, only a short walk from the U-Bahn station at Moritzplatz and a short ride to Tempelhof and their new home. The paraphernalia of a home, the little things that counted to his parents, made an impression on the young boy: 'My mother took the sewing machine, my father took the stamp album.'

(In the summer of 1990 I drove around the area where Sebastianstrasse had once been. I had been there before, in 1981, and seen the frontier line no longer made out of houses. They were long demolished, like those in Bernauer Strasse, and in their place was the familiar ten-foot Wall with its rounded top, designed so that its circumference was too large and smooth for an arm to gain a grip. In 1990 the Wall had gone, as had the concrete sheds of the Heinrich-Heine-Strasse checkpoint. The floodlights were extinguished. There was nothing but a great desolate emptiness, awaiting the contractor to restore life.)

On the night of 12 August 1961 Manne had been with his grandparents to see his father and mother. The grown-ups had all had one or two schnapps and a glass or two of beer, so they came home relatively late, after midnight, changing underground trains as usual at Stadtmitte for the line north to Senefelderplatz. They noticed nothing unusual and were soon fast asleep in bed. It was at seven o'clock the next morning that the neighbour, pressing endlessly on the doorbell, woke them all and told them to put the radio on because the world was coming to an end. Like almost everyone else in Berlin, Manne's grandparents rubbed their eyes and refused to believe the impossible. For him, however, anything was possible. He was ten and the world was a giant adventure playground, even if the risks were real.

As his grandparents sat glued to the radio, and arguments about what it meant, who was responsible and how long it would last echoed up the dark, dank stairwell of the crumbling tenement block, Manne dashed out into the suddenly sinister sunlight. Oderberger Strasse was only a few minutes' run away for a small boy. There, where Oderberger ran into Bernauer Strasse, he saw with his own eyes what his elders refused to contemplate: the barbed wire pulled across the street, the men with guns and stern unsmiling faces. Alex Margan and Heinz Herzberger were standing only a few yards away, but young Manne did not yet know the two serious-looking young men. He turned away. Then he turned again, took a right, then a left and went up another side street to where the work was already done and a high barbed-wire fence blocked the way to the identical-looking street beyond.

Manne examined the fence closely until he found what he was looking for. Without a second thought he was through a boy-sized gap and off to tell his parents what had happened. Of course, they knew. They were delighted to see the boy and wondering how to tell his grandparents he was safely through when he disappeared – to tell them himself what he had done. They did not know when they would see him again, though he managed one more trip through the wire near their friends' old home in Sebastianstrasse. But the shock was total: 'We Berliners could hardly believe it. That I couldn't see my brothers or my parents any more. We couldn't even call them up. Even if we had had a telephone.'

It was Christmas 1963 when the first agreement was signed to allow West Berliners to visit relatives in the East; visits the other way were out of the question, except for pensioners. Manne's mother arrived with tears in her eyes and an armful of Christmas presents. Now twelve, he was delighted to see her, but had no regrets about staying with his grandmother. 'It was as if it had been meant to turn out like that,' he would say as a grown man. 'Yes, I knew I'd be stuck with him,' grinned his octogenarian grandmother. Two years later, in any case, Emma reached pension age and both she and Alfred, by now increasingly frail, could travel when they wished.

Not everybody got used so quickly to the unnatural amputation of West Berlin from the rest of the world. Among those who found it most difficult were the inhabitants of what they thought were the city's outermost suburbs: small villages that had gradually been linked with Berlin by the city's sprawl in the 1920s and 30s. Although they were physically linked, they were bureaucratically still separate entities, outside the lines drawn by the councils to delineate Greater Berlin. So when the Wall went up, they were left out in the cold. It was particularly brutal in the case of the districts of Teltow and Kleinmachnow, in effect no more than extensions of south-west Berlin. But with the Wall, they were suddenly, ludicrously, given the status of rural villages, dependent on nearby Potsdam and sealed from the districts of Berlin from which they had grown, like hands severed at the wrists and left uselessly hurting only inches away from the stumps. They had their share of victims. It was one night, early in 1982, that Hannelore, Bärbel's waitress at Metzer Eck, told me the story of her Uncle Eberhard, nicknamed Pieps.

Pieps lived in Teltow. He had been sitting with two friends as usual in the bar they had had to get used to since the Wall cut them off from their local. It was a quiet night as usual since there was no longer any through traffic, for their street ended in barbed wire, a fence and searchlights. It was as if conscious of a malign fate that one of the three stood up and said: 'This is bloody useless. Let's go for a drink at Franz's.' And the others followed him into the night, with Pieps, half-drunk and totally bamboozled, a few steps behind. Franz's bar was half a dozen streets away, but it might have been a million miles. In between lay the 'death strip'. 'Don't you remember the fucking frontier?' he shouted. But they had remembered it. Indeed they had been planning for the moment when they would make their run for freedom, summed up by the right to drink in whatever pub they chose.

They had planned the escape, not the moment. The moment had chosen itself. As they approached the barbed wire the pair suddenly dived for a hollow in the ground, a section they had surreptitiously snipped away. Within seconds they were through and running like the hounds of hell for the fence and vaulting over as the spotlight from the tower whizzed around towards them but caught only poor Pieps struggling with the barbed wire, trying to follow them but hopelessly stuck, unable to see how they had got through. Just as it seemed he might have found a hole big enough, two crashing rifle shots rent the air, and splintered the bone in his leg. The people in the pub watched silently when they took him away.

He was taken to Rummelsburg, the strict-security detention centre in the south-east of Berlin, where East Berlin's death throes would also rattle a quarter of a century later as the protesters from the streets of Prenzlauer Berg, myself among those caught in the net, were driven into the yards and where a few months later the tyrant Erich Honecker himself would spend a brief time. Pieps was sentenced to a year's imprisonment; but when he emerged it was not only as a political misfit with a mark on his identity card that doomed him to menial work, but as a cripple, one leg an inch shorter than the other. Hannelore's family shunned him; her father was in the National People's Army. Pieps was an unwelcome embarrassment. He was forgettable. But his niece remembered him.

The Wall, like all monstrosities, became mundane. Its existence became part of the everyday reality. Manne Schulz grew up with his split family and his divided city as facts of life. He hardly thought about them. Little people did not make history, they experienced it. Insofar as he thought about it at all, that is what he believed. At fourteen he began work as an apprentice electrician, but it did not quite work out. He became a gardener, or at least a garden labourer. But that did not quite work either. He helped his grandmother in her housework as they took in lodgers in the room that had once been Alfred's workshop and would one day be Manne's adult home. They piled in four or five beds and registered with the state as a lodging house so that they could accommodate the itinerant visitors from the curious world that eastern Europe had become: low-level trade representatives from Vietnam or Mongolia, or Polish labourers working on restoration sites.

'Once we had all of eighteen Poles sleeping in this one room; there were beds stacked everywhere,' Manne recalled, gesturing around the four walls where he now housed his record and tape collection and two video recorders, the first fruits of German unification. 'They were here to do shopping. Compared to Poland, you see, we had it good here. They would come into our shops, down at the Alexanderplatz, and grab the goods before we had even had a chance to look at them. If we complained they would shout at us, "You Nazi, you fascist."'

'It was hard work,' Emma remembered, 'worst of all when they only stayed one night and we had to change the sheets every day.'

'It was no hotel though,' put in Manne, 'they had to clean their own shoes.'

In 1986 Manne got a job stacking shelves in one of the sparsely stocked supermarkets, arranging rows of dusty packets of Soviet instant potato, bottles of Bulgarian tomato juice, jars of Polish beetroot and crates of Berliner Pilsner. He developed a taste for the beer and grew fat, indeed obese, though it was primarily a genetic problem. I once overheard him discuss with his equally enormous father the problems of getting one's knees beneath the water in the bath.

Alfred had retired but the family found life difficult on two pensions and what Manne could contribute. Just as in George Orwell's *Animal Farm*, the state found it hard to keep its promises of a life in clover for those who had exceeded their usefulness. Pensioners in their thousands took advantage of the rules that let them spend thirty days a year in the West. Some just indulged in small-scale smuggling, but many opted to stay and receive the much higher West German pension to which they were automatically entitled. East Germany was rapidly becoming a land without old people; for the young it created a curious perception of a long life's struggle to obtain an exit visa. But it looked good in the international demographic statistics, especially as it seemed West Germany was becoming a land of the old.

Alfred and Emma were not inclined, however, to leave. In any case they had Manne to look after, even though he was now a teenager and bigger than both of them. Alfred got a job as doorman at the Friedrichstadtpalast, the slightly sleazy variety theatre near the River Spree in what was left of Berlin's heart on the eastern side of the wall. Manne would come regularly to see him and was fascinated by the glittery world backstage of acrobats and showgirls. The entire cultural mêlée of eastern Europe passed through 'Democratic' Berlin. There were jugglers from Hungary, singers from Bulgaria and once, a memory that stuck with Manne, a whole theatre troupe who came and stayed in his grandparents' flat: 'Teatro Fantasia Constanta', he recalled, a fragment of adolescent enchantment still to be glimpsed in his middle-aged eyes. It was a temporary transformation of their little

flat amid the smoky tenements of Prenzlauer Berg into an offshoot
of the glittering world of the theatre. Romania sounded as exotic
as the Caribbean.

From shelf-stacker Manne moved on to labourer on the lorries
that moved the goods to be stacked on the shelves. That was not a
great success either. He lasted only nine months. By 1970 Manne
was nineteen and a big, burly man with a barrel chest and belly to
match. He had become one of the regulars at Metzer Eck, famous
for knocking back *Korn*, the traditional favourite North German
clear schnapps. He would drink it in hundred-gram measures,
jovially referred to as '*sto gram*', the only bit of Russian most
East Germans could remember from their compulsory lessons at
school.

In November that year he was taken on by a small firm, still
in private hands despite the growing difficulties placed by the
state in the way of private enterprise, making asphalt to fill the
potholes in the road. It was the toughest of manual labour, out
on the streets in all weather. His job was to mix the asphalt. Even
twenty years later, he could still remember the formula: 'For four
tonnes of asphalt I had to pour in three hundred and fifty kilos
of bitumen and sixteen-hundred kilos of ground chalk, then fill
up each with gravel and turn on the machine that mixed it. In
each shift we used two tonnes of asphalt.' The firm did relatively
good business because the roads were in such poor condition. In
fact, they did so well that the state decided it would no longer
take 'No' for an answer and forcibly nationalized it as 'People's
Own Enterprise: Street Maintenance Company'.

Manne stuck it out mixing asphalt on the streets of Prenzlauer
Berg for ten long years, growing larger all the while. He met a girl
called Karola Bieski and got her pregnant. The child was a boy and
to signify the changing times they decided against any traditional
German names and called him René; the daughter that followed
was Bianca, not after Mick Jagger's wife but after a one-hit-wonder
West German pop singer. Regulations governing visits from West
Berlin had become less strict after the four-power agreement of
1970 and Manne's brother Rainer now came regularly to see him.
He had good reason. They had worked out a useful arrangement:
Rainer had bought a diesel Mercedes that ran on the same fuel
as the heating in the offices of Manne's street-mending firm.
Each time he came over he carried four thirty-litre canisters in

the boot and Manne filled them up. It was hardly theft, scarcely even dishonesty; it was only the state's property and God knew the state had enough. Didn't it own everything in the end, even the people?

The customs officers ignored the canisters; the only contraband they were really searching for was hidden human beings. In return, like a European merchant prince trading with aboriginals in Africa or America, Manne's brother gave him the trinkets of the West: pop records, music cassettes. 'It wasn't really business,' said Manne, 'more a form of barter.' But the idea was already there – in fact he had grown up with it – that so long as this preposterous system and cynical division existed, it was the right – nay, the obligation – of the sensible citizen to make what he could out of it.

In 1980 Manne took critically ill with a perforated appendix. Because of his obesity, however, what should have been an urgent but simple operation became a major surgical task. No sooner was the appendix removed and the wound sewn up than the stitching failed. Then he suffered a rupture. In the end he needed a total of seven operations and was ill for seventy-eight weeks, long enough for his sickness pay to expire. He was still scarcely fit to return to mixing asphalt, but he had only two choices: to return to work of some sort or run the gauntlet of red tape in an attempt to be declared an invalidity pensioner. To take a pension was to take a colossal cut in wages, but it meant freedom from the one right guaranteed to citizens of the German Democratic Republic, the right to work, and its corollary: that not to work was a crime against society punishable by imprisonment. But the invalidity pension also carried one inestimable perk: a passport. It took visits to three doctors and a thorough examination again by the hospital and the state organization known as the ABK (*Ärtzliche Beratungskomission*), an advisory panel of doctors who made the decisions on who was and who was not fit to work.

At last, in December 1981, they gave him the crucial piece of paper. There followed three tense months while the bureaucracy went through its paperwork paces. In February Manne received the certificate declaring him a pensioner; with that he went to the police and applied for a passport. On 17 March 1982 – the date is inscribed in his mind – he was summoned to the police station and presented with the document that to an East German was solid gold: a passport, with an exit visa valid for up to thirty days in a calendar year.

'It was a Wednesday. I went to the police, collected the passport, went to the hospital to collect spare bandages for my wound, which was still suppurating, then jumped on the train and went to see my mother.'

Manne's parents had moved by then to another flat in West Berlin's Charlottenburg district. It was a large flat, on the first floor, but in a nineteenth-century building that in almost every respect was identical to the one in Strassburger Strasse where his grandmother still lived, except that the lights in the stairwell worked and the walls had been painted. Breathing heavily from a mixture of excitement and exertion, he panted up the stairs and rang the doorbell. His mother, by then already suffering badly from arthritis, pulled herself to the door and opened it. 'Here I am then, Mutti,' he said.

But he could hardly wait to get back. For Manne, it was the start of a new life. Until then he had been distinguished in the bars of Prenzlauer Berg only by his obesity. I had met him for the first time in Metzer Eck a few weeks before he received his passport. The change, that little time later, was remarkable. By midnight that night he sat at the *Stammtisch* surrounded by listeners. Alex was there, and Bärbel, her fifteen-year-old daughter Kerstin, and all the host of regulars – Bernd, Uschi, Ulla, the workers and the artisans, the heavy drinkers and the poseurs – all hanging on every word as Manne, overnight Man of the World, showed off his digital watch, handed out a few spare disposable cigarette lighters to grateful clients and told story after story about the Kurfürstendamm – where he had been only for a few brief minutes – and KaDeWe, the Harrods of West Berlin – where in fact he had only glanced at the pop records – and the street stalls full of fruit and flowers and vegetables, and the stereo systems and the videos and the porno shops. Manne was a star. Manne was in business.

Now that he could travel he was inundated with 'small requests'. Could he perhaps just manage to bring over a pair of football boots for a son's birthday, or a music cassette for a daughter, or even a cassette recorder, and how big was a video recorder anyway? There was cachet to be gained to saying 'yes' to a few, but bad feelings to be provoked by saying 'no' to others, and only chaos to be reaped by agreeing to all. Business was not only financially sensible, therefore; it was the only solution. Apart from anything else, he only had thirty days a year. They had to be husbanded carefully.

In May I met Manne for lunch in West Berlin. It was the first time I had been with someone from the East recently allowed into the West. I had expected wide eyes and wonderment, and was quietly disappointed at the measured calculation, the petty concern for the precise cost of items that to me were mundane. It was the same concern, however, that the entire population of East Germany would display in the first few weeks following the euphoria of the opening of the Wall in November 1989: the concern to make the best of what they could purchase for the limited amount of money at their disposal. The West was not just to be wondered at; it was to be dissected and as much of it taken home as possible, in case it might not last.

Manne asked me to bring back a few 'bits and pieces' from his parents' flat. As a correspondent I had a special 'preferential treatment' pass which gave me and my car immunity from searches at the Friedrichstrasse/Zimmerstrasse crossing point (known in the West as Checkpoint Charlie), the only road by which non-Germans were allowed to enter or leave East Berlin. It was, of course, at best an abuse of my status, at worst possibly illegal, to bring gifts destined for East German citizens that might normally incur the punitive duty imposed by the communist authorities to prevent too much of the 'cheap attractions' of the consumer society slipping over. That did not seem good enough reason to refuse to bring over presents from parents to their son; especially when I saw what they were, the second-hand electronic goods that any Western family get through over the years: an old toaster, a digital clock-radio in which one of the liquid crystals had gone on the blink, a ghetto-blaster that was too large for the latest Western fashion. In his parents' flat these things were beginning to gather dust in cupboards or in his brothers' bedrooms; for Manne they were status symbols.

There were a few other things too that his brothers slipped him, that he brought over himself: well-thumbed, hard-core pornographic magazines wrapped in plastic bags. These he smuggled through with ease by slipping them down his trousers, secured with the bandages that supported his swollen stomach. It was still a wound that would put off investigation by all but the least squeamish of customs officials.

He developed another trick. It was possible to buy Western cigarettes in East Germany. They were available in the hard-currency shops at prices that were equivalent to duty-free, in other words some twenty-five per cent cheaper than in the West. But they were also – particularly Marlboro, which were made under licence in Moldavia in the Soviet Union – to be had for East German marks, albeit at over seven marks a packet, almost double the cost of the best East German brands. Manne did his sums, however, and worked out that a carton of two hundred would cost him about seventy-five East marks, but at the black market exchange rate, which at that stage was roughly five-to-one, that was the equivalent of only fifteen West marks, whereas he could easily sell them to his brothers in the West for twenty-five marks, giving them a substantial discount on the West Berlin shop price of about forty marks, and him a profit of ten West marks, which was equal to fifty East marks, or half a week's wages for a waiter. The profit on two cartons gave him the equivalent of a week's wages.

'I can remember the first time I tried it,' he told me. 'In theory we were only allowed to take out one bottle of schnapps and one carton of cigarettes, but in practice they didn't care about us taking out anything that was not in short supply in the East. So I took three cartons of cigarettes in my duffle bag. By the time I got over I was still sweating just a little, so I stopped at a bar on the way for a West-beer. And when it came to pay for it I sold two of the cartons to customers in the bar.'

Although it was theoretically possible for him to convert his West-mark profits back into East marks at any bank or *bureau de change* in West Berlin at the five-to-one rate (it was, however, illegal to bring East marks into the East), that never occurred to him. It was better business by far to buy pre-recorded Western pop music on cassettes, bring these back to the East, copy them and sell the copies for twenty East marks each. It was a flourishing business, in addition to which Manne's collection of Western pop music became legendary in East Berlin. He bought a tape-to-tape recording deck to make the copying easier, and also a Western turntable and record-player, had speakers built to order in the East, which he paid for in Western currency, and before long he was set up as a disc jockey, running a disco for parties in

Metzer Eck and, as his fame spread – strictly by word of mouth – for other bars and private parties. He took care, of course, to remain strictly an invalidity pensioner; the loss of his pensioner status would have meant the end of his business.

Manne's popularity brought him a girlfriend, the first he had had since splitting up from the mother of his children. And he was still swamped with requests to bring over items from the West, by people who had the money, often in hard Western currency, but lacked one essential: the freedom to go over and buy for themselves. Manne had a virtual monopoly. It was clearly time to branch out. He discovered a loophole in the practice of the customs regulations. Whereas any goods considered 'high technology' brought by hand across the frontier attracted punitive duty, often as high as two hundred per cent, it appeared that anything sent through the post was ignored, as long as it was not on the list of forbidden goods: pornography, newspapers and magazines that might contain information contrary to that approved for release by the party, as well as audio or video cassettes that might contain pre-recorded Western propaganda. These were faintly ludicrous restrictions in a society where everyone watched Western television.

For Manne the loophole was both a revelation and a business opportunity. He tested it by sending himself a new cassette deck. To his astonishment, it was delivered within a week with no problems. He picked it up from the central post office and took it home, delighted not just with his new purchase but with his new scheme. He had hit on the solution. A quick tour of the major West Berlin electronic shops produced a bundle of hi-fi catalogues. Armed with these, he soon turned his room in the flat in Strassburger Strasse into a mail-order centre. Like country folk in some remote village queueing at the mobile shop, East Berliners given the nod by reliable friends came to Manne to browse, choose and order. He became an expert, advising on the relative merits of Sony versus Schneider, of separate-component hi-fis against compact systems. He knew by heart the last posting dates for Christmas.

For his customers he had a few simple rules: pay in West marks – or East marks at the going black-market rate – and add the cost of postage and packing, plus ten per cent for his efforts, paid in advance and with no guarantee of delivery. They had also to give him a name of a possible sender from West Berlin; they could give him a real name or invent one, but he could not put his own name on each parcel; there was no point in playing into the Stasi's hands. But no parcel ever went astray. To be sure, there were those who resented his ten per cent. The indoctrination of the communist state created a certain antipathy towards entrepreneurism, that feeling, experienced sometimes even by consumers in the West, that the middle man was making easy money. It was a sentiment easily given the semblance of moral authority in a society where buying and selling at a profit was actually a crime. But even those who affected to disapprove of what they half-jokingly, half-scornfully referred to as 'Manne Schulz GmbH', would often come to him secretly when it got round to birthdays or Christmas time.

In pure business terms Manne made a pretty moderate profit, considering that he had to spend several hours of his precious thirty days a year allowance in the West picking up the goods from the shop, wrapping them, addressing them and carting them to the post office. But for Manne travel to the West was no longer an end in itself, merely a means to an end, which was to support a decent standard of living for himself and his grandmother in the East and, perhaps more importantly, create a niche for himself in the society in which he lived. A misfit for too much of his life, he had finally arrived. The only thing that could go wrong was if they pulled down the Wall. And no one expected that would ever happen.

# 8

# *The Story of the Roofer*

### The Little Fable, by Franz Kafka

*'Ach,' said the mouse, 'the world is getting smaller every day.
At first it was so big, I was frightened; but I ran further and
was happy to see, far in the distance, walls to both left and
right; but these long walls came so quickly together that now
I am already in the last room, and there in the corner stands
the trap I am running towards.'
'But you only have to change direction,' said the cat, and
devoured him.*

The gods first elevate those whom they wish to destroy. On
a balmy, spring-like day in September 1987, East Germany's
diminutive dictator stood in Bonn, at last on equal footing
with his rival, Helmut Kohl. It seemed the climax to Erich
Honecker's career. In Bärbel's sitting room, above Metzer Eck in
East Berlin, the Margan–Falkner family watched the television
uncomprehendingly. Alex tutted aloud.

The two men were like contrastingly awkward allegories of
the Germany each represented. The Chairman of the Council
of State, Chairman of the National Defence Council, General
Secretary of the Socialist Unity Party of Germany, stood, small
and pinched-lipped but militarily rigid, as the brass band played the
anthem of the German Democratic Republic. He did not sing, of
course; there were still those difficult lines about 'Germany, unified
Fatherland'. But his very presence here had surely given the lie to
that. Next to him, large and ungainly, stood the portly figure of
Helmut Kohl, Chancellor of the Federal Republic of Germany,

aware that he was following the best cautious political advice in receiving this arrogant little man who symbolized the division he hated. But he could still feel the ghost of Adenauer frowning over his shoulder. The mass-circulation pop daily *Bild* screamed with banner headlines an all-too-conscious parody of Adolf Hitler's catchphrase: 'Two hymns, two flags, one Fatherland!' An old lady in the crowd, asked if she knew who the little man was, tutted impatiently: 'Of course, he's the Führer of the Zone.'

Back in the 'Zone', the regulars at Metzer Eck would have agreed with her, had they been able to hear. Instead they were puzzled as to why this was happening, why even West German television seemed to be singing the praises of a man they regarded as their jailer.

For an Englishman to understand how a German of Honecker's generation, or even that of Kohl, twenty years younger, felt that crisp September morning requires a leap of the imagination. Picture, if you can, a post-holocaust England defeated and divided, with Durham as parliamentary capital of a re-emergent industrial North, while a war-devastated, impoverished South-east is ruled from the remnants of the City of London as a one-party socialist state headed by Arthur Scargill. A wall of barbed wire and watch-towers has been erected along a line from the Wash to the Bristol Channel to prevent escapers to the freedom of the North. West London, from Oxford Street to Hammersmith and Wimbledon to Wembley, is an enclave in a hostile state of fellow-countrymen, suddenly a million miles from Westminster, Wapping, Bromley or Bow, boroughs of the new English Democratic Republic. Now picture Arthur returning up North on a state visit to his home town of Barnsley.

It seems a joke, but it was a terrible, black practical joke on all of Germany: a farce written in blood. Its props were the Wall, the guards and the guns; and the row of wooden crosses commemorating those who had died. Londoners nickname their socialist inner-city councils 'The People's Republic of Islington', or 'Red Brent', and joke about never crossing the Thames, while New Yorkers have their East Side and West Side, Parisians their Left and Right Banks. Berliners used to make similar jokes about 'Red Prenzlauer Berg' or living 'j.w.d.' (pronounced: yot vay day: a slang acronym made famous in a Marlene Dietrich song and meaning *'janz weit draussen'*, Berlin dialect for 'out in the sticks'). But the jokes lost their punchlines when they became a lethal reality.

The effect on many Germans in 1987 of seeing the Bonn Chancellery fly two national flags, each red, black and gold, but one adorned with the communist puppet state's hammer-and-compasses device, can only be compared to how many Englishmen might feel seeing the House of Commons draped with two familiar Union flags, but one with an additional hammer and sickle, or swastika, depending on your generation, for the insult was not the political orientation but the sight of one's national symbol stamped with the mark of an alien power. In Bonn the scrawl on the wall opposite the Chancellery defined it: 'Betrayal'.

Throughout Honecker's five-day trip to West Germany security was as great as it had been for Ronald Reagan and would be for Mikhail Gorbachev. Yet the emotions evoked by this curious visit – 'official' not 'state', the Bonn chancellery officials took pains to point out – were more subtle, more complex, more tortured. Helicopters hovered overhead and thousands of police lined the streets as Honecker was whisked past in an armour-plated Mercedes. The crowds were curious rather than enthusiastic or hostile. The visit enabled the idealists of German unity to remind the average Westerner of the hole in his heritage. All the television channels carried extensive reports throughout the week from Leipzig, Rostock, Schwerin – cities once as familiar to Germans in the western part of the country as Canterbury or Dover to Yorkshiremen but, with the years, increasingly faded from the collective consciousness.

In unlovely industrial Wuppertal, heart of the Ruhr, East met West in caricature when the drab but dapper Honecker was confronted with his nemesis in the gangling figure of Udo Lindenberg, at forty-one a rock star past his best, pointedly proclaiming the power of rock'n'roll to overcome barriers. Lindenberg had revived a flagging reputation at the expense of the communist state six years earlier with a top-twenty hit entitled 'Sonderzug nach Pankow' (The Special Train to Pankow), a reference to the East Berlin suburb where the party élite had their homes. Manne Schulz had played it to discomfit junior party bureaucrats dancing with their girlfriends at Metzer Eck. It was sung to the tune of 'Chattanooga Choo-choo', and the key to its success was a lavatorial note that went down well with an East Berlin youth that was overdosed on orthodoxy: '*Honi, ich weiss, Du bist ja eigentlich ganz locker, tief in Dir drin, bist Du heimlich auch ein Rocker, Du ziehst Dir ganz heimlich auch gerne mal die Lederjacke an, schliesst Dich ein auf das Kloh und hörst West-radio*' ('Honi, I'm sure you're not really so uptight; deep down inside you're a rocker all right. And secretly you put on your leather jacket, I know, lock yourself in the loo and listen to West radio').

It was a scene even the most dour of teenage *apparatchiks* could associate with and a weapon for those who baited them. Lindenberg had made the record as a protest when he was not allowed to perform in the plate-glass Palace of the Republic on East Berlin's Karl-Marx-Platz. It ended with the line, in sonorous Russian: 'After all, comrade Erich, the Supreme Soviet has no objections to Lindenberg doing a concert in the GDR.' Lindenberg, as fate would have it, was right. East Germany had taken its ideological isolation to extremes that were all the more preposterous given that each and every East German teenager listened to the American forces radio station or the pop programmes of West Berlin's German stations.

As a 'spontaneous' event it was well organized. Security ruled out surprises. They were an odd couple: the puffy-cheeked, straggly-haired singer in pinstripe suit, open-neck red shirt and blue eye shadow, and the diminutive, stiff, elderly autocrat muttering awkward thanks for Udo's gift of a guitar. Both seemed embarrassed. Mostly the background music was a cacophony of shouts: 'The Wall must fall,' from the conservative Young Union and 'Long live' chants from a Communist Party delegation, usually few in number but their apparent strength inflated by a forest of red banners as 'Erich the Red' turned to greet them for the benefit of his own television cameras, playing the game, even though most East Germans watched West German channels. The communists sang pre-war working-class ballads: with one per cent of the vote in West Germany, communism was more nostalgia than politics.

But the Germans who lived under the reality watched as live coverage fed discussion panels in which those who thought the Honecker visit was the beginning of a new era of *détente* argued with those who thought it was dangerous approval of the *status quo*. In reality it was neither: just an odd trick of fate, the tense calm of logic and pragmatic politics before the unimaginable, unanticipated, storm of a revolution that no one knew was brewing.

It is hard to tell in retrospect which straw played the largest part in breaking the camel's back. As Honecker preened himself in Bonn, behind the Wall in East Berlin there were lumps in throats that had little to do with pride; seeing Moscow's number one lackey was surely only tolerable if treated as a joke. Part of the irony was that Honecker was going home. For the first time since moving to Berlin in the 1930s to agitate for the communists – and end up imprisoned by the Nazis – he was about to pay a sentimental pilgrimage to the tiny, grimy villages of the Saarland where he had grown up, played in trade union bands and sold on the streets the pamphlets of the red revolutionaries who were the Nazis' chief rivals. On the road into town a cigarette hoarding proclaimed with unconscious irony: 'Test the West.' Within two years it was to be the most fortuitous cigarette branding in German history as English-speaking television cameramen from around the world looked for a focus for a cheap and easy symbol of the collapse of Erich Honecker's world.

But that misty autumnal afternoon, in Wiebelskirchen, the little industrial dormitory town, Honecker's sixty-seven-year-old sister Gertrud had baked a cake. The old redbrick family home, painted lime green, had stood under police guard for forty-eight hours in advance – just beforehand protesters had built a symbolic paper wall across the front door. The house took pride of place on the itinerary: the Friedrich Engels house in Wuppertal, the Karl Marx house in Trier, the Honecker house in Wiebelskirchen. The implication was that it was ready for its own plaque, when Gertrud would bequeath it to the German Democratic Republic. No one there that day thought she would outlive her brother's country. The rest of the town's enthusiasm was part tongue-in-cheek, part local patriotism. Across the road, a Czech *émigré* sold Honecker-pizza; in the bar next door Monica Hartmann put on a red dress and waved her advert for a 'Honny cocktail' of local kirsch and the aptly named Gorbachev vodka. 'Honny' waved back before posing with an apple for a snap-happy policeman. You could taste the dash of Gorbachev.

But it cut no ice at home. In Metzer Eck the regulars were gathered as usual around the *Stammtisch*. Manne sat with his usual '*sto gram*' tumbler of *Korn* as Alex launched into a teasing diatribe against Hans Busch: '*Na ja, na ja, schon gut.* OK, OK then: let us drink to the wisdom of our political leadership in this historic hour of reconciliation between the German people and the German people.'

'Yes, let's,' said Hans warily, worried as usual that he was walking into a trap.

'Good, cheers to Helmut Kohl and the Christian Democratic Party of Germany,' said Alex, raising his glass, with a cackle at his own mischief. Hans put his glass down firmly with a look of disapproval, then grinned and drank anyway: 'At least they've learned to be reasonable.'

Alex nodded solemnly: 'Yes, we must not underestimate the impression made on Honecker by his lowly upbringing. Indeed he was so impressed by his childhood poverty that he created a country to perpetuate it.' Bärbel roared, and so did Hans, and ordered beer all round. The conversation lapsed again into the banter of people whose feelings are expressed in undertones and asides because their everyday reality is a tissue of lies. What they did not know then was that one day soon they would confront it head-on and the tissue would be torn apart.

No one knew it at the time. History, it seemed, had been taken out of the hands of the common man. Politics was a sport for professionals. The superpower stand-off negated action. Nothing was more wrong. But all that the Metzer Eck regulars knew for certain was that East Germany had failed as a concept. On rainy, cobbled 1930s streets inertia had conquered history: nineteenth-century tenement blocks still echoed to the clank of ancient trams; the railways were still called the *Reichsbahn* and car number-plates still followed the pre-war system, and indeed were often affixed to pre-war cars. Barbed-wire and electric fences, the trappings of a police state, negated attempts to forge a national pride. The majority of East Germany's citizens still considered it a Russian-occupied zone.

Over after-hours schnapps in the pre-dawn twilight, Dieter Kanitz, the plump, jovial barman who in 1981–2 had sold badges of the banned Polish free trade union Solidarity like a surreptitious dealer peddling the drug of freedom, told his version of the story of the Pied Piper of Hamelin: 'It went like this, you see. Down at the Communist Party offices they had a plague of rats. Along came a little girl who said she could get rid of them if they would promise her whatever she wanted. They agreed. So she took a clockwork mouse and trailed it behind her; all the rats followed to the river, where she kicked the mouse in and they all drowned. The delighted communists asked her what she wanted. So she told them: "A clockwork Russian soldier." Ha, ha, ha,' he would boom, not caring whether his hearty laugh would turn the heads of comrades at the counter. They knew how hard it was to find a place to drink.

As their television screens showed Honecker gloating in his underdog's triumph in Bonn, his reluctant subjects back in Berlin were only too aware that this latest phase of East–West *détente* had not changed the fact that there were still three hundred and eighty thousand Soviet soldiers in East Germany. What Honecker did not realize, however, was that since the elevation of Mikhail Gorbachev to supreme power in the Kremlin, the Russians were no longer seen by Alex and his fellow reluctant compatriots as the prime instruments of repression. The elderly cabal of Honecker and his colleagues in the politburo had become the focus of a resentment that was sharpened by their refusal even to contemplate reform.

The splash made by Gorbachev in Moscow had begun to send ripples through Hungary and Poland. Dieter's ancient Solidarity badges were now collector's items; the latest fashion was badges of Gorbachev labelled 'State enemy number one'. The East German leadership, along with that of the even more ruthless dictatorial regime of Nicolae Ceausescu in Romania, was deliberately refusing to see the changes that were coming. Even on a personal level, despite the curiously passionate-seeming comradely kisses that the two men exchanged on airport-runway greeting ceremonies, Honecker did not like Gorbachev. Honecker was twenty years Gorbachev's senior; there was a generation gap. He was so used to being a loyal servant to more elderly masters in Moscow that he found it difficult to take this relatively brash young man seriously.

He could dismiss Gorbachev's talk of reform as a purely Soviet matter. The theory that, thanks to the silver tongue of Soviet Foreign Ministry spokesman Gennady Gerassimov, would within two years become known as the 'Sinatra doctrine' – letting East European countries go their own way – seemed to Honecker, insofar as he believed it was genuinely meant, not necessarily a bad thing. He would use it to avoid reform. It was an attitude that contained more than a hint of the German superiority complex.

Honecker knew the Soviet economy was a shambles. But he refused to believe that that of East Germany was in a similar state.

Nor did he ever seem to understand what he had become to East Germans: a figure of hatred, the leader of a regime that refused to wear a human face. Over almost four decades the communist rulers had, he felt, adapted enough, altering its style and strategy in an attempt to win the loyalty of its citizens. At first the 'workers' and peasants' state' of the Stalinist Walter Ulbricht attempted a blitzkrieg against the past. The old Hohenzollern royal palace in the centre of Berlin had been badly damaged by allied bombing raids but was not substantially worse off than many of the surrounding buildings in the old imperial city centre. It could have been restored, albeit at great cost, as was the squat, ugly cathedral, the Berliner Dom, next to it, although that took forty years and had to be paid for largely by generous aid from the churches in the West.

For the Ulbricht regime, however, the Hohenzollerns' palace was a monument to Prussian militarism and was demolished. The vast expanse where its neo-baroque courtyards had stood became a car park for a country without cars. It was aptly renamed Marx-Engels-Platz. And, in a curious political double take, the communists at the last minute relented, if only to save a section of the stone façade containing the window from which the Kaiser had watched military parades and waved to the crowds. It became a preposterously pompous and incongruous frontispiece for the uninspired slab thrown up opposite its old site to be the office of the Chairman of the Council of State. But he never appeared on the balcony. Bomb-damaged streets were razed and drab blocks of pre-assembled flats hastily built. A main avenue was rebuilt as a virtual carbon copy of Moscow's Lenin Allee and briefly, embarrassingly, named Stalinallee. After the dictator's death it was renamed Frankfurter Allee, because it was the main road out of Berlin to the small town of Franfurt-an-der-Oder, now on the Polish frontier. Alex, who knew the road well, joked: 'Who succeeded Stalin? Frankfurter, of course.'

East Germany had tried to tell the world it had experienced an economic miracle of its own; the impression was successfully created that the land of the champion sportsmen also had an economy that was at least ahead of most of the communist world.

The Russians looked on in wonder; the East Germans knew only that they worked hard. And they despaired when they compared it with the soaring affluence of those who had had the simple good fortune to be on the right side of the line when the curtain fell. It took three decades for the communist leadership to realize that Germans did not want to become Russians. It would take less than a year for the myth of the 'functioning socialist economy' to be exploded by the cold light of unification.

Towards the end of the 1970s Honecker had a sudden change of heart. East Germany, he decided, needed a soul and that meant history. Overnight a bronze equestrian statue of the Prussian king Frederick the Great that had been removed for safe keeping during the wartime bombing and subsequently left lying in a corner of the old king's palace at Potsdam, was reinstalled triumphantly on Unter den Linden. Restoration work began on palaces and churches. It was an attempt to find something to bind East Germans together, a surrogate nationality that was other than 'great German' but had more substance than the official 'DDR-Burger' (GDR citizen).

East Germany was geographically similar to the rump of the old state of Brandenburg-Prussia, but the name of Prussia was tainted with militarism. Honecker's regime tried to get back into what they felt they could salvage of Germany through the back door, praising social reformers, literary figures and architects. Frederick the Great, it was overnight remembered, had not just been a warrior prince, but a man of letters and friend of Voltaire, a classic figure of the intellectual, tolerant Enlightenment. It was like putting Georgian pillars on a bungalow. A statue of the nineteenth-century social reformer Freiherr von Stein was allowed to remain in a prominent position outside the starkly modernist Ministry for External Affairs. Visiting West Germans who had long been burdened with the psychological problem of reconciling their own past between poets, philosophers and Nazi barbarism, were shocked to discover the East claiming sole rights to the better side of the national soul: Goethe, Luther and Handel claimed exclusively by the communists. It was as if English communists had claimed ownership of Shakespeare, Wesley and Elgar and denied the middle classes access.

When new banknotes were issued Goethe featured on the twenty-mark note with a 'socialist schoolroom' on the reverse, while the medieval leader of the peasants' revolt, Thomas Münzer, appeared on the five, backed with scenes of combine harvesters. The message the masses were supposed to understand was: 'See, we have carried history to its logical conclusion.' Other banknotes were given over to revolutionaries: Clara Zetkin on the ten, Friedrich Engels on the fifty and Karl Marx on the hundred. Nobody minded that Marx, like Honecker, came from what is now West Germany. It was an attempt to inject Frankenstein's monster with a soul. Predictably, it did not work.

Nor did the attempt to create a hedonistic, classless society. The Free German Youth, with their blue shirts and camp-fire songs, were strict on adherence to socialist discipline and relaxed about sexual morals at the holiday camps. Here again a totalitarian regime sought to draw benefits from a cult of the body, as the Nazis had done in the Strength through Joy movement. But it was precisely in this materialistic world that differences from the West were the critical factor. East Germans could have beer and sausage from stalls in the street and nudist beaches on the chilly shores of the Baltic, but it was not the same as holidays in Spain, Beate Uhse sex shops in the high streets and the best-stocked supermarkets in Europe, all of which had become the norm for the working class in the 'exploited' western half of Germany. But complaining was done only in known company. The Stasi showed themselves more brazenly than the KGB; their raincoats were more identifiable and the service was more chillingly efficient. Ghosts of the Gestapo lingered, in both memory and practices. It was one of Alex's favourite old chestnuts that the 'brown plague was replaced by the red'.

The communists' chief priority was to contain the damage threatened by those it could not convert. The main method of dealing with dissidents who could not be scared into silence was a one-way bus ride to the West. When the Berlin singer-songwriter Wolf Biermann strummed his guitar and sang 'I am the Prussian Icarus', about a young man who flew over the Wall, the party let him out, but not back again. But he continued to sing to his countrymen in the East on West German television. Those who remained were forced into extreme caution.

Dissent, like everything else in the curious East German half-state, mirrored attitudes in its bigger brother to the West. Thus in the early 1980s the main East German opposition to the government was a peace movement with the Biblical motto 'Smite your swords to ploughshares', which was used on a controversial cloth badge sewn on denims as a symbol of dissent. In other words, at the same time as the opposition in the West, both the marchers on the street and the parliamentary opposition in Bonn, were badgering the Christian Democrat government about its decision to accept new American cruise and Pershing-II missiles, the underground opposition in East Germany was mimicking it, through a glass darkly.

Similarly, when at the end of the 1980s the new craze in the West and focus of opposition to government-establishment policy had become concern for the environment, those who in Poland or Czechoslovakia were openly anti-communist became in the GDR 'Greens'. It mattered not a jot that in the West the Greens and the Left were more often allies; the enemy was the establishment. In the cellar of the parish church of the Zionskirche, a dark, brooding, nineteenth-century Gothic church that was actually in Berlin Mitte but annexed in East Berliners' popular conception to the revolutionary Prenzlauer Berg, was an informal 'ecology library'. In the bleak repressive years that preceded the 1989 revolution, this was a centre of freethinking in Honecker's tightly controlled world.

It was, in theory, a reading-room dedicated to environmental issues. But on the walls were pacifist posters, cuttings from smuggled Western newspapers and, in big red letters, a quotation from the communists' martyr, Rosa Luxemburg: 'Without unrestricted freedom of the press and association, life and public bodies perish.' The latest joke was that Honecker had become a supporter of Ronald Reagan's Star Wars programme – as the first man to shoot down a sputnik. Kurt, a bright young student with round, wire-rimmed glasses and black beard, rolled a cigarette and described the Honecker clique as paranoid: 'They have removed five Soviet films from the list of those allowed on our screens, but the joke is that their fear of the Gorbachev reforms is greater than our belief in them.' Even so, the effect of reform in the lion's den was insidious; one or two of the young men sported perestroika badges from Moscow's unofficial art markets more boldly than they had once passed Solidarity badges from hand to hand. Yet Walesa was still a hero, and on the walls were pictures of mass rallies in Gdansk, as a reminder of how others dared protest. Upstairs, under cover of attending an art exhibition sponsored by the parish, sixty young people sat drinking Hungarian wine in an earnest forum on how to avoid military service and whether they should send letters of support to a jailed Bulgarian pacifist. Posters attacked Nicolae Ceausescu for his plan to demolish Romania's ancient villages, but also, implicitly, his and Honecker's mutual support in vetoing political change.

The ecological movement was certainly a mirror of the West, but it was, if anything, cause for even greater concern in East Germany. It touched a raw nerve to accuse the regime of salvaging an economy that it claimed was a Marxist success story by acting as a paid rubbish dump for the West. Thomas Welz, a member of one ecology group, summed it up: 'Nothing is more feared at present than cultivating an awareness of real problems.' Huge factories had been built for burning imported waste and tips for burying it. 'They have nothing to sell, refuse to change their ways and are reduced to making money by accepting other people's rubbish,' said Kurt. It was a pigeon that would come home to roost after unification, when the West German taxpayer who had paid to ship his rubbish to the East found he had reinherited the cost of cleaning it up.

Axel Grote, a regular at Metzer Eck, was a television producer, and as such obligatorily a card-carrying communist, who had nonetheless tried to make his job meaningful by tackling real issues. Over a beer he showed in despair the documents that detailed his year-long fight with the censor over a programme discussing the pollution of forests and lakes north of Berlin. The battle seemed to end with permission to show the programme, but the decision was reversed two days before the broadcast date. Instead the viewers saw a recording of Demis Roussos, the Greek singer, in concert. For the next year Axel had permission, in theory, for a programme called *Freedom and Democracy*. But he mused that it would probably end up the same way. He little thought that within two years he would film the definitive documentary on the fall of the Berlin Wall.

The communist authorities tacitly acknowledged their captive population's nightly emigration to the West in the privacy of their homes. American and West German views of the world penetrated the Iron Curtain on the ether. East Germans watched *Dallas*, *Dynasty* and *Black Forest Clinic*. In token retaliation the party broadcast its own series, *The Black Channel*, to explain away the 'false propaganda' of Western news bulletins. Its presenter was a classic communist aristocrat, a white-bearded, well-groomed television personality, modelled on an American chat-show host. His name was Karl-Eduard von Schnitzler and he was universally despised as the lying voice of the lying system. He was reputed to be inordinately wealthy, even by Western standards, had Erich Honecker's ear and a liking for the high life that he satisfied by exploiting party privilege. He was known to drive expensive cars and sleep with a large number of expensive, pretty and very young women. He was also the subject of an obscene little ditty, which Alex used to sing gleefully late at night: '*Siehe de Arbeiter- und Bauernsohn, Karl-Eduard von Schnitzler: die linke Hand am Mikrofon, die rechte Hand am Kitzler*', which translates roughly as: 'Behold the workers' and peasants' son, Karl-Eduard von Schnitzler – he keeps one hand on a microphone and the other hand on a clitoris.'

But Schnitzler was just a fig-leaf. Everyone knew the antennae of the population were turned to the West. Western television was a double-edged sword for the communists; even though the display of the riches of the capitalist world could encourage dissatisfaction, the box in the living room was also a panacea: those who could emigrate in their armchairs each night might be less likely to risk their lives. In the end the party admitted as much by taking the calculated risk of permitting cable to bring in Western television to Dresden, nicknamed 'Tal der Ahnungslosen' (Valley of the Clueless), which had been unable to receive it because it lay in a valley. It was an ideological cop-out: soap on the box instead of in the shops.

But in his daily life the average East German was never allowed to forget that he lived in a province of a foreign empire. In the dreary rebuilt centre of bombed-out Dresden the hotels for holidaying trade unionists and party functionaries were named after Leningrad and the Neva, the latter not just the river the city stands on but the scene of the Russians' famous fourteenth-century victory over the Teutonic knights on the ice. Right up to the end the marks of the *Imperium Sovieticum* were everywhere: until the last few weeks before the Berlin Wall was opened there were more red banners in Honecker's Berlin than in Gorbachev's Moscow. 'Long live our socialist fatherland,' they preached in vain. Then the Camel cigarette hoardings came to replace them.

Yet the fact that the state had been a failure did not register particularly strongly in the West until almost its very end. The climate of optimism showed most clearly during the East German leader's visit to Bonn in the tabloid press's attempt to build a wish upon a prayer when Honecker suggested 'one day' the inner-German border could become like that between East Germany and Poland. It was a double-edged comment: the East German–Polish frontier, running as it did through land that had once all been German, had been deliberately hailed by the communists as a 'frontier of peace', but in reality it had been closed to most East Germans since 1981 to prevent the risk of contamination by Solidarity's disease of democracy. 'Our borders can come down,' screamed the headline in West Germany's *Bild*. But the other side of the proffered coin should have been an unpleasant afterthought that largely failed to occur to the popular press: in his analogy with Poland, Honecker was not offering steps towards reunification but rather *de jure* recognition of partition and separate national status for the citizens of the GDR; he was asking for recognition of the division of Berlin.

It was a calculated statement designed to strike a chord. The East Germans had identified in the West an insidious tendency to see the *status quo* as immutable and therefore something that had to be lived with. This was the case particularly among the Social Democrats, whose Ostpolitik of reconciliation under Willy Brandt had been based on making the best of a bad job and dealing with Moscow on a pragmatic basis rather than sticking to an ideal of unity that was a foolish pipedream. Four decades of partition had led many to argue that dialogue was the only alternative to total estrangement, indeed that German division was the best solution for Europe, in that it made Germany acceptable to her neighbours east and west, and, to some more importantly, prevented the economic miracle creating a new industrial superstate based on a bourgeoisie that would never vote socialist. The scare tactic of the Left in postwar Germany has always been to cloak prosperity with the guise of the past. As he was given the full honours of a visiting dignitary in the town hall of Saarbrücken, capital of the Saarland, Honecker could reflect that his authoritarian party, in which 'democratic centralism' was a label that allowed dictatorship to replace discussion, was working out a platform of common aims with the West German Social Democrats.

It was a picture of two happy, smiling men when Honecker posed alongside Saarland premier Oskar Lafontaine, great white hope of the Social Democrats for Chancellor after the predicted defeat of the lacklustre Kohl. Outside in the cold, Siegmar Faust, an exiled East German author, distributed leaflets condemning Lafontaine, with the words: 'Vote now while you still have the chance.' His aim was to imply that Lafontaine was associating himself with totalitarianism, with a regime that would take away the right to vote. Inevitably it was a message that came across better in the East than in the West, and would have its most telling effect when the millions of East Germans were at long last allowed their say in the future of the German dream. In the first all-German elections since the advent of Hitler, in December 1990, the electorate exiled Oskar Lafontaine and his party to the political wilderness. They had failed to keep the faith.

Yet it had been so easy, even as late as 1987, to declare convincingly that faith in Germany as something more than just a geographical expression was a foolish fable for children, an old-fashioned nationalist fairy-tale peopled with more ogres than most. Chancellor Kohl himself felt politically compelled to acknowledge that Honecker was not just gloating when the communist called their political systems 'as incompatible as fire and water' and ideas of unity 'fireside dreams'. It took Munich's Franz Josef Strauss, the conservative stalwart who rejoiced in the nickname of 'Maggie Thatcher in lederhosen', to say as usual what was on everyone's mind but no one else's lips: the embarrassingly pedantically accurate finding of the constitutional court that had flown in the face of all political caution. Strauss reiterated it in ringing tones: 'The German Reich of 1945 has legally never been abolished: the German question remains open.'

But attempts to lay the awkward past to rest were not just confined to legalistic rulings and political positions. There were real bodies too. Up the hill in the small, neat cemetery in Wiebelskirchen, Honecker, the most prominent son of a long communist line, laid red roses on the grave of a member of the Hitler Youth. It was a gesture of atonement. The simple soldier's grave marked with a Maltese cross in the 'Field of Honour' was the last resting-place of Robert Honecker, Erich's youngest brother, naval conscript and Hitler Youth member. Robert Honecker had been captured by the British when his ship went down off Greece, and returned from a prisoner-of-war camp in Egypt stricken with the tropical disease bilharzia. He died aged twenty-four in 1947. In his autobiography Honecker said his brother was drafted into the uniformed Hitler Youth 'virtually by decree'. His brother wore the brown shirt, Honecker maintained, because it was forced on him – the argument used by the father of Horst Klohs. Bärbel Falkner would have reminded him of those words, had she been allowed, when it was made clear to her son Horst that, if he wanted to continue with his education beyond elementary level, he had no choice but to don the uniform of the Free German Youth, the organization Honecker had built up with an iron rod to be the 'vanguard of the party'. Her brother had been forced to wear a brown shirt, her children were forced to don blue ones.

But history had bitter tricks in store for Honecker too. The trip to the Saarland might have been a hint from fate. It was there that he had taken the decision to become a full-time communist activist back in 1935 when a plebiscite under League of Nations supervision had voted overwhelmingly to return the still-occupied territory to Germany even under Hitler, the pull of nationality overcoming political uncertainties. In 1955, after Hitler's war, the Saarland would vote once again the same way and join the new Federal Republic of Germany under article twenty-three of its constitution, the same article that would in 1990 be used by Honecker's own state to reject him and all he had stood for and again follow the tug of national identity.

That chill evening in 1987, up the hill in the cemetery, after Honecker's visit, four old ladies, used to passing their evenings with watering-cans in graveside gossip, gave their verdict on the visit: 'He's an old man who's feeling homesick.' They had no doubt about what 'home' meant and where it was: 'Heimat ist Heimat', they answered in thick Saarland accents and in tones of certainty natural only to those who have never wandered. It was not an alternative Honecker would allow his fellow citizens. In an example of the blindness that often comes with power, he would later plead pathetically, after his fall, that he was being deprived of 'a basic human right – to travel, to go and see my daughter'. She lived in Chile, and the authorities in the new Germany estimated, on not unreasonable grounds, that a man wanted for serious crimes might be tempted not to come back.

It had always been a game based on double standards. Even at the peak of his career, as the chief representative of 'workers' power', Honecker seemed more at home taking coffee and strawberry tart with a capitalist archetype, Berthold Beitz, head of the Krupp industrial concern. Otto Wolff von Amerongen, head of the West German Chamber of Commerce, quipped: 'Fire and water are all right as long as no one gets wet and no one gets burned.'

But back home they were gathering wood for the pyre.

# 9

## *The Thrill of the West: the Messiah from the East*

It was a letter from his brother Norbert, now settled in the spa town of Bad Pyrmont in the Harz mountains south of Hanover, that gave Alex his introduction to the élite ranks of those East Germans who knew what they were missing.

Alex's mother, for whose sake more than his wife's he had remained in East Berlin the day they built the Wall, had become increasingly frail. As a pensioner and so deemed useless to the state, she had never really been imprisoned by the wall that divided the rest of her family. She had been often to see her daughter Renate in West Berlin and even to visit Norbert in Bad Pyrmont, where he ran a modest but comfortable hotel named after Franz Liszt. But travel was an effort for her, as was the emotional stress of passing through the Iron Curtain between her divided children. The long lines of shuffling elderly people at the stations were a bitter testimony to the human cost of Germany's division. The old family flat in Prenzlauer Berg was full of memories but badly maintained and ill heated. The family decided it would be better all round if she moved in with Norbert, and in 1981 Renate drove over to the East and completed the few formalities required to relieve the communist welfare state of an unwanted burden. Alex said he was sure that one day he would be able to come and visit her.

The first opportunity arose four years later. His mother was about to turn eighty-five and the birthdays of the very old were considered a potential reason for the granting of an exit visa. Norbert suggested that Alex apply. He did not need further prompting and at once asked for a temporary exit visa. Within weeks, and after a lengthy period of form-filling, the request was granted; but a request for Bärbel to accompany him was rejected. She was not, the official pointed out, a blood relation; in fact, they were not even married.

At last the paperwork came through, and for the first time he held in his hand, albeit on temporary sufferance, the slight blue document adorned with the hammer-and-compasses motif of the communist state: a passport, and what was more, marked with the crucial stamp, an exit visa. Even though he knew he would be obliged to hand it back on his return, it was a strange, intoxicating moment. Alex boarded the train in East Berlin's Ostbahnhof with some trepidation, aware that the trip he had undertaken so recklessly as a young man was now a leap across the great divide that split the world. He watched with the stoicism of one who has seen it all as the coaches pulled slowly past the watch-towers and the barbed wire, observed through field glasses by young conscripts who were themselves more prisoners than guards.

In Hanover Norbert met the train and clasped Alex in his arms. It was a meeting of fraught emotional energy: two brothers well past middle age who had spent most of their lives apart but were aware of the accidental similarities of their careers on opposite sides of the Iron Curtain. So near and yet so very far. Alex was determined to take in the affluence of the West with a solid stoicism. He had, of course, seen it all on television, but here, in its almost wasteful abundance, it seemed a land of plenty whose inhabitants scarcely appreciated what they had.

Renate came from West Berlin with her daughter, also called Renate but known as 'Renatchen' to avoid confusion. The party was as jolly as such gatherings for elderly relatives ever are. His mother smiled as Alex was fêted. They took him everywhere; he was, of course, the toast of the local *Kneipe*, with more and better anecdotes than anyone else. They took him to Hamburg, where he cruised like a cackling tourist down the Reeperbahn, diving in and out of the pornographic peepshows like a naughty schoolboy and seeing in it all, more than the Hamburgers did: freedom. Alex had no time for moral discussions on whether or not pornography was healthy for a society; for him Hamburg was behaving like any great seaport where sailors came and went. Prostitution and a *laissez-faire* attitude to sex were part of the colour of life that had been snuffed out in East Germany before he was old enough to know about it. To Alex the red lights were the beacons of a free society.

He drank late into the night and in the morning rose at dawn to visit the fish market. That, even more than *les girls*, was the story that he regaled them with later in the after-hours sessions at the *Stammtisch* back in Metzer Eck: 'You should have seen it, alive with people and fresh fish, fish like you wouldn't believe existed and all for sale, as much as you could carry – and pay for, of course,' he added, to appreciative chuckles from his audience, 'and cut flowers too!' Their eyes widened. Fish was one thing, but cut flowers were as scarce as holidays in Spain. 'We bought daffodils and whiting, flounders and mussels and went for breakfast of hot bread rolls, steaming coffee and a plate of salted herring and a glass of schnapps.' There seemed little doubt about it: heaven was in Hamburg.

They took him back to Berlin too, to see the western half, almost forgotten, of the city that had become his home. But he had to fly; his visa was not valid for West Berlin, which the GDR legally insisted was a separate state. Nor did he dare to try to travel on the transit routes across the East German motorways; once back through the border, he could have kissed goodbye to a visit to the other half of Berlin. So he flew – with British Airways, in itself for him a bizarre brief taste of a land that he only remembered as a childhood enemy and now part of the glorious West, but alien, so alien. Renate and Norbert paid for the ticket, and he visited the two Renates' home, a smart flat in a prestigious road off the Kurfürstendamm, and had a traditional breakfast of soft-boiled eggs in the open air on a terrace at one of the cafés. He strolled down the Ku'damm and marvelled at the size of this preposterous enclave with its lakes and forests, its vast villas and run-down tenements, a German New York, a microcosm of Western society that was his city too, even if the communists' maps marked it as blank white, as if this hiving human jungle were empty space. And then he flew back, to Hanover, and caught the train east again through the barbed wire and scatter guns that were the reality of the Iron Curtain, back home to the other Berlin.

It had been a cathartic experience. He found himself taken aback by the blur of commerciality and the overall affluence of the other half of Germany. But he was surprised, even shocked, to see how far it had become self-sufficient, almost to the point of forgetting the existence of the East. The contrived communist fiction of a totally separate state had become even more of a reality for the Westerners, particularly the Rhinelanders and Swabians in the far south-west, far from the frontier, bordering on France or Belgium in the new European Community in which Germany was no longer an enemy but a source of wealth creation. For those who had no relatives or close friends in the East, the GDR was a reality as immutable as any of the medieval princedoms into which the German-speaking lands had once been divided. Hitler's unity had become accepted as an aberration; this was the way history wanted Germany to be. Even his own family said 'Deutschland' and meant only the western part of it, albeit with apologies in his presence.

And their new Deutschland was doing very nicely, thank you; as long as you avoided the difficult question of what Germany, new or old, was or should be. Bonn's bit was, after all, the big bit. It had its madmen in the Baader-Meinhof terrorist gang, which from the late 1960s onwards called a plague upon this smug society and embarked on a bombing and assassination campaign. But it was like trying to dent a BMW with a peashooter, so solid was the prosperity and so rugged the determination of the citizenry to hold on to it. The brief glimpses Alex had in Bad Pyrmont, Hamburg and West Berlin of the reality behind the world he had watched on television offered a depressing confirmation of a society that found East Germany at best a topic for nostalgia, at worst irrelevant.

Up in the densely wooded hills above the Rhine between Bonn proper and the pleasant suburb of Bad Godesberg – where Hitler had humiliated Neville Chamberlain, though no one talked about that – the functionaries of the second German democracy, a model state compared with the catastrophe of the interwar Weimar Republic, were fond of their role as 'managers' of this new Germany of unthreatening affluence. They took afternoon walks, particularly on summer Sundays. The afternoon walk was almost part of the national culture, encouraged as an integral component of the German dream, like the strong coffee and sticky cakes afterwards, the Mercedes that brought the family to the forest and the glass of golden beer, brewed according to the medieval Bavarian purity law, topped with its 'crown of foam', a celebration of hard-earned well-being.

'Well-being' – in German, Wohlstand – was the buzzword; it summed up all those material comforts. West Germany had come close to its own socialist miracle: achieving the workers' dream by making everyone middle class. The politicians dressed for the part in expensive but durable country clothes, with strong walking boots and often knee-breeches or even lederhosen if they hailed from Bavaria. Regional differences were, after all, in this proudly 'federal' republic, something to flaunt. Everyone in the hemicycle of the Bundestag parliamentary chamber was as aware of his regional roots and obligations as he was of his party affiliations.

The *Länder*, or provinces, were not only autonomous in many areas of daily life, but they had created a situation where the man in the street perceived Germany as more a composite of the *Länder* than a nation-state with subdivisions. For Germany was not a nation-state; rather, there were, in the official formulation of the Ministry for Intra-German relations, two states in Germany. But West Germans had come to accept the size and shape of the country they lived in. Few visited the East and the very different accents of Brandenburg and Saxony were seldom heard along the Rhine. A return to regionality had disguised the bitter pill of national division and affluence had sugar-coated what was left.

But fate and time conspired to provide catalysts; 1989 saw the fortieth anniversaries of both states. It was, of course, simultaneously the anniversary of division, the process that had started in May 1949 with the passage through parliament of the West German constitution. That event, by decreeing Western values in the western zones, had made division inevitable, but the anniversary was to be the spark that would set off the trail towards unification of which the document itself would be the instrument. Anniversaries are essentially occasions for remembrance; on this occasion they jogged West Germans' memories about events and realities they found it easier to ignore. The fortieth anniversary of the constitution saw a number of passionate discussions about the fate of the nation. For example, Professor Dr Hartmut Bookmann, writing in the *Frankfurter Allgemeine Zeitung*, warned about the dangers to a healthy understanding of Germany's difficult history that could come from assuming the Federal Republic was its end-product: 'The old south-west German provincialism is alive and thriving and in danger of getting itself accepted as not just a part but the whole.'

It was an astute, if unappreciated, comment. The fact that the quiet revolution in the eastern half of Germany should have ended up in reunification was to come as quite a surprise to those who initially followed it on their television screens with much the same sort of enthusiasm – no more and no less – as they felt for events in Poland and Hungary. The tears of joy shed on the night of 9 November, when the Berlin Wall was opened, surprised many of the people who felt them trickling down their cheeks. Over the preceding four decades the Federal Republic had come to be an easy home to live with, a handle to being German, a definition that the younger generation could live with without the stigma that their parents had grown up to encounter abroad. It was a definition that did not include the GDR; the seventeen million people who lived in the area that had once been known as *Mitteldeutschland* (central Germany) but had now just become the 'other Germany' were in effect consigned to a mental out-tray, considered as much part of history and therefore separate, as were Silesia, Pomerania, the Sudetenland and the other territories that had historically been settled by German-speaking people but after 1945 were amputated from the body politic, and through time, increasingly, from the national consciousness. Until the end of 1989 the topic of reunification was deemed by many to be a preserve of the right wing, and its lunatic fringe at that, the domain of the *Ewiggestrigen*, 'the eternal yesterday's men'.

'Yesterday', otherwise referred to with the equally oblique euphemism 'our recent history', was something Germans were profoundly uncomfortable with. The Hitler legacy not only pre-scribed West Germany's relations with the rest of the world; it had warped internal political thought. It was a difficult thing in the Federal Republic of Germany to be a conservative nationalist. Only a few months earlier, on a date that had been one of the most evil in the German calendar and was paradoxically before the end of that year to become one of the most joyous – 9 November – Philipp Jenninger, the Christian Democrat speaker of the Bundestag, the Bonn parliament, chose to make a remarkable surgical probe of his country's conscience. The occasion was the fiftieth anniversary of Reichskristallnacht, the 'Night of the Broken Glass', the brutal beginning of the Nazi pogroms against the Jews, a night Alex as a young boy – scarcely aware that he was part-Polish and part-suspected Jew – had remembered cowering beneath his grandmother's bed in the Dragonerstrasse in Berlin's Jewish quarter as the Nazi thugs in the street hurled bricks through the windows of the makeshift synagogue in the flat above.

The Bundestag was filled with the worthies of what remained of German Jewry, led by the venerable Heinz Galinski, dignitaries from Israel and every deputy in the parliament. The eyes of the world were on Bonn. What was expected was a ritual act of breast-beating, a *mea culpa pro forma*. Jenninger did something different, something shocking. He forced Germans to try to understand how the generation that had lived through Nazism acted as they did. He tried to force a younger generation that now held the reins of power but preferred to live with generalities, to do what they could not and would not: understand that they too could have made the same mistake. Instead of reciting a catalogue of atrocity to allow sombre nodding of heads, Jenninger delved into the psyche of the nation in 1938 to reproduce the paean of praise for Hitler that the average German might then have felt:

The years from 1933 to 1938 even today with distant hindsight exercise a fascination, insofar as there is scarcely another period in history that offers a parallel to the triumphal procession of Hitler's early years: reincorporation into the Reich of the Saar, introduction of general national service, an enormous armaments drive, the signature of an accord with Great Britain on the size of fleets, the occupation of the Rhineland, the Olympic games in Berlin, the 'Anschluss' of Austria to the Reich, and finally, only a few weeks before the November pogrom, the Munich accord allowing the dismemberment of Czechoslovakia. At last the Versailles Treaty was indeed no more than a scrap of paper and the German Reich was the dominant power on the European continent.

For Germans, who had seen the Weimar Republic as little more than a series of foreign policy defeats, all this must have seemed a miracle. And that was not all: mass unemployment had been transformed into full employment, mass poverty had been turned into something approaching decent living standards for broad levels of society. In the place of doubt and hopelessness, there was an atmosphere of optimism and self-confidence. Had Hitler not done what Kaiser Wilhelm II had only promised, brought the Germans wonderful times? Was he not really chosen by providence, the leader a nation receives only once in a thousand years?

Perhaps one did enjoy fewer freedoms in certain spheres of life, but one was personally better off and the Reich was undoubtedly great again, indeed greater and more powerful than before. Had not the leaders of Great Britain, France and Italy danced attendance upon Hitler in Munich and helped him to one more success among a series already thought impossible?

By this stage the walkout was unstoppable. They poured out in their droves, muttering disgust: the Greens and the left wing of the Social Democrats, even some of his own Christian Democrats and their coalition partners the Free Democrats. They had forgotten one of the key rules of democracy: to listen to the end. Philipp Jenninger was in the process of delivering one of the most intellectually compelling and rhetorically structured damnations of Nazism ever heard from a Bonn politician.

The Jewish representatives in the chamber were embarrassed, not by what the man on his feet was saying – that they listened to gravely, nodding – but by the walkout, which marred the solemnity of the occasion. They resented such a gruesome anniversary being made the stuff of party politics. Yet it had been an instinctive reaction. Nazism could only be dealt with in black and white. Even the television cameras managed to lie, recording for the superficial spectator around the world pictures of some of the older Jews, survivors of the Holocaust, in tears. Alex, watching on television at home in East Berlin, felt there was something wrong, a misrepresentation somehow, particularly when the East German commentators began to exult in the 'crazed Nazi outpourings from Bonn'. But in a society starved of free information he was unable to read the whole text, to see for himself if this 'scandal' from a widely respected politician was really as naïve as it seemed.

It was not. The mass media of the West had also preferred simplification to reality and had jumped to their own conclusions rather than wait to the end of the oration. Jenninger had chosen to read one of the most moving eyewitness accounts of the Nazi terror. It was a harrowing document:

The people who had got down from the trucks, men, women and children, had to follow the commands of an SS man clutching a horse- or dog-whip to undress and put their clothes in separate piles, shoes in one, underwear in the next, outer clothing in the next . . . they undressed with neither cries nor tears and stood together in family groups, kissed and said goodbye to one another and waited for a sign from another SS man who stood by the ditch and also carried a whip . . . I watched one family of about eight people, a man and a woman with their children, one about a year old, one of about eight and another of ten, along with two grown daughters between twenty and twenty-four. An old woman with snow-white hair was holding the one-year-old baby in her arms, singing to it and tickling it. The child gurgled with pleasure. The parents watched with tears in their eyes. The father held a ten-year-old boy by the hand and talked quietly to him. The boy was fighting back his tears. The father pointed with his finger to heaven, stroked his hair and seemed to be explaining something to him. Then the SS man at the ditch called something to his comrade. The latter separated some twenty people and told them to go behind the mound . . . I went behind the mound and found myself before a mass grave. The people lay pressed so tightly together that only their heads were visible. Blood ran from almost every head down the shoulders. Some of those who had been shot still moved. A few raised an arm or turned a head as if to show that they were still alive. I estimated there were about a thousand people in there. The ditch was already three-quarters full. I looked round at the guard. The SS man sat on the ground by the narrow end of the ditch, with his legs hanging into it; he had a machine pistol on his knee and was smoking a cigarette. The row of naked people went over to a step cut into the wall of the ditch, shuffled over the heads of the bodies to the point the SS man indicated. They lay down before those who had been shot, some stroking those who were still alive and speaking quietly to them. Then I heard a series of shots . . . then came the next group and climbed down into the ditch and were shot.

The power of Jenninger's speech lay in the classical rhetorical device of building up in order to knock down. The horror of the Nazi atrocities became the more chilling when one understood how the ordinary, decent German man or woman was seduced into believing he was a messiah. It cost Jenninger his political career.

No one wanted even to try to understand the phenomenon of Nazism; it was easier to apologize. West Germany was like a psychiatric patient prepared to rehearse and repent the horrors of his past endlessly, but not to examine and exorcize them. For the same reason there was a tendency to forget the GDR, to avoid the unpleasant fact that seventeen million Germans had suffered for their geography. It was easier to think of them as another nation. Anything was easier than thinking about Germany. Public opinion was more incensed by lead levels in car exhaust or the fate of the Black Forest, dying under acid rain; in itself this was a national issue, one that affected all Germans in a peculiarly strong, emotional way, as did the pollution of the Rhine, precisely because both touched such powerful totems, symbols of the nation; yet it would have been hard to find a Green to admit that. It was easier to reduce them to scientific, ecological terms; environmental catastrophe was an easy issue, involving much scope for self-flagellation and almost none for raising the deeper, more fraught issue of who was and who was not a German. The easy answer of the Left was that it did not matter. The time for such 'grand questions' was past.

But it was not quite so, seen from the other side of the electric fence. Berlin had remained the thorn in the side of those who wanted to come to terms with the reality of the Cold War; they called themselves realists, others called them defeatists. Were it not for the city's particularly brutal division and the consequent anomaly of West Berlin as an enclave, a *de facto* if not *de jure* part of West Germany, deep within the communist state, it would have been all too easy for the division of Germany to have slid into history as yet another manifestation of the political statehood of the German-speaking peoples, as natural as Austria.

The Right, ranging from those who still would have preferred Austria to be part of a single German state, via those who wanted Silesia back from Poland to those who simply believed in self-determination for the citizens of the GDR, were therefore curiously thankful for the Berlin Wall. They took care not to express it. The Left, ranging from those who felt that accommodation with the Soviet Union and reassurance for the Eastern Europeans was the only way forward, via those political masochists who so disrupted their own nationality that they wanted to see it powerless, to the crypto-communists who secretly wished the

Russians had advanced to the Rhine, had cause for regret. And they also took care not to express it. The last thing anyone expected right up to the summer of 1989, when both German states began to mark their anniversaries, was that West Berlin would swallow up the GDR.

West Berlin, as both Moscow and the West had always known, was an unexploded bomb. The curiosities of its position as a city clearly part of West Germany yet cut off from it and treated by Moscow and its allies as a separate, quasi-independent political entity, were a matter raised by protocol every time a Russian came calling in Bonn. Over the years that had been a more and more frequent occurrence. Leonid Brezhnev had become a regular visitor. It was becoming clear to the Kremlin that Moscow stood to gain a lot from West Germany, as the industrial powerhouse of Western Europe, particularly when it had something Bonn was committed to caring for: East Germany. It was, as Alex goaded Busch, like paying a kidnapper for locks from a captive loved one's hair.

Willy Brandt, Mayor of Berlin when the Wall had gone up in 1961, had, as Chancellor, introduced Ostpolitik, intended to be a reversal of everything Hitler had done, recognizing the loss of the eastern lands to Poland and the Soviet Union and finding a workable accommodation with the existence of the GDR. Initially there were some who called it treason. My school penfriend, at fourteen a gangly lad called Reinhard, who lived in a Rhineland village, sent me a scathing verse sung to the melody of 'O my darling Clementine'. It ran: '*Auf der Mauer, auf der Lauer, mit 'nem Knuppel in der Hand, steht der Konrad Adenauer, wartet er auf Willy Brandt*' ('On the Wall – up in heaven – with a truncheon in his hand, there waits Konrad Adenauer, waiting still for Willy Brandt'). Even in the afterlife there was a wall.

Brandt's Ostpolitik led to the 1970 'Four-Power Agreement', which in effect was a truce over the status of Berlin, whereby the wartime allies agreed to differ and left the Germans to lump it. It was a masterpiece of oblique wording, a semantic compromise to comply with both the Soviet insistence that East Berlin was no longer part of the occupied territory but the sovereign capital of a sovereign state and the Western powers' insistence that the postwar occupation status continued to apply to the entire city. All references to either part of Berlin had to be replaced with euphemistic circumlocutions; West Berlin easily became the 'western sectors of Berlin'; East Berlin, more obliquely, became 'areas of Berlin contiguous to the western sectors'. The practical result was an agreement that allowed West Berliners thirty days a year in the East and the possibility of special extensions, plus an accord on easing the regulations for transit travel by train and along the designated autobahns between West Berlin and West Germany. All it meant for Alex was that his sister Renate, now divorced, came over more frequently and he saw more of his niece Renatchen.

By the mid 1980s West Germans had drifted off into a complacent daydream as far as Western European politics were concerned. They had salved their souls by wholehearted engagement in the European Community, happily accepting tutelage from the same French who had now for more than two decades played moral and political giants as if they had not crumbled in every sense before the German onslaught of 1940. The other, more complicated, side of the coin was Russia.

The appearance of Mikhail Sergeyevich Gorbachev was studied in greater depth in the Chancellery in Bonn than anywhere in the world, Washington included. Yet the rune-readers were no better. As Gorbachev moved towards accommodating reform in Hungary and reaching an arms accord with Ronald Reagan, the men in Bonn agonized about what was the best they could make from it. In May 1987 Gorbachev held a summit of the Warsaw Pact in East Berlin. It was a week when the Russian bear danced on Germany's fractured nerves. Gorbachev's visit aroused great expectations. Alex argued late into the night with Busch about whether the new Russian messiah's visit would or should provoke some changes from their own fossilized leadership. The mass-circulation *Bild* suggested, more as a circulation gimmick than an act of serious prophecy, that he might pull down the Berlin Wall. More realistically Eberhard Diepgen, the then Christian Democrat Mayor of West Berlin, called for an end to the notorious *Schiessbefehl*, the command to shoot at would-be escapers.

This was the instruction that would haunt East Germany's leaders even after the extinction of their state. The wording was alleged by some to be ambiguous; it was actually crystal clear to anyone used to the complex formulations used by communists to conceal laws that embarrassed them. It authorized the use of firearms 'in order to prevent the imminent commencement or continuation of any act which under the circumstances prevailing might be construed as a crime against the German Democratic Republic, the common security or the order of the state' and further: 'to prevent the escape of or to recapture anyone who was seriously suspected of a crime or had been arrested for a crime'. As it was a crime to leave the German Democratic Republic without the correct, almost unobtainable, passport documentation, this was pretty well *carte blanche* to the border guard, who faced disciplinary action if anyone got away.

The opportunity to rub in this abominable law to the man who claimed he wanted to change the barbarous image of Soviet communism was too much to resist for any mayor of West Berlin worth his salt. 'Anyone who is serious about *détente* and disarmament should prove it first in Berlin,' Diepgen challenged Gorbachev obliquely. The mere presence in East Berlin, behind the bloodstained Wall, of the Soviet leader who had changed the world's perception of Russia as an evil empire was enough to stir the quagmire of the German question. More than they had been for a long time, Germans were aware that they had some sort of common identity that had been divided by outside forces stronger than its own deep-rooted but forgotten desire to be itself.

Even though reunification was on no one's agenda, the impending fortieth birthday party was perceived in the West as a belated coming of age, a time when it should no longer be necessary for a German to apologize for his nationality. The American presence had never been universally popular, despite what the politicians said. No German liked living in a front-line state, particularly when the other side was also German. The concept of an atomic strike launched by foreigners against foreigners but killing primarily Germans and destroying only German property was a hard one to sell to the man in the street, whether in Düsseldorf or Dresden. The new, medium-range arms race in Europe based on cruise and Pershing missiles had made West Germans think again about what their country was.

The growing fear along the Rhine was that the US generals increasingly saw nuclear weapons merely as something that would make an enemy think twice about war, but in the worst case might not stop him launching it. The German word *Abschreckung* is more clear-cut: it implies restraint through terror; it does not encompass the potential for such weapons to be used. The critical, anti-war constituency sharpened in the universities and liberal press by the scions of the Allies' own postwar re-education programme began to pose awkward questions. What were Germans doing in an alliance whose policy no longer seemed clearly to favour the interests of Germany? What was the point of NATO if it reduced Germans to nuke-fodder, buffer zones for both sides?

Alex travelled west again at a moment that was in theory more sombre: his mother's death. The harsh realities of German division, however, lent the affair an extra touch of the macabre. By the summer of 1988 old Margarete was seriously ill and it became clear to Norbert that she had not long to live. They knew that, if they could produce a doctor's certificate that she was near death, Alex might be allowed out again to be by her side, but most importantly, to take Alexandra, his fifteen-year-old daughter by Bärbel, a leggy, pretty blonde with wide eyes that Alex longed to expose to the wonders of the West. Although there was still no likelihood of a visa being granted Bärbel, Alexandra, as a blood relative of the old lady, had a good claim to be allowed to travel to her deathbed. But disaster struck doubly. Margarete took a sudden turn for the worse and died at the beginning of the summer, before Alex could submit the visa applications; worse, she died when he and Alexandra were up at the cottage on the Baltic, totally out of touch. In the summer heat it was considered unwise to delay the old lady's burial too long, with the result that the funeral, which also might have served as a pretext for a visa, had to take place before Alex was even back in Berlin. He would later recall that, when he heard the news, he was heartbroken more on account of what he feared Alexandra had missed than because of the long-awaited death of his mother.

But his sister Renate had an ingenious answer. Quickly warning Alex not to say too much on the telephone, she indicated she would be in touch soon about 'their trip to see mother'. It was time for a visit to the local doctor. Using her utmost persuasiveness, and the great excuse of the Cold War's inhumanity, she managed to get a postdated death certificate. Thus armed, Alex could now apply for an emergency visa to attend the funeral. It was granted, and to his joy, Alexandra was given one too.

So it came about – in one of the cruel paradoxes that Ger mans have never forgiven or forgotten – that for Alexandra her grandmother's death was to be the occasion for the most exciting event in her young life. She fretted about what clothes to take so that her cousins would not laugh at her impoverished provincial 'Eastie' style; she did not sleep at night; she was sick in the waste bin on the way to Friedrichstrasse station. Then, in the station itself, it seemed as if everything might come unstuck. At the customs desk, the stone-faced officer insisted on a thorough search of Alex's bag and discovered eighty Deutschmarks, a set of East German coins commemorating the seven hundred and fiftieth anniversary of Berlin – a jamboree held the previous year – and a hunk of uncut amber. None of it had been declared. The grey man tutted. It was not a big haul – in total worth perhaps a hundred and fifty pounds at most in the West – just enough for Alex to maintain a little self-respect there so that, particularly in front of his daughter, he would not be forced to rely all the time on their relatives' charity. But it was against the law, and that was that. The lot was confiscated – though fortunately Alex managed to palm a further hundred and twenty Deutschmarks, but he argued long enough for them to risk missing their connecting train.

Then, with the bureaucrat's addiction to the exercise of power over the powerless, the customs man announced he would carry out a body search of each of them individually. Alex protested that he had no right to search a teenage girl, which the embarrassed officer quickly conceded; but he still insisted on taking her into a closed cubicle to search her bag. When she emerged after a few minutes Alex wanted to make a scene, but more than anything else Alexandra wanted to catch the train. They boarded the Hanover coach, she exhausted, excited and trembling; he, brimming with indignation and smarting at what he considered state theft of his property.

In Bad Pyrmont, where there was, after all, no funeral to attend, the welcome was ecstatic. They paid their respects at Margarete's grave, and then went window-shopping. Alex delighted vicariously in his daughter's thrills: at the vegetable shop, 'What's that?' at an aubergine; at the bakery, where she spent fifteen minutes counting the different types of bread. They flew to West Berlin again – Alexandra speechless at the wonder of British Airways' in-flight goodies; the stewardess, a German, loaded her with extras: towelettes, disposable cosmetics, carrier bags and the usual airline trivia, all of it magic to a young girl on her first excursion into another, richer world. In West Berlin even the punks and the tramps sleeping rough on the streets were part of the fascination: 'Imagine, papa, at home – over there,' she gestured to the familiar landmarks of home – the television tower and Red Town Hall tower visible beyond the Brandenburg Gate, 'they would be sent to work, or jailed even.' She was not shocked, but rather entranced by the freedom to sleep in a doorway.

They strolled along the Ku'damm in a dream, Alex delighted to be able to show off his knowledge of 'how the other half live', now and then indulging in the sheer extravagance of a cup of coffee – 'bought for West marks!' – in a pavement café, to watch the fashion parade that was everyday life in West Berlin. Alexandra collected her few marks and stretched to the limit her innate skill as a teenage shopper to choose just the right few small accessories that would leave her friends back home green with envy. But the clock was ticking fast. Her one-upmanship was not destined to last long.

Back home, her mother peppered her with questions, but the experience had taken her powers of expression away. It was two weeks before, in dribs and drabs, she was gradually able to tell Bärbel what she had seen. Most of the impressions that settled in her mind were those of the consumer glitter, rather than the great human and political freedoms, but they had reinforced the idea that the society she had known from birth was a lie from beginning to end.

There was a codicil to their trip that reinforced her feeling of disgust. As the autumn days began to draw in, and East Germany began preparing for its last Christmas as itself – as yet unaware of the impending storm – the state organizations began looking around for venues for seasonal parties. As ever, Metzer Eck was booked to saturation level, so that the *Stammtisch* regulars began complaining that they could never get in because there was always a private party. One evening the telephone rang and Alex answered. It was the chief of the Berlin senior customs officers' social club; he wanted to rent Metzer Eck for their Christmas party. His tone was hearty, full of goodwill, and he promised to pay well, with the customary nudge and wink that he had a bottle or two of the good stuff for Alex on the side. Alex's voice turned to ice: 'I'm very sorry but we are completely booked up. Besides, I regret to inform you that I am lodging an official complaint against one of your officers who behaved incorrectly to my daughter, taking her into a private cubicle without a female chaperone – a girl of fifteen! It is disgraceful.'

There was a stunned silence, then a nervously jokey 'I'm sure there's some mistake. We must meet and have a chat about this. What else happened?' It took a long time, a verbal fencing game around the stated and unstatable conventions of life in a totalitarian society, but in the end Alex dropped his complaint and the customs men got their party.

And he got his coins, his amber and his eighty Deutschmarks – or at least the equivalent in vouchers to be used in hard-currency shops. 'Ha, ha!' he cackled. 'They're not even honest by their own standards.' Alexandra shook her head with adolescent disapproval at the corruption of the world. Her father had beaten the bureaucrats at their own game. But what a game! No one as yet had any idea that the game was up.

By the spring of 1989, Gorbachev decided it was time to put the goods in the market-place. What he offered to West Germany in return for technological aid and economic cooperation was first and foremost the promise of a lasting *détente* that would eliminate the need for the further armaments that the United States and Britain wanted to station on German soil. Gorbachev damaged NATO's credibility. He offered the possibility of a world where there would no longer be a front line in Europe. The official formulations contained nothing that could be interpreted as injurious to the sovereignty of East Germany, a state that had after all been a signatory to the 1975 Helsinki accord on European Security and Cooperation. But the front line between East and West was synonymous with the division of Germany; if one was removed, surely . . . It was a piece of logic that could be jeopardized only by an untimely utterance.

Gorbachev's state visit to West Germany in June had the atmosphere of a triumphal procession. In the great rolling-shed of the giant Hoesch steelworks in Dortmund, the massed ranks of the Ruhr proletariat in their hard hats roared the chant of allegiance 'Gor-by, Gor-by' with intimidating enthusiasm. Not since Adolf Hitler had a leader been so spontaneously and unquestioningly adored by the German people. Never a foreigner, let alone a Russian. The comparison was unfair but not inaccurate. Kennedy, de Gaulle and the Queen had had enthusiastic welcomes but not on this scale. The conservative *Frankfurter Allgemeine Zeitung* saw in

Gorbachev's reception the roots of a national trait that has always scared Germany's allies: 'A bias towards the irrational.'

Even Gorbachev himself seemed taken aback; he spoke of having witnessed catharsis, a 'movement of the soul' among the crowds. *Moscow News* said old enemies had become friends; it was more like lovers. Gorbachev had the magic not only of his undoubted charisma but also that of offering the one thing that had always entranced them: hope at a moment of self-doubt. For four decades West Germany within NATO and then in the EC had been content to play the role of a junior partner. But in May the country had marked its fortieth anniversary; a generation had grown up since the end of the war and it was tired of being saddled with an inbuilt need to apologize and do itself down. Gorbachev played to a neglected sense of pride, dubbing West Germany an 'industrial great power'. He cited the Bonn government as proving that true greatness for a modern nation was attained not by territorial expansion but in achieving prosperity. He could not have said anything more pleasing to a people whose pride was based on dragging themselves up by their bootstraps.

Gorbachev was offering the Germans a chance to carve a new, worthwhile world identity by doing what they are good at: making money. He had tapped into a West German vision in which Germans would again play their historic role of honest tradesmen across the frontiers of Eastern Europe, spreading efficiency and modernization while winning respect and influence. This philosophy was there beside the business horse sense at the heart of the mushrooming trade agreements with Poland, Hungary and the Soviet Union. Already Kohl's insistence that there would be no *Sonderweg*, no 'special way', for West Germany separate from its EC and NATO partners, was by reverse logic an admission that Germany's position was different. Whatever politics might dictate, geography and history were more powerful factors. It would have been against the grain of a millennium for Germans to turn down the offers of trade and cooperation coming from Moscow.

Hans Klein, the government spokesman, was at pains to dismiss as Anglo-Saxon fantasies the ghosts of Rapallo, where, in 1922, the fledgling Weimar Republic scared the West by signing a friendship treaty with Soviet Russia, and the Molotov–Ribbentrop pact by which the Nazis radically altered the nature of that friendship. Everyone was at pains to insist that West Germany was not going its own way in a fatal flirtation with Russia. But opinion polls showed ninety per cent of the population trusting Gorbachev as against fifty-eight per cent for President George Bush, and a sound majority for West German neutrality and the removal of all foreign troops. That Kohl would eventually, in a meeting of minds with Gorbachev in the Caucasus just over a year later, win acceptance for the reunited Germany to remain in NATO was a remarkable political feat.

Only a few die-hard conservative commentators in the euphoria of that June 1989 visit pointed out that Gorbachev had not actually offered them anything. Despite the dramatic developments in Poland and Hungary, East Germany had remained rigid; but the Berlin Wall was an abomination that blighted Gorbachev's 'common European home'. Amid the throng who mobbed 'Gorbi' on Bonn's market square were Berliners with a banner urging him to 'make love not walls', and posters stuck by students on the railings where his motorcade flashed by read: 'Dear Gorbi, you like to travel wherever you will, but Gaby from Dresden can't go too far.' But the real-life Gabys and Günthers in Dresden felt in general like Alex and Bärbel in Berlin: this was a state visit that left their own geriatric, Stalinist leadership looking like a historical anomaly. And no ill could come of that.

There has since been much analysis of the comments that Gorbachev actually made about the partition during that visit: 'Anything is possible . . . time has created the present situation, time alone will bring change.' 'The Wall can come down when the circumstances that led to its construction have disappeared.' 'I don't see this as a big problem.' Even now, each of those phrases could be interpreted pedantically either way; but with hindsight it is hard not to see that the man who regarded the postwar division of Europe as just another of Stalin's crimes and a mistake that had isolated Russia from the world, was carrying in his head a half-formed vision of a better world. Such was the impact of his very presence that in the bar of the Stern Hotel in Bonn four middle-aged civil servants speculated, over their beer, whether they would get relocation costs if they had to move to Berlin.

It was a hallmark of the Russian's political astuteness to be able to seem to be all things to all Germans. On the European parliamentary election posters of the Social Democrats he was the realization of their Ostpolitik dreams of reconciliation; in the electoral adverts

of Chancellor Helmut Kohl's Christian Democrats the summit
was the recognition that they had put Germany again on a footing
with the great powers; Foreign Minister Hans-Dietrich Genscher's
Free Democrats reminded voters that he was the man Gorbachev
had breakfast with. To the steelworkers of Dortmund he said he
was not demolishing socialism but rebuilding it in human terms;
to the businessmen in Cologne he painted a shrewd picture of
economic *realpolitik* and the profit potential. Only the communists
felt left out.

On the day Gorbachev flew in, the main attraction in Bonn's
cathedral square was the West German Communist Party's makeshift Café Glasnost. Red helium balloons floated by the spires of
the eleventh-century minster and a rock'n'roll band performed
against a backcloth of red stars, hammers and sickles. The statue
of Beethoven, Bonn's most famous son, looked on, distinctly
unamused. But even the razzmatazz could not heal the split
between those who saw at long last a vote-winner in the Kremlin
and the party's Stalinist leader Herbert Mies, whose allegiance and
political existence were due to the Honecker regime; for Mies there
was only 'democratic reform nonsense' coming out of Moscow.

And some writers had begun to say so. Fritz Raddatz in a seminal
article in *Die Zeit*, the weighty Friday liberal intellectual weekly
published by, among others, Helmut Schmidt, gave a trenchant
indictment of the whole comfy fabric of West German society:
'We've all become so terribly cosmopolitan and know facts such
as: the martini in the Rainbow Room of the Rockefeller Center
is the best, the tiles on this particular gate in Fez are the finest
and anyone who is given a table upstairs instead of down at
Harry's Bar in Venice ought to commit suicide.' Raddatz did
not shrink from damning the men of power outright: 'It is
simply not true that history is pushed forward by the doers, the
"Real-politicians". This thesis is used to hide an intellectual laziness
and faintheartedness that sums itself in the sort of "I proceed from
the assumption that" speech that is good only for settling the
cost of milk, car-exhaust levels and EC chicken quotas . . . [our
politicians] have only managed, more or less incompetently, to
administer the possible. They have never thought the unthinkable.
But it is dreamers who change the world, whether they are called
Rousseau or Lech Walesa.' And the dreams were about to come
true, though some would call them nightmares.

# 10

## Unhappy Birthday: The Narrator's Tale

*Oh fatherland, fatherland,*
*Show us the sign your children are waiting to see.*
*The morning will come when the world is mine.*
*Tomorrow belongs to me.*

On a frosty October evening in 1989 the leaders of an already
shaky Warsaw Pact gathered on a tribune along Unter den Linden
to mark in ritual fashion the fortieth anniversary of the creation
of East Germany, the front-line state that was in every way
coterminous with the communist alliance. It had been a difficult
year for the communist world, but scarcely anyone present that
evening suspected they were about to witness the beginning of
the end of the most recent partition of Germany.

As they gathered like so many wooden idols breathing clouds
into the frosty night air and waiting for the march past of troops
bearing flaming torches, it was like a last performance of an
old, familiar pantomime; all it needed was the unheard voice of
tomorrow's children to shout at Erich Honecker: 'Look behind
you.' There, like a pantomime ghost, was Mikhail Sergeyevich
Gorbachev, smiling his inscrutable smile and mulling over in
his head the words he would use the next day in reply to the
hollow, boastful rhetoric of his hosts: 'He who acts too late will
be punished by life.' The emperor himself was preparing to point
out that his courtiers had no clothes.

I stood opposite the tribune, stamping to keep warm on the
steps of the State Opera as the stony-faced troopers at the old
Prussian royal guardhouse – now the anachronistically named
Monument to the Victims of Fascism and Militarism – performed

their military ballet, pirouetting in jackboots as the new shift took over for the final act. It was 6 October, the eve of East Germany's final birthday party. Alex Margan had been waiting for it a long time. So had I.

Yet we did not know at the time how close the end was. No one that evening realized how potent would be the magic of truth at this critical moment nor how fragile the edifice of totalitarianism. The troops of the guard of honour of the National People's Army paraded as usual in their ceremonial uniforms of grey with white braid, their jodhpur-clad legs kicking high in the rigid march invented by the Prussian general Yorck, and in German named after him but everywhere else known as the goose-step. Tongues of orange flame licked into the night air as they carried their torches high, as deliberately blind as ever to their parody of the immense spectacles organized by Hitler against this same backdrop of neoclassical Prussian palaces. Next came a display by the Free German Youth, the regiments of young people dragooned into the party's vanguard. They wore their blue shirts over black jumpers to keep warm and waved their own, smaller, firebrands with the jovial enthusiasm of any group of provincial adolescents organized *en masse* by their elders for a night out in the capital. Most had been brought in buses from Cottbus or Rostock, bleak industrial cities whose inhabitants' view of the world was even then still shaped by an awareness of being on the edge of communism rather than in the middle of Europe.

Yet the authorities were tense. Almost every East German in the preceding months had seen a brother or sister, friend or neighbour leave for ever. In Leipzig particularly, there were problems; in the classrooms indoctrination had been replaced by argument; some of those 'chosen' to join the great birthday parade refused. Alex and Bärbel told their daughter Alexandra not to go even though she was a member of the Free German Youth, the 'vanguard of the party'. Their prohibition was inspired more by parental care than politics. They had an inkling there might be trouble. They were right.

Earlier that evening we had sat together around the *Stammtisch* as the first few late-afternoon drinkers began to be replaced by the 'night shift', as Alex called the regulars, and mulled over the change in the world since I had left Berlin six years earlier. I had not realized it then but the occasion for my departure was the first knot to come undone in the tapestry of life as we knew it across half of Europe: the death of Leonid Ilyich Brezhnev. I was posted to Moscow. This occasioned great hilarity among our East German friends. 'How about that,' quipped Alex inevitably, 'the whole world is open to them and they go into the lion's den.' We had a farewell party in Metzer Eck with a vodka bottle frozen in ice and lavatorial humour from Dieter the barman: 'Why does a Russian take three pieces of wood when he goes for a shit? One to balance on, one to lean on, and one to keep the wolves away.' German jokes at Russian expense were based on millennia-old stereotypes. Russia was the land of ice and idiots. That was why it was so humiliating being in thrall to them.

But my departure for Moscow was not the interruption I thought it might be in my relations with Berlin. For the ice was melting out there. The changes in the Soviet Union were to be far greater than anyone dared imagine. The death of Brezhnev was only the beginning of a process that would snowball as the gerontocracy that had held Stalin's empire in thrall more out of inertia than malice succumbed to mortality. His successor Yuri Andropov was already ill. It would take another two years for the tide to turn after the death of Andropov and his doddering, incompetent successor Konstantin Chernenko and the accession of Mikhail Gorbachev. Only then did the protracted end of the Soviet Empire, which had long hung just below the horizon, begin to heave into a still misty view.

The beginning of the 'Gorbachev effect' in the satellite countries could be noticed already when I returned to East Berlin to cover his visit in May 1987. Clenched fists punched the air as the hastily mustered plainclothes rent-a-crowd greeted the Soviet leader with the traditional Prussian salute of a triple cheer: 'Hoch! Hoch! Hoch!' But the remainder of the three-thousand-strong gathering clapped with genuine enthusiasm rather than the obligatory ritual applause rehearsed for past Soviet leaders, as the glamorous Gorbachevs tripped up the steps of the Schauspielhaus theatre, totally, if belatedly, reconstructed from the ashes of 1945.

For that was one of the curiosities of the years leading up to the apotheosis of 1989: over the preceding decade East and West Berlin had been growing together. The desolate waste ground in the centre of the former German capital, scarred and razed first by the bombers and then by the builders of the Wall, was bit by bit reclaimed by the developers. Paradoxically, the reason for this was not any prescience but rather a blind belief that the division was permanent and therefore there was no longer any point in preserving the centre for some future reconstruction. But the result was that when unity finally came much of the groundwork for repairing the heart of Berlin had already been laid in both East and West. Under Honecker East Berlin – long one of the shabbiest East European capitals – was gradually reconstructed as part of his plan to re-establish a national identity, absorbing what was usable from the Prussian past. This ideological about-turn happily coincided with the impending seven hundred and fiftieth anniversary of the city's foundation, a largely artificial anniversary that fell in 1987 primarily because Hitler had decided he wanted to celebrate its seven hundredth anniversary in 1937.

By the spring of 1989 the rot that had permeated the communist system began to have serious debilitating effects on East Germany. Alex and Bärbel sat transfixed by the scenes coming over on West German television in Bärbel's upstairs flat – in the room where Horst had been seized by Russian soldiers forty-three years earlier – and relayed for discussion around the *Stammtisch* downstairs in the bar. When the semi-democratic elections in Poland in June were followed by the Hungarian decision to open the frontier to Austria, only slowly did understanding dawn among either the rulers or the ruled in East Berlin that the plug had been pulled – deliberately or negligently – on the whole Soviet imperium of totalitarianism in Eastern Europe. Hungary, after Czechoslovakia, for which they did not need a visa, was the most popular destination for East German tourists, whose tiny Trabants were a familiar sight parked around the shores of Lake Balaton in summer. Now, suddenly, a trip to Hungary meant the sheep could leave the fold, and the signs from Moscow were that the shepherd was no longer wielding his Kalashnikov to stop them. Thousands of East Germans fled to the West, as Budapest, keen to re-enter the international community as quickly as it could before the Kremlin changed its mind, declared it would no longer honour its pact of dishonour by which it was obliged to send East Germans back home if they tried to leave the country illegally. It was a breach in the dam.

By September everyone in East Berlin agreed about one thing: the communist state's most redundant employee had become the border guard at Checkpoint Charlie, who used a mirror on a stick to check for escapers clinging under cars. 'Why get covered in axle grease when you can book a coach trip via Budapest to Vienna and Munich?' joked Saxon Uschi, who for years had sat at home while her musician husband toured the world on trips from which she was expressly barred. 'Did you hear about Margot Honecker going to visit Erich in hospital only to find him packing his bags and checking out? She asks him where he's going, and he says: "To my people – west."' Another hoot of laughter goes up and another round of schnapps goes down. If it was a tragedy for East Germany, it was a marvel for East Germans, who watched and wondered, in the words of the famed graffiti on the side of the Wall they had never seen, who would be the last to turn the lights out. Alex examined the new paintwork on Lothar's beer bar across the road: 'What are you looking for?' shouted Lothar. 'We had the microphones taken out.' Hoots again and the clink of beer glasses.

'If we all tried to leave, it wouldn't be the Russians who'd invade, but the Chinese,' grumbled Hans Busch at the table.

'Ach, that's not so bad – at least you can walk on their Wall,' Alex replied with his characteristic cackle. It was a difficult topic to joke about. In the basement of the church-sponsored 'ecology library' in a crumbling block near the Zionskirche, a focus for disaffected youth, notices on the wall complained of harassment by the Stasi, of young people interrogated about friends, threatened into silence or shunted out to the West. Pinned to the church noticeboard was a copy of an open letter to Honecker asking him to condemn the Tiananmen Square massacre, which only a few months earlier had seemed to put a brutal end to hopes for a global lifting of repression; in fact, he was first to defend it and no one reading his mind that evening would have been so willing to joke.

Alex's greatest public worry was a new ban on off-sales of imported wine; he feared it heralded the end of imports from Hungary, and with it the beginning of a new isolation of East Germany even from those who used to be its allies – a new Cold War, a new closing of doors. This was astute political rune-reading, as meaningful to the uninitiated as guessing election results from tea leaves in the bottom of a cup. Back at the table they were talking about pensions. 'I heard,' said Gerd, 'that a painter in the West gets a thousand marks a month pension.'

'Well, well,' countered Busch, with a wary glance to show that he was going to make a joke, 'to think I've been reporting these conversations to the secret police for fifteen years and they'll only give me two hundred.' Hoots of laughter again, but most at his bravery for striking so near the knuckle.

The regulars were passing from hand to hand a copy of the manifesto signed by New Forum, an embryo protest and civil rights group set up only a few days earlier. I had been to see one of the organizers, Bärbel Bohley, a forty-four-year-old painter. An intelligent, articulate woman, she lived in a book-lined flat in a building with peacenik and Green Party stickers on the door. In January 1988 she had been arrested for taking part in an illegal demonstration and 'sentenced' to exile abroad for six months 'in the hope I wouldn't come back'. Instead of going to West Germany and staying, as the authorities hoped, she went to England, helped by Paul Oesterreicher and CND, and came back, just in time for her fifteen minutes of glory. She had mixed feelings about the exodus that on the one hand had drawn world attention to the need for change in the GDR but, on the other, had 'robbed us of just the people we need: intelligent, educated, young and, most importantly, willing to take risks'.

New Forum, loosely modelled on the Hungarian Democratic Forum, had little hope of gaining legal recognition. When it did, it would be too late. Bohley and her colleagues, notably Jens Reich, would play a courageous role in proving that free speech could make itself heard and give a chant for the demonstrations so imminently to come. I brought Alex a copy of New Forum's appeal to the government for talks and recognition. He dithered about who they were and what good it would be, but signed in the end. Bernd, the musician, to Uschi's disgust, declined. It was, he admitted, cowardice, but he did not want to jeopardize two expenses-paid foreign trips a year. It started a family row. Uschi declared that if he was not a man, she was. 'I've had it up to here,' she proclaimed. 'My son, he's with the army; they guard one of those missile bases and you know what they wanted him to do: give the others a lecture on friendship with the Soviet Union and the evil West. And him with his father [her first husband] in Frankfurt. He told them where to get off.' Her outburst started another round of gloomy discussion and complaint. In came Michy, a cabaret artist, to announce: 'Walter's gone.' Walter

Plathe, a popular television actor allowed out for a performance in the West, had decided not to come back. On Monday night there was a sullen silence to watch Karl-Eduard von Schnitzler's *The Black Channel*, the government counter-propaganda show, as it attempted to refute with half-truths and misinformation Western news reports about the stream of East Germans still leaving daily for the West. It had become masochistic cult viewing.

But no one was to be allowed the luxury of experiencing the dramas of that autumn at second hand. On an unnaturally balmy October evening I turned into Metzer Strasse, parked on the corner and strolled over to the pub, only to see Bärbel leaning out of the window as if it were a summer's night. It was not that warm. I looked up and asked what she was doing. But her voice was too choked to answer properly. I waved cheerily and went in downstairs. Horst, by now long returned from the army and working behind the bar with his young wife Sylvie, followed the rituals quickly and perfunctorily with a cautionary glance. He wiped his hand, dried it, then shook with me, motioned to Sylvie to pour my beer and said the words that explained everything: 'Kerstin's done a runner, gone west.' As I swallowed the bombshell he dropped another: 'Mother's upstairs. She's a bit upset, in a mixed-up sort of way. We've just seen them on television.'

Bärbel's first indication that her eldest daughter was about to vanish from her life had come on Tuesday. The news was just beginning to sink in that East Germany's communist rulers had closed the border to Czechoslovakia, the last open door. Kerstin called her mother and said in meaningful tones that she and her common-law husband, Andreas, had decided they would, after all, take that holiday in Poland. She would leave the keys to the flat with her father-in-law. And then the fateful phrase 'He'll know what to do with the furniture.'

The exodus of young East Germans to the West had touched the lives of everyone who remained, leaving empty spaces at dinner tables, silent toasts to absent friends in corner bars. It still came as a shock to experience it at first hand. I had seen Kerstin grow from a chubby schoolgirl to a sophisticated woman of twenty-two who took a coquettish pride in her resemblance to the young Shirley Maclaine. She had everything to stay for. Kerstin had begun living with Andreas, eight years older and divorced, the previous year. She worked as a waitress in a bowling alley while Andreas was manager of a state-run bar in the pleasant suburb of Köpenick. They got a flat near his work and had gifts showered on them: a colour television, new furniture, crystal glassware. Andreas's age brought one advantage: at last, off the production lines in Eisenach, came the car that he had applied to buy thirteen years earlier. It had cost thirty-three thousand marks, a small fortune.

On Tuesday afternoon they packed only as many clothes as they could reasonably expect to need for a two-week holiday and headed east into the unknown. It was 3 October 1989; they were taking the risk of a lifetime, saying farewell to family and friends they expected not to see again for many years; it was inconceivable that in exactly one year Germany would be united. The Poles had made it clear that East Germans were being allowed to leave the country for the West only if they had entered legally in the first place. Andreas and Kerstin had visas because a Polish friend had invited them months ago to visit. But they had had a busy summer and Andreas's visa had expired, which required a last-minute visit to a police station for an extension.

At home Bärbel fought mixed emotions. She feared they would be found out or turned back at the border on some technicality. She feared they would get through and it would be years before she saw them again. But on Wednesday night, as she and Alex watched the black-and-white television in their flat above the pub, suddenly there they were in the crowd scenes around the Warsaw embassy, grinning happily. Bärbel burst into tears. Within the hour Andreas was on the phone from Warsaw; just a quick call to say they were registered at the embassy and had been given bed and breakfast privately until their fate was decided. But they would not be sent back.

Bärbel fell back on the sofa and pulled on a cigarette happily, her eyes brimming. Alex pretended to fume: 'Have you ever heard anything like it? That thickhead has sold the car to a Polish policeman. And what did he get for it? A lousy one hundred American dollars. It won't be enough to buy him breakfast in West Berlin!' But he was grinning broadly. Seconds later the phone rang again. It was Renate; she had seen the TV, too, and thought she recognized Kerstin. 'How wonderful, yes, but how awful. I must go out and get some shopping in for their dinner. They can stay with me as long as they like.'

'But Renate, they're still in Warsaw. We don't know how long it will be before they're allowed out.'

Barely a few weeks earlier people had been careful what they said on the phone to the West. Now, in crisis, no one cared. In the event, it was less than twenty-four hours before the next train rolled out of Warsaw. Alex and Bärbel slept fitfully, aware that somewhere out there in the dark Kerstin and Andreas were passing through the suburbs of Berlin. By three a.m. the train was going through Köpenick, a few hundred yards from their home, the station dark and lined with police to discourage anyone who might be thinking of hitching a ride to freedom. Then on to Helmstedt and West Germany and the return flight back to West Berlin to Aunt Renate's, avoiding the dangerous transit routes that would give the communist authorities a second chance to change their mind.

Pondering, we all sat late into the night at the *Stammtisch* over beer, the last of the Hungarian wine and token Czech apricot schnapps, drinking the health of the fraternal republics who had indeed turned out to be brothers in the end. Between the tears they hoped against hope and joked. 'Why is the socialist hell better than the capitalist hell? Because they keep running out of boiling oil and hot coals.' I promised to see Kerstin next time I was in West Berlin. 'Give her my love and tell her to send a photo,' Bärbel said. She had no idea when she would see her again. Least of all did she imagine it would be in a mere couple of weeks.

Yet the signs were there for those who could read them. The real candles for East Germany's fortieth birthday party were the ones impaled on railings outside the Gethsemane church a few streets north of Metzer Eck. They had been lit, one by one, by young people as tokens of solidarity with those arrested after the democracy demonstrations that had become a weekly event on Mondays in Leipzig. Across the road in dark doorways, uniform in their plain clothes, anoraks and slacks, the *Bonzen*, or bully-boys, of the Stasi took notes, and were joined by phalanxes of uniformed police as demonstrators converged on the church after marching from the centre of the city.

The youth of East Berlin, the spiky-haired punks and smart young girls in imported designer denims, trooped in and out of the old redbrick Lutheran church, guided not by devotion but by the politics of disaffection. One after another, young men and women came to a microphone to speak a few words: 'Pray for my boyfriend in jail since July.' 'Forward to freedom. We have a great future.' Yet none of them knew what that future was, other than mixed-up, half-understood equivalents of the popular revolutions happening in Poland and Hungary. The choir sang 'Kyrie Eleison' between each testimonial for a land in the throes of rebirth; no one seemed to realize that East Germany's salvation was synonymous with its death; in this state, unlike Poland or Czechoslovakia, there would be no resurrection. But the opposition had attained critical mass; those who did not go west no longer went underground.

The official candles were elsewhere on Unter den Linden, the triumphal neoclassical avenue that was the Kaiser's pride and joy, which had until recently been a road to nowhere, running into the Berlin Wall. The sixth of October 1989 had come upon us and we strived to guess its meaning. In the columns of the *Sunday Times* that night I wrote: 'Setting East Germany on the road to pluralism is the act that really would break up the Soviet imperium in Eastern Europe . . . Gennadi Gerassimov, Gorbachev's spokesman, acknowledged the true state of the relationship yesterday, when he told reporters that East Germany was Moscow's "strategic ally". It was a way of saying that the binding factor is the presence of Soviet troops, and that any change in the relationship would have to be part of a wider agreement . . .' But precisely that wider agreement was the goal Gorbachev was aiming for. He had decided retreat was the way to advance. Of the men who stood alongside Mikhail Gorbachev that night, Erich Honecker would be deposed within days, Czechoslovakia's Milos Jakes toppled within weeks and Nicolae Ceausescu, the dread dictator of Romania, ousted and shot by a firing squad before the end of the year. Life was preparing a fearful punishment indeed for those who had failed to move with the times.

Honecker's vanity had already sparked confrontation: in Dresden a week earlier. He insisted that to allow the refugees in West Germany's embassy in Prague to be released, they must be shipped in sealed trains across East German soil and 'expelled'. As the West German media broadcast that news, streets around Dresden station filled with those wanting to jump on board and those who just wanted to watch the interface between history and humdrum. The man in charge was the party boss of Dresden, Hans Modrow: an opportunist communist bureaucrat destined to be a footnote in the history of the demolition of the GDR, as the first communist to allow free elections and therefore the last to stay in power. The events of that night were not to be trumpeted in his later election campaigns, which would see him into honourable defeat in East Germany and later into the Bundestag in Bonn, an outcome he would have scarcely credited even as late as October 1989.

Police with megaphones and dogs came on to the platforms, ordered the crowds back, cleared the tracks, but still the people surged forward. Water-cannon were brought in and the trains held in Prague, to roll only hours later, at dead of night, through a station ringed by armed police. The anger had been repressed, not defused. For the first time since Soviet tanks had crushed the workers' uprising on the streets of East Berlin in 1953, the traditional weapon of the working class, the cobblestone, was back in use.

The dilemma of the East German opposition as the police state began to flounder was its fear of espousing the nationalism that had moved the masses elsewhere in Eastern Europe. Nationalism was confused with Nazism and *de facto* taboo, but in its place was no more than a Green–liberal mishmash of ideas cobbled together more from Western television than from genuine commitment. Solidarity-style worker power was missing, while attempts to develop a real intellectual opposition had been crippled by the government's policy of shipping out troublemakers to the West. 'We are not afraid any more,' declared Bärbel Bohley before leaving Berlin to avoid house arrest over the anniversary that she and her New Forum colleagues still thought would be a communist show but would in fact be their missed opportunity, the evening when their names would be called and no one would answer. Perhaps it was just as well; their answers, insofar as they had any, were not the right ones. For through it all, like some hitchhiker's guide to the galaxy of collapsing communism, appeared one face: that of Mikhail Gorbachev. 'Don't panic,' he told a young man in the crowds that turned out to greet him. But as another youth in the Gethsemane church put it: 'What else can we do? Leave?' But they did not leave. They took to the streets.

Every good reporter likes to let it be understood he witnessed every important development from the beginning. In fact, when the first riots in East Berlin since 1953 began that evening I was inside a police station. It might have been a brilliant ploy to see the instruments of repression prepare for action, but I was simply complaining about a missing car. I had driven up to Metzer Eck in the late afternoon to hear if there was any word of Kerstin and Andreas. Alex and Bärbel had had a phone call to say they were already in West Berlin and staying with Renate. I hurried off back towards the International Press Centre for a briefing by Gerassimov. But on the way my car gave out. For reasons that have remained a mystery to me the engine failed on Prenzlauer Allee. I coasted to the kerb and left the car there, intending to come back for it after the briefing. But by the time I got there three hours later, after watching several hundred young people gather to shout 'Gor-by! Gor-by!' outside the windows of the Palace of the Republic where the distinguished guests were saying their farewells, the car had gone. A policeman on special duty at the corner said it 'must have been towed away; the convoys are due to pass here, you know'. He could only direct me to the local police station, *Volkspolizeirevier* Berlin Mitte, tucked away behind the drab flat blocks that lined the Alexanderplatz.

My banging on the locked door of ribbed grey metal eventually brought an abrupt response: I was ushered inside to face iron gates and to the left, a harassed-looking policeman through a grille. 'What do you want? How dare you make a noise here?' I tried to explain that my car was missing, possibly stolen but presumed towed away. Coming to the police seemed not unreasonable. In fact, it was. In East Germany the police did not exist to clear up crime or give directions to the public. No, he could not help me. No, he did not know where my car was and if I was from the Western press this was probably some kind of provocation, especially 'under these circumstances'. I looked blank for a moment, puzzled, then noticed the groups of *Bereitschaftspolizei*, the special units supposed to deal with civil unrest, filing into lines on the other side of the barred gates. I was about to ask why they thought they were needed when a sharp look from an advancing lieutenant cautioned me that it might be more prudent to make my excuses and leave.

Outside, through the archway beneath the flat blocks, the

sodium lights glowed orange in an atmosphere that crackled with a different, human electricity. People were milling about in unusual numbers, straying into the middle of the wide road and across the vast expanse of Alexanderplatz. They were moving with animated gestures and just that extra touch of speed to their walk that signified unusual excitement. The police were already lining up in solid, dark-green lines along the northern side of the square. From the direction of the Palace of the Republic came the first large groups of several thousand, strangely quiet at first, then chanting again the name of the man of the moment: 'Gor-by! Gor-by!' Some wore Gorbachev badges and joked that their communist rulers had declared him 'public enemy number one'. The police frowned in confusion at a Soviet leader's name being used against them. In the last days of the Soviet Empire the symbols had become confused.

The demonstration, for that was what it had unconsciously become, flowed up to the headquarters of ADN, the state-run news agency, before there was trouble. A first snatch squad of plainclothes Stasi men, no older than a few of the marchers, dashed in to grab a couple of young men. One teenage girl tried to pull them off, only to find herself toppled to the ground, her legs lashed by a pencil-thin cosh produced like an evil magic wand from beneath a nondescript anorak. But it was as if the sheep had overnight developed a strong will and left the sheepdogs snapping angrily at their heels. The police tried first to pen them in, then to split them up; neither tactic worked properly as the masses, now swollen to some ten thousand, spilled over the tram lines, evoking tuts and waves in equal measure from elderly passengers. As the Stasi charged at one junction a young girl was pulled through the windows of a tram to safety and the driver speeded up.

Inevitably the tide flowed back up the hill into Prenzlauer Berg, down the blackened streets between the cavern-like walls of the six-storey tenements, where grannies leaned from balconies to wave and drop eggs on the heads of the police.

It unfolded like a scene from *Les Miserables*: a red flag snatched from one of the communists' own flagstaffs and waved against them, again the banner of revolution rather than orthodoxy, the Internationale sung with heart and soul on the streets compared with the dutiful rendering given hours before by Honecker and his cronies. I took the risk of leaving the marchers for long enough to get to Metzer Eck to use the telephone to file a report for the front page of the *Sunday Times*. Horst was behind the bar and the *Stammtisch* was full of the usual gang: Manne, Busch and Alex deep as ever in joke-swapping political repartee. They had heard the noise outside but looked out too late. The revolution was passing them by. Like too many others that night, they assumed it was a flash in the pan, a youthful exuberance that would have vanished by the morning. They were surprised to hear that the marchers were still assembled in a body only a few streets away. I left and said I would be back soon.

It was only when the exhilarated protesters had arrived at the Gethsemane church that the masses for the first time wavered; some wanted to continue, but did not know where to go. The steps to the church door offered a prime opportunity for someone to address the crowds; they called for speakers, but nobody came forward. In the streets they had chanted 'New Forum', the most broadly based of the new, still illegal, popular organizations, but no spokesman appeared. A figure with a sense of occasion and minimal rhetorical ability could have moulded them to his whim, sent them where he wanted, turned them into a mob and directed them to the Central Committee buildings, to the Brandenburg Gate, anywhere where they would have forced themselves before the blind television cameramen who served the world for eyes and were still reporting mechanically on the summit. But the lingering bogeyman of the little Austrian corporal with the Charlie Chaplin moustache still exercised his black magic: a powerful disincentive to demagoguery in Germany.

Inside the church Bishop Gottfried Forck told them to go home. Outside they grumbled that turning the other cheek invited crucifixion. But nobody had any alternative. In the end it was the police, acting on orders and instincts, who stopped the demonstration evaporating, by attempting to disperse it. In the back of everyone's minds was the fact that their government had been first to endorse the massacre in Tiananmen Square. It was with tongue in cheek and heart in mouth that the protesters, sitting on the ground before lines of armed police by the entrance to the Schönhauser Allee overhead-railway station, chanted '*Volkspolizei, steh dem Volke bei*' ('People's Police, stand by the people'). The People's Police stood by their orders. Water-cannon and dogs drew up, the demonstrators fled into a side street. On the right were high fences and railway tracks, on the left tenement blocks. Eventually they would have their backs to the Wall, the hated edifice itself barely three hundred yards away. Then, from that direction, a line of truncheon-wielding police began to advance, the classic sandwich manoeuvre.

An interlude of farce followed: the police charged from both sides, but the demonstrators, on their home ground, disappeared into doorways to scuttle through back yards and reappear, hooting with laughter, leaving two sets of scowling People's Police with raised truncheons facing each other. Three young women of eighteen to twenty went up to the grey line of young men their own age and pleaded: 'What are you doing this for? We're all in this bloody mess together.' When the empty trucks backed into the street, wire gates gaping like jaws, they were the first victims, snatched by the licensed thugs of the Stasi. Within minutes a blanket operation had seized almost everyone in the street, myself included. Bundled roughly into the lorry, forty of us with seats for thirty, we bumped off into the night. A couple in a car at traffic lights looked aghast at a truckload of incarcerated fellow citizens. The boy next to me held up his fingers in a victory sign. The woman in the Lada behind us bit her lip, looked at her husband and then made the same sign back. The police looked away, embarrassed. Martha, a fifty-year-old bar landlady, nagged the young policemen: 'A fine way to behave, this is. I suppose you'd do the same to your own mothers. You need your rear ends spanked.'

As we rattled over the cobblestones in a prison van, armed police watching from the tailgate as sirens screamed in the distance, there seemed little cause for high spirits. But Berliners are a tough lot and the banter continued: 'I'll tell you one thing. I'm not going to work tomorrow.'

'Don't you worry, they'll claim their fortieth anniversary record production figures without you.'

'Oh, we're slowing down – nice to know the cops are economizing on fuel too.' As the truck passed the district police station, my fellow passengers erupted into song: '*Völker, hört die Signale, auf zum letzten Gefecht, die Internationa-a-a-le erkämpft das Menschenrecht*' ('Nations, rise to the call, on to the final fight, the Internationa-a-ale will win our human rights'), the German version of the communist anthem flung in the communists' faces.

At Rummelsburg interrogation and detention centre we waited an hour in the truck before they decided the cells were already full. It was an hour of suspense and working-class humour: 'Hey mister, let me out,' called a bubble-gum-chewing girl from the back, 'I'm dying to go for a wee-wee.'

'I can't help that, love. You'll have to hold on.'

'It's all right for you, big boy; I've got nothing to squeeze. Oh shit, I've just ruined my last pair of tights.'

'I wonder where that boy of mine is,' said Martha. 'I bet they've got him too.' We asked the police. They had. He was in the next truck. His disembodied but still sarcastic voice came through the night air: 'Hello, Mum, got you too, did they?'

Then we shunted off again into the dark, still in convoy. This time the laughter stopped when the truck did, in a high-walled, floodlit courtyard, ringed by People's Police in jackboots and jodhpurs. They clasped lethally thin truncheons, the same as I had seen the Stasi man whip across the fallen girl's legs. Through the chicken-wire that caged us inside the lorry, we faced a brightly lit room, like a carwash, with white-tiled ceiling, walls and floor. Around the edge of the floor ran gutters to take away urine and vomit. Young men stood spread-eagled, legs apart, hands high against the wall, quiet, subdued and sick. Truncheons were run up the inside leg of anyone foolish enough to complain. The man next to me in the lorry sighed deeply in despair. The infectious collective euphoria that had survived our arrests evaporated into the cold night air that swept from Siberia across the north German plain. This was Marzahn police post, a forbidding fortress amid the drab tower blocks on the eastern edge of East Berlin. 'Out, one by one,' ordered a blond officer with a crew cut, and pushed us to a neat, bureaucratic desk where identity cards were taken away and the men were separated from the women and shoved into the white room to join the miserable line. It was a scene from every German's nightmare about Germany.

# 11

## Remember, Remember, the Ninth of November

Alex did not sleep that unquiet October night; even after the sounds of the police sirens had faded and the trucks had stopped lumbering down Schönhauser Allee with their human cargo. He stayed downstairs in the bar drinking lemonade and schnapps with Manne and Busch, all the while aware that my bag and coat lay unclaimed in the kitchen. Later, when the last one left, tottering down the steps on unsteady feet, he went upstairs quietly and paced the room, waiting, worrying that any minute he might hear the knock on the door, the same door at which the Russian officer had called to collect Bärbel's brother forty-three years earlier.

A realist, Alex was not over-concerned for me. He knew I had a foreign passport and press pass and at worst would probably face a tough time and maybe expulsion. But I had telephoned from his bar and they would not have missed that. If this was the beginning of a Stalinist clamp-down, then they could collect him and Bärbel at any minute. They already knew, obviously, about Kerstin and Andreas. He had a sense of premonition that things would get a lot worse in East Germany before they could get better.

Out at Marzahn, as I had been unloaded from the trucks with the other tired and frightened remnants of a night of defiant protest, I too had had more than a moment's trepidation about the immediate future. When my turn came to present my ID card to the cold-faced clerk sitting sorting humanity at his card-table, my Irish passport and press card caused him to raise his eyes for the first time and summon a superior. It was the man in the white crash helmet and jodhpurs, like a caricature of the blond beast. He snarled in annoyance and shot bayonet glances at the already unhappy police escort, who had not known the fate awaiting their catch. They were now to suffer for having brought a crab in with their haul of tiddlers. For the presence of a Western reporter was one of the things the security men most wanted to avoid.

I was hustled away, out of the glare of the blinding white lights into a welcome darkness, then through a courtyard and into a drab administrative building, like a 1960s school or local government office except for the electric doors that opened only when the buzzer was pressed and the stern-faced sergeant accompanying me showed his pass. What followed was more like a Teutonic TV-cops soap opera than a secret police interrogation. There were, predictably, two interrogators: a hard man and a soft man, though both mellowed as the weary hours dragged on. Neither would give me his name. The shorter, dark and with a crisp police haircut, was supposed to be the hard man. He was curt, tough, casting sniggering aspersions at my explanations; he had heard about the 'Western press', he sneered. But he had not read any of my stuff.

His colleague was the closest thing East Germany's secret police produced to Joe Cool. He had shoulder-length blond hair, a leather bomber jacket in the latest fashion and tight blue jeans. I asked, was he Stasi? He looked surprised, shocked even, and said, 'No, of course not. Criminal police.' But I had never met a Stasi man who admitted it and he looked very much as if he had just come from the ranks of one of the demonstrations. He would have fitted in perfectly. (I later learnt that among the Stasi men who had joined the demonstrations, partly as spies and partly as *agents provocateurs*, there were some who started taking the slogans seriously and converted – at least that is what they later said, but you can never tell, as Germany knows to its torment.)

They wanted a statement. So I gave them one: a detailed description of my night's adventures, from my missing car to the back of the police van, though I saw no need to let them know where I might have stopped off for a swift beer or to use the telephone. The lad in jeans, who was obviously in charge, took it all down, fairly and neatly, allowing me to see it in case I wanted to alter anything, which was just as well, for his German grammar was worse than mine. He went over the night's proceedings at least half a dozen times while my documents were taken away and my history cross-checked, I had no doubt, against a substantial file that existed somewhere from my days as a permanent correspondent in the GDR, with the Kremlin knew how many additions sent back from my time in Moscow by the large fraternal service.

Gradually, it seemed, he was accepting my story that I was merely caught up in the net while reporting, which was substantially true, though I lied when he asked if I had joined in any of these 'anti-socialist protests'. 'Of course not,' I said. My mission, I told him, was like *Star Trek*'s Captain Kirk's: not to interfere in the civilizations I reported on. It raised a chuckle for half a second. Even in East Germany there were *Star Trek* fans. In fact, I had surrendered to the mood and been shouting '*Auf die Strassen*' ('On to the street!') with the best of them. It is not every day, after all, that you get the chance to join in a revolution you believe in.

The interrogation was followed by seemingly endless waiting in an ante-room. Compared with Western police stations, it was bare: no posters warning about casual theft, no adverts for the Christmas police ball, no 'No smoking' signs even. The sergeant who had brought me in and the hard man took turns to sit with me. Their main task, it seemed, was to stop me looking out of the curtained window into the courtyard below where they were still bringing in and unloading the vans. The sergeant was about fifty and looked tired. He lived nearby, he said, when I squeezed a few words out of him at last, in one of the tower blocks of Marzahn. He wanted to get home to his wife. He had little taste for the night's work, but blamed the 'rowdies'. Then he went silent. Perhaps I was trying to provoke him.

After an hour or two, as the clock hand crept round and the sky edged towards a still-distant autumn dawn, the hard man grew more chatty. They had established that there was no real reason for holding me; sooner or later I would be set free, so I seemed, I suppose, less of a risk. He too was tired, though he was only twenty-nine. He also wanted to get back to his wife. He had been on duty almost continuously for three weeks. It was the first indication I had had of how much the exodus, the anniversary and the Gorbachev visit had strained both the manpower of even East Germany's overstaffed police force, and its nerves. Close to, he looked exhausted. 'I have had only a few hours' sleep this week,' he admitted. 'My wife has hardly seen me. I had only just got to bed two hours before I was hauled out again for this emergency. What sort of characters are they out there anyway? Hooligans,

I'll bet.' I explained that they seemed to be just ordinary people, decent Berliners who were fed up with their lot and had thought things might be changing enough for them to shout about it on the streets without being locked up and beaten.

This was too much. He looked offended, shocked, suspicious, then just tired again. '*Na ja, gut*, perhaps they are right.' Then I could see that he instantly regretted having uttered a private thought. He turned on me, the hard man and the soft all at once: 'This is just chit-chat, right, between us? I mean, you being a reporter and all? You wouldn't publish this in some West rag just to get me into trouble? If you did, I'd run into you again some time, you know.' I smiled and reassured him. Anyway, I did not know his name. But he was more afraid of the ability of his own side to trace even the most trivial leak. Today it is less than irrelevant.

By six-thirty a.m. we were both restless. His denim-clad colleague came back. They were, he said, trying to locate my car. They might have been, for all I know; they never found it. That was left to the hire firm, who, although I reported the inconvenience to them, did not get too worried for a couple of weeks, then sent their own man to find it and presented the *Sunday Times* with a thumping bill. At the time I was more worried in case the delay had been to allow the Stasi to search my hotel room. What concerned me most was that they might find a carrier bag in which I had left social security papers Alex had asked me to take to Kerstin and Andreas in West Berlin. They were of little intrinsic importance, but because West Germany would honour refugees' contributions made to the state welfare system in the East, they would help them speed up the bureaucratic side of settling into a new life. But they might have been used by the Stasi if they had wished to trump up charges against me.

It was still on my mind as shortly after seven o'clock I was driven through empty streets, shining in the autumn sun reflected in puddles I suspected were left by water-cannon rather than street cleaners or rain. We pulled up at the Grand Hotel and my suspicions deepened when the reception said they could not find my key. I asked for the floor manager to open my room, expecting the worst, particularly when I heard hurried grunts and movements inside. I edged into the door only to find the room occupied by a journalist colleague and his girlfriend who had seen me carted off by the police and assumed I would not be needing my room.

I had been given until midday to leave East Berlin, though I was assured that this was not an expulsion that would prevent my return. That morning the authorities were saying anything to get rid of the huge international press corps they had invited for the birthday party that went wrong. We drank beer and coffee for breakfast in the hotel dining room as I briefly reversed roles and gave an impromptu press conference, as one of the few eyewitness sources for the number of people who had been arrested during the night: I had seen at least a dozen vans, thus putting the figure at over four hundred within a few hours in one part of town. The final figure was several thousand. The protocols and documented evidence of their mistreatment, collated by the churches, were a further nail in the coffin of the German Democratic Republic.

Fearing that I might be searched on going back through Checkpoint Charlie, I had to decline to take the documents for Kerstin and Andreas, and hastily returned them to Alex, who was dozing fitfully after his sleepless night. 'Thank God, you're back,' he exclaimed, answering with some initial hesitancy the knock on the door he had been dreading. I recounted the night's adventures to a steady stream of 'Well I nevers', before saying quick farewells to meet my noon deadline.

After such a departure it seemed unreal to be meeting Kerstin and Andreas a few days later in West Berlin. We met at Café Kranzler, the place to see and be seen in West Berlin. They had been out of East Germany barely two weeks and spent part of that time in Poland, but looked as if they had emerged from a glossy fashion catalogue rather than the drab world beyond the Wall. Both were sporting what for Germans, East and West, was the symbol of the good life: a designer leather blouson. Kerstin combined satin-pink lipstick with a spiky-slick hairdo and tight, tapering trousers. Andreas's fashionably faded new blue jeans offset exactly his pastel-green leather jacket.

The waitress smiled politely as she took our order; nobody was a refugee in those heady weeks, provided of course that they looked as if they could pay the bill. After all, Café Kranzler was itself a *Flüchtling*, an economic escapee to the West's glitzy Kurfürstendamm from its pre-war Marlene Dietrich days on the corner of Friedrichstrasse and Unter den Linden. Kerstin giggled.

'It's all so colourful,' she said. 'Such consumerism,' said Andreas, sighing happily. What had impressed the pair was the food hall at KaDeWe (an acronym for Kaufhaus Des Westens: Shop of the West). It was the first stop for West Berliners showing off the riches of capitalism to relatives from the East. Kerstin and Andreas went there with Aunt Renate. Their smart clothes were bought with money scraped together by Andreas's father before they left East Berlin.

Kerstin had been offered a job as a waitress at the Argentinian Steak House in the Ku'damm at twice the salary she earned at the bowling alley in the East. Andreas was trying to decide between taking up an offer of a waiter's job in the Wienerwald fast-food chain and a trial as a *maître d'* at the Old Nuremberg sausage restaurant in the basement of the Europa Centre, directly beneath the skyscraper with the symbol of captalism: the Mercedes star itself. 'They have only offered me a three-month contract to see how I do, but that sounds fair enough,' he said. Their biggest problem was finding a flat, but Andreas was hopeful. 'It all works through strings, you know,' he confided with a grin, 'just like *drübeno*, over there,' he laughed, jerking his thumb in the gesture East Berliners always used to indicate the West. I thought they had settled into a new world with disconcerting speed. But then they had only moved a few miles across town, hadn't they?

It was the calm before the storm. West Berlin had seen the fewest of the stream of refugees leaving via Hungary, Czechoslovakia and Poland. Most of those who escaped wanted to taste their new freedom to the full and were unwilling to return to even the relative restrictions of living in the enclave of West Berlin. There were some exceptions. Petra, a twenty-two-year-old dentist, friendless, was excited but nervous on her second day in West Berlin. She had, like Kerstin, moved only a couple of miles, in spite of a lengthy exit route via Prague, Budapest and Bavaria. But geopolitics, reduced to the family level of who was where on the day they built the Wall in 1961, meant that instead of finding herself surrounded by relatives, she knew nobody. 'I had to come back to Berlin . . . at least to understand the mentality, the accent, the sense of humour. Bavaria was beautiful but more foreign than I'd imagined. It would be very hard to fit in there. The only problem here is that I love the landscape but access to it is still restricted by the bloody Wall. It's hard to see the rest of one's past so near yet so far.' She had been warned by the West Berlin authorities not to use transit routes through East Germany, nor the few underground railway lines, which, run by the West, passed below the East and therefore were for a few miles nominally under communist jurisdiction.

I introduced Petra to Günther Zschäckl, an actor friend from the East German Volksbühne whom I had met in Metzer Eck in the early 1980s, when he would deliver bursts of opera as he poured the beer behind the bar for the after-hours crowd at the *Stammtisch*. He laughed at all this. He had been in the West for over three years, and was working at several theatres. He had little good to say about the communist regime even though life as an actor in the West was a lot less certain than in the state-sponsored East German arts world. But he had asked on several occasions for permission to visit West Berlin for the birthday of his ageing mother and been refused without reason. When she died they let him out for the funeral. He did not go back: 'Their stupidity is matched only by their thoughtlessness.' 'But it's the friends I still miss most. Last month I became a grandad (he was only forty-four) but I cannot visit my grandchildren. They would let me move back permanently, which I don't want to do, but not for a visit. It's funny, you know; there I felt locked in, unable even to go to Poland without a visa; now I can travel wherever I want in the world, but the one thing I'd really like to do is get on a train and nip up to Alex's place for a drink.' He had no idea how soon his wish would be fulfilled.

We had met in a bar in West Berlin's Charlottenburg district. It was called Dicke Wirtin (The Fat Landlady) and was run as a student bar with the proviso that in Germany students are often into their mid thirties before they finish university. One of the barmen was Jürgen, who looked on the whole business of escaping from East Germany with a cynical eye. He later told us why: he came from Erfurt in Thuringia and had himself been an East German border guard when he decided on one early patrol some twelve years earlier to make a run for the West.

It was only a few days later that Kerstin, on her way to work at the steak-house, noticed the dramatic news on the electronic billboard at the Ku'damm Eck crossroads. It displayed a giant electronic picture of an elderly man in glasses and the legend 'Bye bye Honey'. Erich the Red had gone, pushed by his own crown prince, Egon Krenz, the man they called Horse Face. By some delicious mischance the announcement of his appointment as the new leader of East Germany had interrupted a programme on the state-run television called *Everyone Dreams of a Horse*. Krenz was to be a nine-day wonder, but will go down in history as the man who opened the Wall. That, at least, is the image he has tried to foster since then in quiz shows and his ghost-written autobiography.

With swept-back, iron-grey hair and curling lips that revealed a mouthful of sharp teeth, Krenz at fifty-two had the sort of 'kind uncle' leering smile that makes adults cringe. In his first televised address as ruler of East Germany he sat hunched over his script, reading slowly, his head moving from left to right as he followed the words, looking into the camera with sunken but penetrating eyes at the end of each paragraph. His assumption of power reassured nobody. Wolf Biermann, the satirical singer-songwriter expelled from East Germany in 1976, described Krenz as the 'nastiest possible candidate'. Several thousand East Berliners formed a human chain across the Alexanderplatz to express scepticism about the promise of a more human face.

Michy, a Metzer Eck regular who was a cabaret artiste from the Reiz'zwecken (Tin Tacks) cabaret troupe, lamented that popular wit was outstripping their scriptwriters. They had just rehearsed a new sketch with Krenz as the wolf in a version of Little Red Riding Hood when he saw a banner on the street showing the new leader's face with pointed ears and the caption 'My, grandma, what big teeth you have.' 'They don't laugh any more,' Michy despaired. 'We used to have to fight the censor for every bloody comma. Now we can't even keep up with the jokes on the streets.' Alex laughed and poured him another beer.

The situation was crumbling. Reforms that only a few weeks earlier had been deemed unnecessary were suddenly declared ripe for discussion. Krenz acknowledged that the tide of emigration was an 'open wound'. Rumours emerging from the communist ranks said Krenz had been given only until the party congress – May at the latest. Talk was already of Hans Modrow, the Dresden party boss, a self-billed Gorbachev despite the violence that had occurred in Dresden. But there was no real strategy, in East or West; just hastily convened pragmatism. In the East the small parties that had legally existed as lackeys slowly began to find their voices as they had done in Poland; old corrupt leaders were ousted and new ones, with apparently impeccable credentials, were elected to replace them. This was the rise of the nondescript, lisping Lothar de Maizière as leader of the East German Christian Democrats still tainted by years of collaboration with the communists. He would rise to become East Germany's last prime minister, the job finally having regained meaning with the abolition of communist monopoly on power and fully free elections. It was to be the bitter lesson for East Germany that after forty years of a police state nobody was squeaky clean. After the euphoria of unification he too would be hit by mud-slinging and allegations of cooperation with the Stasi.

Krenz hinted he might open the border if only Bonn would finally recognize a separate East German citizenship. That would have removed the right of East German refugees to claim West German passports. It might have saved East Germany, but it was against Bonn's hallowed constitution and was rejected, not without some dissenting voices on the Social Democrat benches. But it had all gone too far anyway. Even without the assurances he so desperately wanted, Krenz caved in. On the afternoon of Thursday, 9 November, exactly fifty-one years after the Reichskristallnacht anti-Jewish pogrom that had shown the world the true face of Nazism, behind the grey walls that once housed the state bank of the Third Reich – now the headquarters of the East German Communist Party – Egon Krenz, like a gambler with one life left, decided to go for bust. It was a final attempt to salvage the East German state, to relieve the pressure and stem the tide of refugees from communism whose euphoria was spreading and now also threatening the communist regime in Prague as they passed through. It worked like pulling a cork from a champagne bottle.

The events of that night are history. Günther Schabowski, Berlin party boss and *de facto* number two to Krenz, broke the news at a press conference in East Berlin almost by accident. From then on it was a media event as the radio and television cameras of the West bounced the still unclear formulation of the new relaxed travel regulations back into the GDR. Key among them was the simple fact that no hindrance would be put in the way of East Germans wanting to cross to the West.

Much has been speculated about what the principal parties involved intended – Krenz, Schabowski, Modrow, the others in the East German leadership and even Gorbachev himself in Moscow. They, least of all, are now reliable sources as each in one way or another tries to improve his own role and take credit for an historic event that all the sources now concur was essentially an accident. I personally have no doubt that what was intended by the new regulation was simply an end to the practice of issuing passports only on special occasions and demanding exit visas from citizens. Information pieced together from a wide mixture of sources suggests that the scenario that should have happened was as follows: the borders were to be opened in the same way as, say, the frontiers of Britain or Spain; that is, the border police, in a reduced role, and the customs officials would remain. What might have happened to the electric fence through Germany and eventually the Wall itself in Berlin is an open question. It was not on the agenda that night.

What mattered was to meet Prague's demand and end the stream of refugees by guaranteeing everyone the right to come and go as they pleased. It was intended that East Germans, from the Friday morning, should go to their local police station and request a passport, which would be granted them automatically and as quickly as possible, perhaps within a few days for bureaucratic delays. The hope was that the refugee exodus would stop immediately, that there would be a large number of visitors to the West in the coming weeks, but in numbers controlled by the bureaucracy needed to issue passports; of these, many would defect, but these probably could not now be prevented from doing so anyway; the rest would taste the West but still come back; the scenario would then be open for a series of internal reforms that would create democratic change in East Germany in much the same way as had happened in Hungary, but not create difficulties on the international level. It was a stopgap policy; in the long term the results would most likely have been identical; but the invariable confusion of human affairs wanted a swifter solution.

Because the regulation itself was unclear, the media reports on it were unclear and the public perception was only that it was now legal to cross. Schabowski has freely admitted that he opened the door to the first major misinterpretation when, asked when the regulation came into effect, he replied, 'Immediately.' It is understandable how it seemed academic whether or not one might request permission to travel that night or next day; but what was not explained was exactly what documentation was needed. The first East Berliners began to hurry to the checkpoints. The first to be seriously besieged was that at Bornholmer Strasse, where Prenzlauer Berg touched on Wedding in the West. In Metzer Eck Alex and Bärbel had heard the news on television but, like many others, at first discounted it as misrepresentation. The version given out by the East German state-run channel was markedly more fudged. It later emerged that no one had given the state television instructions and they made up their version of the truth as they went along. Axel Grote, the Metzer Eck regular and television producer who had been sacked for political unreliability, made it his job in the months that followed to piece together how the orders to the border guards got confused.

By coincidence the nearest bar to the Bornholmer Strasse checkpoint was that run by Dieter Kanitz, Alex's former barman. He and his wife Hannelore had set up on their own managing a state-run *Kneipe* in the middle of a colony of allotments with weekend *Lauben* that abutted the railway tracks and the Wall.

The commandant of the contingent of border guards at the crossing was Manfred Sens. He was later to complain that they felt betrayed, they who for years had done a thankless task only to have it made a mockery overnight for no clear reason and without proper explanation or clear orders. He had had no instructions about any change in border regulations other than those that came over the public radio, by which time several hundred East Berliners were clamouring to be allowed to cross. He had a veritable arsenal in his stores, allowing for every degree of retaliation to any attempt to force a passage: rubber bullets, gas grenades, water-cannon and, of course, live ammunition. But he was reluctant to start an incident without orders from above, especially when everyone was telling him that to prevent them crossing would be against the orders he would shortly receive. He stayed on the telephone trying in vain to get a clear response. He got through to Fritz Streletz, Chief of the General Staff in Stalsund on the Baltic, who could not give him a definitive answer either, other than to remind him that he had been chosen for his experience as a man who lived in the political world and must be aware of the importance of avoiding serious incidents at the country's frontiers, especially in these critical times. It was too much.

Eventually Sens lifted the barrier and let the first of his whooping fellow citizens, on production only of their national identity card, cross into the West, a street away. Sens and his colleagues had no idea if they were letting people out for the night or for ever; at one stage the instruction came to put the exit stamp across the photograph in the identity card – for identification purposes. Within twenty-four hours tipsy teenagers coming back from West Berlin simply waved identity cards at bemused border guards who only weeks earlier might have shot them. In the bar only a hundred yards away there was a rush for the door. Dieter would have gone too, but he had lost his identity card, and Hannelore sat with him, doing good business anyway serving those who came back home for a drink at prices they could afford after the adventure of a lifetime in the next street.

It was so obviously, in retrospect, the beginning of new, more difficult times for those who had gone through mental and emotional cartwheels to create a tolerable life for themselves within the pattern of the GDR. In Metzer Eck Alex was torn between disbelief, scepticism and confusion about what it might mean. He refused to leave his *Stammtisch*; at a time of crisis he preferred to hold firm to what he knew. There was anyway no excitement for him, as he had last been to West Berlin only weeks earlier with Alexandra. Bärbel, however, had not been since 1961, and her daughter, whom she thought lost to her, was now once again within reach. Ominously, she and Alex had a row. They ended up squabbling and neither went, but Horst and Sylvie headed for Bornholmer Strasse.

Up and down the crossing points, literally set in concrete, between East and West Berlin, the frustration of millions of lifetimes were played out in a grand stage denouement of the Cold War. I was stuck in the crowds at Checkpoint Charlie, battling with a notebook and tears of excitement. I had been on my way back from a demonstration in Rostock when I heard the report of the Schabowski press conference. Accelerating to over a hundred and seventy kilometres per hour, I headed straight for the Wall. At Invalidenstrasse there were already thousands. I spoke to the border guard in charge, who confirmed that they were letting GDR citizens through, but he would not let me through. As a foreigner – even in the depths of the Cold War East German officialdom did not use that word for West Germans – I would have to go to Checkpoint Charlie. Cursing Prussian pedantry to the last, I ran back to the car and drove the kilometre or so, taking with me a group of East Berliners who had despaired of the Invalidenstrasse queue.

There it was every bit as chaotic. I drove into the middle of the wide expanse of the East German control area. The obviously harassed border guards completed my formalities in a few minutes, but would not let the East Germans come with me in the car. They had to go on foot. So, in the end, did I. For the scene on the other side was chaos. Guards with megaphones ran to and fro, shouting preposterously at photographers to stop taking pictures as families streaming tears kissed and hugged and Western revellers climbed on to the electrically controlled metal barriers. From the eastern side it genuinely looked like an angry, drunken mob. The other side of the checkpoint was Kreuzberg, home of West Berlin's disaffected squatters and anarchists, and some in the crowd were hurling abuse and beer cans at the border troops, suddenly transformed from sinister silhouettes behind searchlights into a close-up enemy (any uniform was a target for some Kreuzberg characters). The control area had meanwhile filled with cars. One party of Third World diplomats fumed at the helpless troops for not opening the gates, which, although pedestrians were coming through, remained closed against the teeming throng.

Frenetic, confused, at last they opened the gates. My car was first in the line. 'Go on then if you want to tackle that lot,' shouted one now angry lieutenant. I didn't. I was not sure if the crowds dancing in the gap ahead of me were angry or happy, but I knew one thing: I did not want to be responsible for the first casualty of the night by running over someone. It would be much later that night, when the mood of celebration had been firmly established, before the first little box-like Trabants began to trundle through and the curious welcome custom of 'Trabby-bouncing' would occur. At that moment I made my own decision; I turned the car round and drove east, leaving the diplomats fuming as the troops closed the gates again to stop an influx of partying drunks set on invading East Berlin.

I crossed on foot. It was a memorable, if bizarre, experience: stepping through the pedestrian gate I had used a thousand times before, to have my hair ruffled by a forest of outstretched hands, be kissed at random by unseen lips and find a can of beer thrust into my hand with the emotional cry 'Herzlich Wilkommen im Westen'.

Dazed and probably looking as emotional as if I had indeed set foot for the first time in West Berlin, I muttered '*Danke*' and stumbled on through the crowd, who were already embracing the next arrival.

I went to the Adler Bar, recently opened in a building that had long lain derelict and now doing the best trade it ever would, and phoned Alex in Metzer Eck. He told me he was not going to come over. 'Guess who has just turned up? Günther Zschäckl. He says it was only the other week he was telling you his one wish was to be able to drink in Metzer Eck. Well, now he can. There's progress for you.' He said he did not know about Bärbel, but Horst and Sylvie had gone and would probably, he guessed, turn up at Renate's. For a couple of hours I dithered, drinking in a scene I had thought impossible.

Remembering somehow that I would have to compose an article for the paper, I talked at random to some of those who had just come over. Most had their hearts in their mouths. Petra Lorenz, a dumpy, middle-aged mother-of-two, had travelled two hours by bus and tram from her flat in Marzahn, leaving her husband to look after their children. 'Don't be daft, it's a lie,' he had said. She wandered in a trance for twenty minutes on the western side of Checkpoint Charlie, and went back with a newspaper as a souvenir of a dream. The burning question in everyone's mind was answered by a bus driver from the East, smiling with a crisp uncertainty: 'Can they take back their decision? Close the wall again? Never. We'll see them sink in ashes first.'

It was time to go to the Ku'damm, the centre of West Berlin night-life, where it seemed likely most of the more adventurous would head. But it made sense to take some East Berliners with me. The obvious candidates soon presented themselves. Running a cheering gauntlet of beery West Berliners dancing on the Wall came a ready-made party. Their names were Christiane Schulz, Janna Meyer and Andrea Fleischer, waitresses from the Hotel Stadt Berlin, and they came whooping into the West, spraying Rotkäppchen (Little Red Riding Hood), the fizzy party plonk of the East, at grinning policemen. I grabbed a taxi and offered them a lift to the Ku'damm in exchange for the story of their evening.

Until eight p.m. they had been serving pig's knuckles and mushy peas to Russian tourists. Then came the news that the

Wall was open. They bit their lips and looked at each other but with that characteristic devotion to duty that even the Germans call *deutsche Gründlichkeit* they worked until the end of their shift at two-thirty before Andrea turned to the others and, with a nervous giggle, asked, 'Anyone for the Ku'damm?' For the first time in their lives, three girls from the East could go up West for the evening. When we piled out of the taxi in the middle of the carnival that had spread across the centre of West Berlin, Andrea looked longingly at a telephone box that would work only with the Western cash she did not have. I handed her a few marks and she woke her parents in the East: 'Mutti, I'm on the Ku'damm. It's mad. It's marvellous. Oh, don't be cross. I'm coming back.' Then 'Yahoo!' and into the mêlée.

For one delirious night most of East Berlin took a walk on the wild side: two-stroke 'Trabbies', the fibre-glass midget cars soon to become an accidental symbol of a revolution based on middle-class values, raced Mercedes along the glitzy avenues littered with broken bottles beneath a sky ablaze with fireworks; it was as if a long-awaited marriage had occurred; Berlin embraced Berlin. Policemen from the West kissed bus conductresses from the East. 'Berlin is again Berlin. Germany weeps with joy,' screamed the headlines on special-edition tabloids handed out free on the streets of the West.

I stood and watched, stunned, then startled when I was suddenly grabbed round the neck by a tall man in a leather jacket with cropped hair: Andreas, an improbable *deus ex machina*, but profoundly welcome. He had just met Kerstin after work and they were still reeling from the news. We dived into a phone box and called Renate to find out if she had heard from Horst and Sylvie. They were with her. We arranged to meet them as soon as they could manage it on the Ku'damm Eck, probably the most confused spot in Europe at that moment. But we managed it. 'We've . . . uh . . . just popped over for a drink,' said Horst, looking exaggeratedly nonchalant before he whooped with joy and swung his sister into his arms. At five-thirty a.m. we were sitting over tall beers while Kerstin wept quietly with happiness; Horst touted for custom for Metzer Eck: 'Better pig's knuckles than any you get here,' he shouted. As we left, he asked the waitress if he could perhaps buy two of the tall, elegant Warsteiner Pilsner glasses, just as a souvenir. She laughed and told him to take them and not ask silly questions. As an unimaginable dawn broke on the first day of a new Germany, we staggered off to bed, the East Berliners in Renate's West Berlin flat, and I, the Westerner, to my East Berlin hotel. Life would be different from now on.

At nine a.m. on Friday 10 November, when the luxury department store KaDeWe opened its doors, the East Berliners flooded in to stare at the electronic miracles on offer, at the mountainous meat and fruit display on the 'Gourmet Floor'. But with West marks still like rare gold, most only window-shopped and made their purchases at the cheaper supermarkets and discount electrical stores.

Alex and Bärbel came over in the afternoon and we all met at Renate's flat and went out for a celebratory Chinese meal. Bärbel had spent hours wandering the Ku'damm, which she had last seen as a little girl, and caused laughter when she returned, still daydreaming, with the single comment: 'The streets don't seem as wide as I remember.' On the Wall the East German police and border guards abandoned trying to understand what was really intended by the new border regulations. They were again insisting on stamping documents and issuing visas, but of random validity from three days to six months. Manfred Sens, the commandant at the Bornholmer Strasse checkpoint, would later testify that on 14 November he received the order again to 'secure the frontier'. 'That was a joke,' he snorted. 'By that stage it was all we could do to ensure an orderly flow of traffic.' The stream of honking eastern cars continued to flow down the Ku'damm, over the border and along Unter den Linden. The wall before the Brandenburg Gate looked more redundant than ever. Within weeks it would be breached in dozens of places, within seven months consigned to archaeology.

It was perhaps understandable that the full significance of what had happened only sank in slowly. The Berlin Wall *was* the Iron Curtain, a point graphically illustrated by the rapid chain reaction that now raced through Czechoslovakia to the bloody overthrow of Nicolae Ceausescu in Romania. A Soviet spokesman billed the superpower summit about to take place in warships on the choppy seas off Valletta as the progress of history 'from Yalta to Malta'. It was a more than broad hint that Moscow no longer claimed the advantage Stalin had wrested from Churchill and Roosevelt as they partitioned the world in the elegant drawing room of Livadia Palace in the Crimea in February 1945.

But not in Washington, not in London, not in Paris, nor even Bonn – and least of all Brussels – was there a blueprint for Europe to replace the strategic certainties of the Cold War. Wolf Biermann was right 'We had already half-swallowed the lie that the sun could never rise again in the East.' In Bonn Chancellor Kohl prepared his 'ten-point plan', a steady, long-term timetable for progress towards German unity; in Washington George Bush paid lip-service to the idea; in London Margaret Thatcher implied that even consideration of such a topic was 'destabilizing'. US Secretary of State James Baker told reporters that talk about German reunification was premature.

But the East German communists had played their last card, gambling on a scorched earth policy, yielding every demand in the hope of exhausting the enemy. It was one of the founding fathers of communism, a high deity in the crumbled East German pantheon, Friedrich Engels, who, a century earlier, had written their epitaph: 'Everyone strives for his own interests, but in the end what emerges is something no one intended.'

# 12

## *Tomorrow!*

It is also true that there is no fire without smoke. The conflagration that consumed the decaying corpse of East Germany left scorch marks across the whole of a nation that was now once again to be nervously predominant in Europe. The stain was the Stasi, different in detail but similar in substance to the smear left by the Nazis, which West Germany after much public and private *angst* had hoped to be rid of after four decades. Now its ghost, or at least its mirror image, had returned to haunt a nation once again trying desperately to see a clear vision of itself.

The bonfires started sporadically. It was the people of the sleepy medieval city of Erfurt in Thuringia who were first to recognize the dark wisps curling from the chimneys of the drab office block for what they were: smoke from the funeral pyre of communism. 'The bastards are burning the evidence,' shouted a man in the crowd. Throughout East Germany in the first week of December 1989 the men of the Office of State Security, still an organ of the state, if overnight no longer a ministry, were doing overtime to destroy their lifetime's work. Files and documents, films and tapes, all were shovelled into ovens and incinerators; in Erfurt, Dresden, Gera, Suhl, Leipzig and other cities. The people in the streets now terrified the men who had terrified them.

At the congress where the Communist Party narrowly avoided suicide and changed its official name from SED (Socialist Unity Party of Germany) to PDS (Party of Democratic Socialism), a factory worker from the port of Rostock said he was afraid to support the party under any name: 'My mates don't talk to me any more.' Delegates complained that hairdressers and bus drivers had put signs in their windows declaring 'SED members not accepted.'

Democracy became a devil in disguise, a label for recriminations and score-settling; yet there were genuine grievances to be redressed and there was an equally genuine need to remove the *apparatchiks* if the danger of a sudden reversion was to be averted. Alex found his daughter was closer to the front line than he was himself. The pupils in Alexandra's school, after years of indoctrination to the Marxist–Leninist line, were suddenly invited to contribute to changing the curriculum, to commenting on the past performance of their teachers. Alexandra was elected to a group of 'pupils' representatives' and to her own surprise found herself shoved to the fore at a meeting of parents, pupils and teachers.

Surrounded by shaken totems of her childhood, she felt as if in the company of wolves; adults had been transformed from pillars of righteousness to lying cowards who said one thing one moment and another the next. As the meeting, for the sake of compromise, continuity and a quiet life, was about to re-elect to a position of authority a woman teacher who had been an unrepentant die-hard communist until the last minute, Alexandra stood up like the child who declared the emperor had no clothes, and said the woman was a fraud, a phoney and a fascist and she would cast the pupils' vote against. The adults followed suit, like the sheep they still were.

Purges spread even to the church, which for so long had sheltered the opposition; Horst Gienke, Bishop of the Baltic city of Greifswald, who was on first-name terms with Erich Honecker, was forced to resign. Outside the Volkskammer, the parliament, a group of artists erected a banner written in the same runic script as the 'S' on Alex Margan's long-lost childhood trumpet: 'SED=⚡⚡'. Everyone demonstrated about something. Three dozen children of former Stasi officers carried banners complaining that their fathers were being persecuted. Passers-by laughed.

The scale of the fury among East Germans against the greedy *apparatchiks* who had so long exploited and oppressed them shocked the Germans on the other side of the fast-fading frontier. Bonn joined the communists in East Berlin in calling for calm. The West Germans preferred not to remember their own painful cure from schizophrenia. The fear in West Germany was that the outpouring of rage against the erstwhile repressors could mutate into *Volkszorn*, the 'wrath of the people', an uncomfortable phrase because it was coined by the Nazis as a Wagnerian euphemism for anti-Semitic pogroms. Bonn had spent forty years sanitizing the international image of the German nation. It did not want to have to start again because of some overenthusiastic debt-settling, even against acknowledged criminals. No one wanted lynchings, though at times it came close, as when the crowds sacked the Stasi headquarters in Leipzig, a symbolic hate-object that had been whistled and booed as every Monday march passed its barred windows.

The conservative newspaper *Die Welt* commented in a front-page editorial: 'The boisterous enthusiasm with which some people under suspicion in the state, party, justice and media are being condemned without investigation, made non-persons and even driven to suicide has more in common with purges. Legality needs practice.' In the meantime it had become *laissez-faire*. On the bumpy 1930s autobahn from Berlin to Leipzig two traffic policemen who stopped me for speeding apologized for demanding an instant fine, then could not decide whether it should be paid in East or West marks: 'It's not easy these days, you know,' said one of them. 'I grew up in the Young Pioneers. We were taught all that anti-fascist stuff and how it was great to protect the achievements of socialism. Now it seems it was all a load of nonsense. We could all be out of work, or I suppose even be on patrol outside Munich in a few months' time.'

Restoring legality, from faith in the police to trust in judges, was to be a long and painful process. An entire legal profession needed to be re-educated or removed, a process that would go on long after the blitzkrieg unification, hampered by Stasi files that continued to disgorge dirt. Most of what emerged was against politicians, but only because that made news. Totalitarianism was what it said: it embraced everything and everyone. After forty years there were few people who could claim their hands had never touched muck.

In Berlin, in the canteen of the formerly feared Normannenstrasse Stasi headquarters, after it had been taken over by the new citizens' groups, visitors could stare at a trophy case in the canteen that contained a large, red, plastic plinth with a figure of Felix Dzerzhinsky, founder of the KGB, inscribed in Russian with his recipe for the perfect secret policeman: 'A cool head, a warm heart and clean hands.' It was a wonderful recipe, the opposite in every particular from the truth. But then to turn truth on its head had been their job.

The mere existence of the vast pile of material that constituted the sum of the Stasi's massive surveillance efforts, in neatly filed pieces of paper and the more sinister, less accessible banks of computer memory, was a source of national paranoia. In Metzer Eck Hans Busch confided his own fears to Alex: 'Someone is going to have it in for me. I know they are. After all, *they* came to me, you know, once every month or so, just to check, of course. But I had to cooperate, didn't I? I mean, I didn't dish dirt on anyone, but they had to have reports on the apprentices, didn't they? I mean, the party was paying for their training.'

'Of course they did, Hans; of course they did.' There was no sarcasm in Alex's voice, no gloating. Everyone knew what the rules of the old game had been. Among close friends all across the country, the tone was that of the confessional.

But there had been a revolution in the media. A passion for investigative journalism caught on like a schoolboy fad in a country where a reporter's job had been to say what his superiors told him. The youth television programme *Eleven-99* devoted an episode to the secrets of the dread Stasi headquarters in East Berlin's Normannenstrasse. *Eleven-99* was an accident of the Honecker era, a programme that began with a series of pop-art images, including a winking Karl Marx, and was meant as a controlled safety-valve for youthful rebellion. With the end of censorship, its latent anarchy surfaced. Even Angelika Unterlauf, a woman in her late thirties who as newsreader for twelve years parroted the stock phrases of the dictatorship, admitted she found it embarrassing. Would she have been able to read the doctored news calmly if Honecker had sent in the troops in Leipzig? No, she replied, she would have reported sick. Unterlauf described the crude way in which the old regime had exercised its power over television: 'There would simply be a telephone call to the director's box. Sometimes the whole broadcast would be in chaos because the Central Committee was still debating what we should say.' Now, the East German press published West German television listings, while the (East) *Berliner Zeitung* published a city map including West Berlin's transport system, no longer just blank white space labelled obtusely 'WB'. The editorial board of *Neues Deutschland*, the party newspaper, sacked the editor, pledging a new, open policy.

When Lieutenant-General Manfred Schwanitz, head of the Stasi after the deposition of the evil octogenarian Erich Mielke, announced he had given the order to burn documents that 'did not fit in with the new attitude to security', the reaction was an insistent demand, reluctantly granted, to allow a handful of reporters and 'citizens' groups' representatives' into the Stasi headquarters. Accompanied by a military lawyer, the group was shown ashes in the ovens where the documents were incinerated. A sheepish official in an anorak said he normally burnt papers here but admitted the volume had grown. 'By how much? Are you burning ten per cent more, twice as much or a hundred times?' pressed Margitta Hinze, the small but determined spokeswoman of the citizens' group. 'Well, um, uh,' he hesitated, looking in vain for guidance, 'about three times normal, I guess.'

One Friday night in Metzer Eck I met Axel Grote, the television producer who had been sacked the previous May after resigning from the party in protest over the notoriously falsified local election results – the last the communists were to control. He was preparing to drive his beaten-up Wartburg hundreds of miles to Nuremberg in West Germany, a trip that in itself had been a fantasy only a month earlier, to gather information on a Stasi 'front firm' used to launder money. He then drove back through the night to set up an interview with the deposed Krenz to challenge him with his evidence. Within weeks he had set up with a cameraman as an investigative news team and swapped the Wartburg for a second-hand Golf. He was already planning the documentary on how the Wall came down.

There was much public smirking, such as when the head of Deutrans, the state road-transport firm, was forced to defend himself in a television interview, claiming an unblemished record of honesty for himself and his truckers: men long envied in East German society because their regular foreign trips provided them with stockings, cassette recorders, videotapes and condoms to upgrade their social standing. Like all black-market princes, including Manne Schulz, overnight their magic powers had become commonplace. Manne was no longer to be seen so regularly at the *Stammtisch*. His adoring girlfriend had suddenly grown bored with his company and found someone slimmer. His music collection, though still exceptional, was no longer unique. And everyone had digital watches.

The changing economic climate had other emotional casualties:

Alex and Bärbel separated. The events of the past year had already put severe strains on their relationship. Now, among other things, they disagreed about plans for the future in the united Germany they both clearly saw approaching fast. Each knew the new freedoms that had been won had a down side; in the wider world that had now opened on their doorstep Metzer Eck would no longer necessarily be the rare and special place they had made it. There was already the attraction of the myriad bars of West Berlin to compete with; eventually there would be more competition close to hand. They had opposing answers. Alex wanted to expand, to apply to take over new premises and open at least one more bar, if not an entire chain. At fifty-nine he wanted to employ the entrepreneurial drive that had been frustrated for most of his adult life. Bärbel preferred to hang on to the bird in hand. Horst was keen to work more in the bar with the aim of taking it over one day. Bärbel saw risky, hard times ahead and wanted to consolidate what they had in the unfamiliar new world of real money and sharp business practice. The arguments grew more frequent and more bitter. Alex moved out. It was a radical move. He left not just the woman he had lived with for the best part of twenty years, but their doted-on daughter, Alexandra, and his livelihood. He found a small flat a few streets away, in a gloomy *Hinterhof*, and a part-time job bundling newspapers while he looked for financial backers and a site for the new pub that he hoped would be the key to a new life.

Meanwhile the East German state around them was crumbling by the second. The new coalition government of Hans Modrow, trumpeted by the last-ditch communists, had humiliatingly failed to squeeze more money out of Bonn for 'restructuring and transitional arrangements'. The lumpen Kohl had suddenly become a political vulture and he scented blood. The Modrow government had, in any case, already been dismissed on the streets of the provinces by workers chanting, 'Modrow, you have no legitimacy without free elections.' It was agreed that elections would be held in March. As new parties sprang up, old ones rehabilitated themselves and forged links with their big cousins in the West, and it was increasingly clear that the only real issues were the ifs, whens and hows of unification.

Yet there were still a million uncertainties. Willy Brandt, not sure whether he was witnessing the fruits of his Ostpolitik or just its end, told an East German newspaper what it would once have wanted to hear but now doubted: 'The existence of two German states remains a basic consideration'; Eberhard Diepgen, another former mayor of West Berlin, then leader of the Christian Democrat opposition in the city senate, declared that on the contrary 'sooner or later the people of East Germany will decide for unification'. It was all to be sooner, much sooner. On the eve of its December congress the SED had publicly accepted responsibility for 'the worst crisis in the history of the German Democratic Republic'. It was a typically mistaken analysis: the communists were responsible for the entire history of the GDR, its very existence and its lack of democracy. Now democracy destroyed it. The communists had made themselves the state; when they went, so did it. A banner I glimpsed on the streets of Erfurt said it with a cartoon and the slogan 'We need the Communist Party like a fish needs a bicycle.'

The tone of the continuing street demonstrations had decisively altered. One Monday in freezing fog on the steps of the now empty Stasi headquarters in Leipzig, I had watched four lads in leather jackets burst into hoarse refrain: '*Deutschland, Deutschland über alles*', the first verse of the old national anthem, now not even sung in the West for fear of any associations with Nazism. In the crowd a small man with a neat scarf and fur hat barked: 'Stop it. That is not what it's about at all.' But it was. The banners on the demonstrations now read: '*Mit Herz und Verstand – Deutschland einig Vaterland*' ('With our hearts and our reason, Germany, unified Fatherland') or '*Einigkeit und Recht und Freiheit*' ('Unity and law and freedom' – the first line of the words now sung in West Germany to the national anthem).

I met a burly, middle-aged man with a beard and beret who told me he taught musicology but, for the moment, the revolution came first. The message from Moscow that reunification 'is not an issue at present' had changed, after Chancellor Kohl's February meeting with Gorbachev, to 'go ahead'. As the new Christian Democrat-led government after the March elections negotiated terms for the now inevitable imminent currency union, there were queues outside antique, jewellery and household goods shops in East Germany as people translated paper money into durable items such as furniture, fridges or gold. It had had a creeping inevitability about it. The opening of the frontier had convinced East Germans that those on the other side were different in only one important way: they had more money.

In the bar of the Schwarzer Adler (The Black Eagle) in the snow-hung Bavarian hamlet of Tettau one sunny afternoon in March, I came across two apparent locals, Dieter and Siegfried, arguing in the same impenetrable Thuringian mountain dialect about the relative virtues of different types of market economies. 'Funny, I'm a member of the communist party, and will remain one, but it's more fun drinking here with you,' conceded Dieter as he fell off his stool, picked up his carrier bag (East) full of vegetables (West) and toddled off merrily north towards the meaningless frontier and his home village of Grafenthal three miles away. For four decades it had been 'so near, yet so far'; now they were having to learn to be neighbours again. Since 1946 Tettau had got used to being a dead end, a picturesque place of tile-hung gabled houses in a thickly wooded valley that ended in barbed wire, an electric fence and armed guards. Then one day the border guards made a hole, set up a ridiculous tiny caravan and began issuing visas, then just checking papers, and by March they were simply leaning out and waving, happy to pose for pictures leaning over their caravan half-doors like downmarket holidaymakers on an abandoned campsite.

It was in these isolated areas, East or West, on the Cold War front lines with roads that had once led in only one direction but where old people still remembered when they were in the heart of Germany, that the knitting-together process came as such a culture shock. As Rosie Nussbaum, the hard-drinking, robust manageress of a state-owned beer garden in the small town of Gross Breitenbach, twenty miles inside the frontier, put it: 'Bloody nowhere, that's where we were.' Rosie was a rumbustious woman who had been born in Pomerania, now Polish, but grown up in Saxony to share the same rolling vowels as her lifelong friend, Uschi, one of the regulars in Metzer Eck, who had sent me to stay with her. For five years Rosie had been trying to get permission for her elder daughter to open a hairdressing salon in their house. She had met a blank wall of indifferent bureaucracy, until overnight all walls fell together: 'Suddenly they fell over backwards when I told them if they didn't give us permission we'd move down the road and open up in the West.'

# TOMORROW!

The entire life of Gross Breitenbach had been transformed. Posters nailed to trees invited entries for the fancy-dress competition at the carnival ball in the West German village hall across the frontier. The pub in the village of Spechtbrunn in the East held a cross-border Skat competition, the equivalent of a whist drive. Unheeding of the great powers' deliberations, unity was being forged at parish council level. Yet slowly but surely the differences of forty years of separate development were becoming noticed: 'They have everything,' laughed Rosie, 'but they've forgotten the basics. They open tins instead of cooking. I had a meal in Bavaria that cost a king's ransom in our money but was barely edible.' But she was in no two minds about the political necessity of unity: 'I got a trip to Moscow once. It was twenty years ago; me and my girlfriend, we were young and pretty then. The Russians wouldn't let us into the hotel bar because we were from the East. Two lads from Stuttgart offered to take us but our group leader said we couldn't mix with the "class enemy". For twenty years they wouldn't let me visit my parents in the West; by the time they agreed, my mother was dying. Now they say sorry, it wasn't our fault, give us another go. Bloody see if I do.'

The Christian Democrats had won free elections and signed an agreement on unification in two stages. Suddenly, it was over. On a sunlit July afternoon I climbed to the top of a watch-tower on the western edge of the now unified city of Berlin, where once it had ended abruptly. The countryside within and without the Wall, now hacked and holed, was once again knitting back together. I watched small children kick balls to and fro along the former death strip. In a ring round West Berlin and for nearly a thousand miles in a wound cut through Germany the watch-towers stood empty, each one a *Marie Celeste* of the Cold War, abandoned in shame by its crew, graffiti-scarred and soiled, reinforced-glass windows shattered by stones. Even in the summer heat a chill pervaded the concrete columns within which a vertical iron ladder led to a spartan metal chamber where young soldiers had shivered, under orders to kill their countrymen.

At Metzer Eck they held a party on the eve of the currency union that would consign millions of banknotes with Karl Marx's head to the bottom of phosphorus mines and landfill sites. Horst wore a black armband as the regulars gathered to hold a mock wake for

189

the unlamented Ostmark. Hermann handed out black-bordered mourning cards with a single, almost weightless aluminium one-pfennig coin glued to each and the words 'In solemn remembrance'. The last Ostmarks went on the last old-style Ost-beer. 'We've only half a barrel left,' moaned Bärbel. 'When the new stuff comes on Monday we'll have to pay real money for it.' Heinz had spent all his East marks too soon. He asked if he could pay in D-marks. Bärbel laughed and said: 'Charge the idiot half price.'

It was the infectious, nervous gaiety of those whose dreams had come true too fast; anticipation tinged with uncertainty. At midnight there was not only a single currency throughout Germany, but the border guards of a GDR that was by now barely clinging to life would pack up their bags and retire. As if befitting the end of the collectivist ideal, the communal experience of instant German unity came as a separate shock to each individual. Mine had come twenty-four hours earlier: driving back to East Berlin's Grand Hotel, I took a wrong turning and found myself suddenly in the West. It was a moment of almost blinding, elated panic. In terms of street names, communist hero Otto Grotewohl had been transmuted back into Kaiser Wilhelm. The dingy café hard against the western side of the Wall had been bulldozed, the floodlights replaced with street lights, the asphalt relaid; and the Wilhelmstrasse, former site of the Reich Chancellery, resurrected as a thoroughfare as if it had never been interrupted.

I accelerated, turning left and left again and back through Checkpoint Charlie, where amid the giant hangars that housed the East German border troops a yellow cigarette hoarding read: 'Camel, rediscover good taste.' The guards were still there, smoking – East German Club cigarettes, not yet Camels – and watching the passing traffic. I recognized one and called out: 'How are you?' He waved cheerily back. I said: 'After ten years of crossing here, you know all about me: name, date of birth, passport number, profession and perhaps much more. I don't even know your name.'

He gave a bitter-sweet grin: 'We don't need names.' (The public prosecutor is considering charges against border guards who might have killed, even in duty.) 'Oh, all right,' he lapsed, 'my first name's Uwe.'

At midnight on 30 June Uwe and his comrades sauntered into West Berlin and cracked bottles of Beck's beer in a bitter-sweet celebration of their own redundancy. In an unexpected final moment of glory they became celebrities, as television teams from Italy and Japan queued to interview them in pidgin German: 'You are from where please?'

'Cottbus, on the border with the People's Republic of Poland – oops, I mean the Republic of Poland,' he corrected, suddenly remembering that he had entered the post-communist age.

'What will you do now?'

'Work. One has to work. I'll find a job.'

The papers called it New Year in midsummer. But Germany had not had a New Year like it in half a century. Along Under den Linden the firecrackers exploded and champagne corks popped as the cavalcades rolled from West to East, back again and round and about and across reopened streets, car horns sounding as Berliners rediscovered Berlin. On East Berlin's Alexanderplatz, again declared the centre of Europe, ragtime bands played Dixieland jazz and traditional oompah music as the beer glasses clinked, despite their contents being paid for in hard D-marks. On the great empty expanse of Potsdamer Platz, where the death strip had been, a combined East–West orchestra played Mahler's 'Resurrection' symphony.

The streets of East and West Berlin were fusing back together like severed nerve endings seeking reconnection after an operation; here and there the bulldozers pushing through the streets in the East found themselves crashing into pedestrian precincts or gardens. The capital of the espionage war had become a spy-thriller adventure playground. Wandering around areas that had been no man's land was like exploring behind Hollywood movie sets. On a suitably atmospheric drizzly night at Oberbaumbrücke, the pedestrian bridge where John le Carré's Smiley waited for his Karla to defect, I watched the drunks whistling as they kicked tin cans into the River Spree, reeling across the bridge unheeding of the grey sniper post, now a vandalized anomaly in the rain.

Not everyone was happy. The Kreuzberg squatters had erected a sign on their last piece of Wall in idiomatic English: 'Fuck off tourists.' It had a political subscript in German. 'Down with the stinking unity of Trabant and Golf.' But there was nothing to be done about it; the Kleinbürger, the little men, had won.

Already, out in the East German provinces, where the division had no concrete symbol, the new values initially seemed to fit like an old glove. The superficial transformation of the towns and villages were speeded by the West German advertising agencies, which suddenly found themselves with more 'greenfield sites' than they had ever dreamt of. There was soon hardly a pub that had not added a Western beer to its cellar and a neon sign outside; no supermarket or small shop still in thrall to the centralized state economy that was to be handed over to Bonn's receivers that did not have its windows plastered with stickers for Western radio stations or special introductory offers on HB cigarettes.

It was more of an *Anschluss* than anyone liked to admit. Only two days after the currency union, Schwerin, thirty miles from the border, could, judging from appearances alone, have been on either side of it. Before, East Germany had smelled of brown coal; now it smelled of fresh paint. In Schwerin the red, yellow and blue ancient flag of Mecklenburg was waving, as was the green-and-white banner of Augustus the Strong over the square in Leipzig now once again named after him instead of Lenin. The shoppers calmly and calculatingly contemplated the new washing-machines and breakfast cereals in shop windows.

Yet again there was a certain amount of concealed trauma. The influential Hamburg weekly *Die Zeit* speculated, however, that half of East Germany's sixteen million population could need therapy to get over the feeling of inferiority after devoting half a lifetime to a system abolished within a few short months. For most East Germans life was turned topsy-turvy. Luxuries, once expensive or inaccessible, were now easy to come by and cheap – a colour television cost one tenth of what it did – while daily necessities soared – potatoes, meat, bread and beer all rose roughly threefold from the level at which they had been subsidized by the communist state.

The situation was not helped by the overnight disappearance of almost all East German consumer goods from the shops. What had been worth having was snapped up in the dying days of the Ostmark. What was left was considered unsaleable at worst, undesirable at best. It created a general impression that East meant worse and damaged the already limited ability to compete of the industries in the East. The spirits wholesalers supplying the bars produced a ten-page catalogue but by midweek could not deliver half its contents. Butchers found that promised supplies of meat from disintegrating collective farms failed to materialize and instead ordered from the obliging West. So did barkeepers.

TOMORROW!

Bärbel had closed Metzer Eck the day after the wake for the Ostmark. With Alex gone, she wanted to sit down with Horst and work out how they would operate before her first day open under the D-mark regime. I joined them and we sat late into the dark capitalist night debating what the mark-up should be on a sausage and whether it was worth continuing to make meatballs or import them from Western wholesalers. As it turned out, on day one the bar was half-empty, but the turnover was more than enough to live on. But they bought factory-made Western *Bouletten* and decided that they could no longer afford to keep on the extra waitress.

For the man in the street in Berlin or Dresden, unity was an economic fact, but in Washington, Paris, London, Moscow and Bonn the statesmen were hurriedly working out the strategic mechanics of restoring the German sovereignty the victorious allies had assumed in 1945. The anachronism of two imperfectly fused states was riddled with risk. As the German national football team beat Czechoslovakia in the World Cup a gaggle of skinheads halfheartedly ran amok in East Berlin in celebration, pouring scornful derision on a police force robbed of all self-respect or moral authority. West German teenagers used to be able to flout parental authority with the bitter jibe: 'What did you do in the war, Daddy?' Fate now allowed a new – East German – generation to challenge its parents with: 'And what did you do under the occupation?' There was no easy answer. East Germany was well and truly dead. It was time to bury the corpse before it began to stink.

In July Kohl went to see Gorbachev in the Caucasus and sealed the deal on the last critical element: the new Germany could be part of NATO and would pay for the gradual withdrawal of Soviet troops, as well as becoming the major Western partner in Gorbachev's drive to transform the Soviet economy. In September in Moscow the 'two plus four' talks, which had brought together the two German states, plus Britain, France, the United States and the Soviet Union, with Poland butting in occasionally from the wings, were concluded. The deed was done. At midnight on 2–3 October the partition of Germany was over.

Yet on Unity Night itself, as Kohl and Brandt and Lafontaine and Schmidt and, almost as an afterthought, one or two outgoing East German ministers gathered to toast the fatherland in the

Reichstag – now again bidding to become the seat of the German parliament – the old bars of East Berlin's Prenzlauer Berg had closed their doors to outsiders, their patrons, like so many members of a disintegrating club, holding a final, final reunion. I met Alex at Quelle (The Source), on the corner of Metzer Strasse and Prenzlauer Allee; he no longer felt he could go to Metzer Eck, barely a hundred yards away, and had collected a small coterie for a separate party. Renate and Renatchen had come from what we were learning just to call 'the other side of town'. Over beer and schnapps we struggled for metaphors to understand what was happening. The most popular analogies were marital. 'It's like a wedding where the bride has no dowry,' suggested Heinz.

'And when she isn't a virgin either,' added Alex.

'No, it's more like a divorce, because it's painful and expensive.'

In the end we settled on a wedding, but decided it was marriage for the third time to the same woman, definitely a love match but without much of the excitement. It was accurate enough; the first passionate embrace had been the fall of the Wall; the second, the real consummation, came with currency union in July; in comparison this seemed just like another rehearsal of a familiar act.

But even that did not quite quell the sense of disbelief. As the throngs pressed past the beer and sausage stalls and the statue of Frederick the Great towards the floodlit Brandenburg Gate, Alex turned and said with a deadpan face: 'In this crowd we won't have a chance when the Russian tanks move in.' Then the loudspeakers that had once played communist anthems boomed out Handel's Fireworks Music and we watched the reflections of the firework display on the windows of the monolithic Soviet Embassy, now no longer the secret government of half a country but a diplomatic mission – almost like any other. '*Wilkommen Deutschland*' – 'Welcome, Germany' – screamed the red, black and gold posters for Radio 100.6, the self-proclaimed 'new station for the new capital'. Alex was one of three men who had fought their way clear of the crowds to relieve their bladders in a side street, only to be joined by a fourth who set them laughing with: 'At last, a wall!'

The jokes were a safety-valve for feelings that ran deep and bitter. The enthusiasm of most East Germans had been tempered not just by fears of the rough-and-tumble Western economic system, but by a smouldering resentment against the system that psychologically crippled them. At Checkpoint Charlie the vast concrete sheds were already derelict. They have since been pulled down to make way for rebuilding of the missing section of the Friedrichstrasse. But that night they were inanimate victims of the physical expression of East Germans' resentment. Shortly after midnight, in the early hours of the first day of the new Germany's existence, I wandered in the dark around these abandoned buildings, where people were locked up or strip-searched, where guns were stored. Every window was broken, every door forced, every wire ripped out. In one room, where interrogations took place, I found an unbroken pane of glass. I thought twice, then with a smile I smashed it; I knew how they felt.

# 13

# The Day After

After the euphoria came the reckoning. It was as if all of Germany
suddenly woke up with a hangover after a year-long night on the
town.

There was reason enough for sore heads. After the unexpected windfall of the one-to-one exchange rate came the cost in
unemployment as firms in the East found their goods no longer
marketable and the price of supplies soaring. Journalists, writers
and politicians juggled their metaphors in an attempt to describe
what had happened to the people in the eastern regions now
known officially as *'die fünf neuen Bundesländer'* – the five new
federal states. It was time warp and jet lag and culture shock, a
cold bath and post-coital depression; all at once! The East Germans
were in effect required to make a lightning leap in lifestyle from
1938 to the 1990s.

In the West there was concern about the cost of it all in
increased taxes. Had Kohl lied? Oskar Lafontaine, the SPD's
candidate for chancellor, said he had. But Kohl got the victory
he wanted in the December 1990 elections, though without the
absolute majority he would have dearly loved. The new political
climate was blotted by violence, raising the unwelcome spectre
of the instability that had so dogged the Weimar Republic, the
last united German democracy. Oskar Lafontaine was the victim
of a knife attack; Wolfgang Schäuble, the interior minister, was
shot. Both survived, but Alfred Herrhausen, the chairman of
Deutsche Bank, was blown up in his car and Detlev Rohwedder,
the head of *Treuhand*, the government agency acting as receiver
and executioner for bankrupt East German firms, was shot dead
in his living room by a sniper.

In Zwickau the comic, unloved Trabants that had been East
Germany's worst standing joke until they became the symbol of

the revolution, rolled off the production lines for the last time. The factory closures, violence, strikes and industrial unrest took much of the gloss off the new toy of nationhood, but it was tempered by the realization that, for better or worse, Germans now had to live with Germany. The gut feeling on both sides was that, for all the trauma, unity had been both right and inevitable; and sooner had been better than later.

Alex, in his one-room flat in a back courtyard in a back street with living-room furniture looted by friends from a former hostel of the disbanded Free German Youth, working late at a print works that was itself now moribund in the face of competition from the glossy Western magazines, never had a moment's doubt. He was surprised to find himself a patriot. He had for years considered himself only a religious humanist, a believer in tolerance and justice. Now he found he believed in Germany too, that there could at last be a Germany that would be a framework for the lives of himself and his children and let them be part of the wider European community. It was an idealism that no amount of doom-mongering could deflate.

When we met over lunch in the restaurant of the Grand Hotel, the showpiece of the old regime, from which its citizens were all but banned, over salmon and pheasant that cost a week's wages for the passers-by outside, Alex expressed his amazement at the subtle osmosis of unification. The little things told the real tale: the traffic news on the (West) Berlin radio warning of roadworks near Halle; the weather forecast given for Berlin and Brandenburg (the city restored to its historic hinterland); and most of all the West Berlin police badge sewn on the cap of a pretty female 'Vopo' – I could see where the stitching from the hammer-and-compasses symbol of the People's Police had been carefully unpicked. Spluttering Vopo Wartburg cars repainted in the colours of the West German police dashed down the wide streets blaring the same sirens they had used when we were rounded up like cattle in meat wagons in that now distant October of 1989. 'You always need policemen,' said the Eastern partner in the new 'mixed double' – one West, one East – that stood on patrol outside the Soviet Embassy on Unter den Linden.

Alex and Bärbel hardly saw each other any more, though they were on friendly enough terms when he called to speak to Alexandra. In Metzer Eck itself, the clientele had changed.

The bakers no longer came from the bakery next door to fill their buckets with beer for the overnight shift. At the new prices it was too expensive – sobriety by default. The camaraderie of resistance had perforce evaporated. Bärbel sacked her casual staff; capitalist customs had to be learnt fast. Now Horst and Sylvie ran the bar most nights and Bärbel came down to play hostess at the *Stammtisch*, though Alex had taken with him his sign reading 'For anglers, hunters and other liars'. And indeed, who needed the shelter of mutual conspiracy when anyone could say anything? Democracy had dealt a death blow to political repartee.

One night we were shocked to encounter a group of English CAMRA beer freaks on a whistle-stop tasting tour of liberated Eastern Europe. Horst tried with some difficulty to explain the difference between East beer and West beer. 'Remember when I only had two of these,' he smiled, looking at the stacked shelves of tall Warsteiner Pilsner glasses identical to the ones he had humbly asked a waitress in West Berlin for on the night the Wall came down. 'I still keep those ones at home, though,' he acknowledged, before switching on the digital Coca-Cola can that danced in time to the rap music from the new hi-fi.

They still ran special dinners, of course, but no longer needed Manne's once-unique music collection. He, for his part, hardly came any more. 'The beer's too expensive, you know. I can buy from the supermarket and drink at home.' He had bought a small puppy and took it alone for quiet evening walks, not too far, perhaps the few yards to the end of the street, to let it urinate between the rubbish skips brought in by the reconstruction men, now all with shiny plaques and the names of Western firms.

Hans Busch came less often too, particularly now that Alex was no longer there to bait him. He realized too late how much he had enjoyed the cut and thrust. Sitting in the Working Men's Club near his home in the suburb of Weissensee, he was prone to wax philosophically melancholy about the collapse of the communist dream: 'When I think of the years we spent training the young generation I can only reflect how little we achieved. They were all brought up in our schools, our apprentice homes, our youth organizations; they even served in our army. And it all obviously meant less than nothing to them.

'We had half a million men under arms, what with the factory militia, the border guards and the regular army; yet it all fell apart as if it were made of tissue paper . . . I knew things were wrong. I'd had enough experience myself, but we could have corrected them, given a chance. It wasn't my problem. I just wanted to bring up kids to think less selfishly.'

Hans had left the party. The kids from the home were headed, most probably, for unemployment, not because of the anti-communist victimization that he feared, but because they had spent years learning skills for a print industry that was outmoded. The jobs they had learnt had – in the brave new world they had been thrust into – been made redundant years before they began learning them. 'And now, just look,' he added, pointing with an expression of wry, bewildered amusement at a well-dressed young man downing a glass of dark bock beer a few tables away. 'He's a rubbish collector, head of a local trade union. They've just more than doubled their salaries overnight by going on strike.'

Alex, meanwhile, had set about taking capitalism seriously. Sitting amid his books and clutter in his tiny, light-starved flat, he pushed aside the coffee cups to lay out a map of Berlin. Excitedly, like a child at a new school showing off his homework book, he explained to me how he had found the ideal site for a new pub and got together enough friends and savings to take out a bank loan and set up in business. He pressed into my hand his new visiting card, proudly engraved: '*Alex Gaststätten GmbH*' (Alex Public Houses plc).

At first he had been approached by a group with connections to the reformed communist PDS who asked if he would like to take over the management of a substantial property they could offer him. It was in the basement of a former Communist Party district headquarters. They nudged and nodded and said finance would be no problem and 'of course' he would give priority to 'any comrades who might want to organize a function'. Afterwards he was not sure if it was a sudden aberrant fantasy about 'beer-hall putsches' or just the newspaper reports of continual scandals over laundering of communist funds embezzled from state property, but he said, 'Thanks but no thanks.'

The pub he had found instead was a dilapidated, long-closed ruin of a bar that had once been called, with a singular lack of inspiration, Zur Molle, which translates roughly as The Frothy Pint. It was situated in Cothenius Strasse, a small street in the Friedrichshain district of East Berlin, a short tram ride away. It was abysmally lacking in character and had no goodwill left among the local population, for whom it had long been little more than an eyesore. But Alex thought he could make it work.

The street's curious name fascinated him. His research in libraries had revealed a certain Christian Andreas Cothenius, born in 1701 and personal physician to Frederick the Great. It was the theme he had been searching for. The little table was littered with obscure reference books from which he had put together the scant facts about the life of the doctor who had encouraged Frederick in his enthusiasm for potatoes, a copy of an etching – the only known likeness of Cothenius – and further books from the libraries of Potsdam and Berlin. Alongside lay the plans for the interior décor of a pub that he had decided would be called Zum Leibarzt (The Personal Physician). I sat entranced as he reeled off the patter he had already prepared for the first guests from the Rhineland.

On offer would be not just beer and sausages but their Prussian past. What Germany still lacked, Alex had decided, was a soul it could live with. It was the revelation that had come too late to Honecker, that ideas could change the world, that revolutions could overturn existences, but a sense of history strengthened and gave form. Familiarity, correctly handled, bred not contempt but contentment. Germany as a nation needed collectively the same as any individual: a sense of dignity that came through a moderate pride in the past and a sense that both present and future were part of a pattern, that the life of the nation was not a tree without roots.

That, Alex had realized, had been part of the key to the success of Metzer Eck. Bärbel and he had emphasized continuity, beneath the political storms and above the hurricanes of human brutality. With his old pictures of the windmillls, Zille's letter, the collection box of the working men's savings club and the market cart, he had delved unashamedly in the trough of nostalgia. But what he had offered was gold dust to people whom politics and history wanted to reshape as ciphers, as production units on a conveyor belt to a socialist heaven that was a human hell. Already he could see that neither the West German state nor the new, united fatherland were perfect. There were capitalist versions of hell too. The important element was the human, the little man with his little dreams of a home, a family, a job and a beer with friends at the end of the day. The key to tomorrow was in living today and coming to terms with yesterday. It was more philosophy than he cared to admit, even to himself.

On the opening night the place was packed and they drank the small hours away as they had done in the old days. But Alex knew that now it was down to business with fingers crossed. He had seen enough euphoria to last a lifetime. Twice in his life the world around him had fallen apart and he had survived it. It was time to give the world another chance.

# 14

## Deutsches Land – Pax Germanica?

*This age of ours has required us, Germans, to become political
animals. It has taken difficult years for us to awaken from a
fuzzy dream of indifference which almost threatened the demise
of the German name. God be praised we have again been
shown a Fatherland that all Germans as a nation can look to,
and die and work for.*

Ernst Moritz Arndt, after the defeat of Napoleon in 1814

Fifty years to the day after the German warship *Schleswig-Holstein*
pulled into the port of Danzig and, training its deck-guns on a
Polish artillery emplacement in the cold light of dawn, fired the
first shots of the Second World War, the passenger ferry *Rogalin*
docked in a steady, night-time drizzle against the opposite quay.
It had previously been a Finnish ferry, then British, and now it
was back on the Baltic, managed by the Polish state shipping
agency for the long trek from Travemünde near Hamburg to
Danzig and on to Soviet Estonia.

Across the narrow waterway, barely a hundred yards away,
the monolithic, Soviet-style monument to the Poles who had
died defending the narrow strip of land called the Westerplatte
on 1 September 1939, stuck into the night sky like a sore thumb.
There were few on board, this night of all nights, who missed the
poignancy of the anniversary. Many had come on that account.
For a few it was a sombre occasion, but for others it was a
once-in-a-lifetime return to a never-never land; back to the future,
without a vengeance.

Short, stocky, his wavy hair swept back like a 1930s matinée
idol, seventy-year-old Siegfried Rosenberg hugged his wife and

pointed excitedly ahead: 'Look darling, the *Heimat.*' Rosenberg was a professional Danziger, a publisher of replica pre-war maps that gave an overlay of the old German street names for those in search of their private past; he was also co-organizer with a Hamburg businessman of pilgrimages for the growing trade in nostalgia trips to Germany's lost territories. Most of the Germans on board the *Rogalin* were deep in memories. All were from the West. Until almost the final moment of East Germany's difficult history the communist state reserved the right to refuse its own citizens permission to cross the 'friendship frontier' to Poland.

We had embarked at Travemünde nearly twenty-four hours earlier on a 'memory cruise'. Those who had memories were narrating them to anyone who would listen. Karl-Heinz Seidel, a solid, bearded, sixty-two-year-old, recalled the events of half a century earlier. He and his schoolmates had come out on to the streets, he recalled, all in their Hitler Youth uniforms, to watch the Stuka dive-bombers roaring overhead. He remembered thinking: Now those Polaks'll get theirs. Five long years later, in 1944, when Alex was still practising his trumpetry, Karl-Heinz, then a strapping lad of seventeen, was conscripted into the raggle-taggle remnants of the retreating Teutonic crusade. With more than a touch of irony he would later come to call it the 'glorious retreat'. But he knew it was really a rout. In its aftermath he ended up deposited with the other flotsam for a while in the lands that would become the Soviet occupation zone, and later East Germany. He almost joined the church. But his vocation failed him and he went west to end up as an accountant in a Dortmund brewery. He was seeing Danzig again for the first time.

By the ship's railings two elderly sisters, Erna and Dora, held hands and bit their lips. Erna had made a sentimental pilgrimage to Danzig in 1973, but for Dora it was the first trip since that cold, grey morning in 1946 when they were given one hour to pack a few belongings and leave the family home. 'We were herded into a camp in town, then put on goods trains and shipped west,' she recalled. Their first encounter with the victorious Polish and Russian troops had been a year earlier in the Götterdämmerung of 1945. 'They were officers, I think. They ripped our blouses off and told us we had two choices: to curse Hitler or stand and catch pneumonia in the freezing rain,' she recounted. 'What did we do? We stood in the rain, of course,' she roared, laughing.

Erna and Dora, like many other sentimental pilgrims, wanted to seek out the old family home. In their case this was a farmhouse in the village of Wesslinken just a few kilometres along the Weichsel (Vistula) from Danzig, now Wislinka a few kilometres along the Wisla from Gdansk. I hired a taxi for them and went along for the ride. Nervously they scanned the landscape for recognizable features. The old road had gone in part to make way for an oil refinery. Even the Polish taxi-driver noticed as we suddenly began to bounce in and out of potholes on the new stretch. He shouted with typically Polish good humour: 'See, Polski road shit, Deutsche road gut.' Poles in those days still managed the psychological tightrope act of claiming their national achievements for the people and blaming the disasters wholly on the communists.

At the far end of a rough, unmade track that ended on the banks of the Vistula they found the little farmhouse, instantly recognizable from Erna's old sepia photographs. But it was the preservation of neglect: Dora's eyes welled with tears at the dilapidated paintwork and crude, breeze-block outhouse that had replaced the neat, well-kept barn. The owner was found: a big, bluff Pole with a warm smile and dirty boots who insisted on kissing the ladies' hands and inviting them in for tea. Dora's husband, Toni, a bluff Bavarian who had met her on a tram when his battleship, the *Prinz Eugen*, was in wartime Danzig, nudged his wife mischievously and pointed: 'Isn't that where the couch used to be, next to the stove, where you and I . . . remember?'

Our Polish host had gone off to make strong, sweet tea – apologizing for the lack of coffee, which he had not seen in months in the shops – and to fetch the next-door neighbour, Lotte Kwela, who against all odds turned out to be an old school friend of the girls. Her father had been a Pole and her family had never been forced to leave. The women hugged and set about gossiping: about who went where and who was dead, how Lotte's Polish father had, with a few words of Russian, saved the life of an SS man whom nobody liked; about who got raped: none of them, they had us know. Lotte hid under cushions while her mother barred the door. Erna and Dora hid in the coal cellar, wore old women's clothes and dirtied their faces. 'They told us to wash; they said, "Germans don't have dirty faces." But we were too skinny then,' laughed Dora. 'Those Russians were looking for meat.'

There were fewer laughs at Lotte's stories of life among the Slavs under communism for those who had stayed on: she told of her cousin who went to the dentist and died from a tooth infection; she explained the poverty of living on a Polish pension. Dora gave her a hundred Deutschmarks (thirty-five pounds sterling), which was just enough to make her feel she had made a little sacrifice, though for Lotte it was a small fortune. Had she converted it into zlotys at the then rampant black-market rate, it would have been a couple of months' average wages for a worker. Outside, beneath the grey Pomeranian skies that were in themselves part of the soul of their *Heimat*, the three women hugged again: Lotte, grey-haired, grandmotherly, in hand-made skirt, jumper, thick stockings and worn canvas slippers, for all the world like a Russian *babushka*, flanked by her contemporaries, blonde and black with hair rinses, trouser suits and shoulder bags, carbon copies of American matronhood. On the way back to town Dora had another sob and told herself: It was hard but I had to do it, at least once before I die, see the *Heimat* again.

Rosenberg was familiar with such reactions among those returning for the first time. 'When I first came back in the 1970s I went to our old family house. I was in a state of shock – five hundred years of family history rushing past me. There was actually the same old bed, the bed my grandfather died in, the bed where in 1879 my father was born and in 1919 I was born.' The Germans were impressed by the Poles' rebuilding of the ancient city centre, the Teutonic knights' fortifications, the skyline of Gothic pinnacles and mammoth brick churches, that Grass in his denial of description nonetheless described as 'multi-towered, bell-clanging, ancient, honourable, still suffused with the breath of the Middle Ages'. But it was the everyday world below that depressed these middle-aged pilgrims from the cosy affluence of Munich and Stuttgart: the squalid 1950s blocks of flats, sparsely stocked shops, queues for sausages and shoes, the lack of bustle on ill-lit streets. 'They've done a wonderful job of creating a dead museum city,' Seidel summed up.

They were guests of honour at a ceremony in the city's oldest church, the thirteenth-century St Catherine's, like the others substantially reconstructed, for the consecration of a new set of bells, paid for by public subscription in West Germany, to replace those taken in the war. The Catholic Bishop of Gdansk spoke of the need for reconciliation and understanding, but on the walls the Germans could see the modernist series of paintings of the stations of the cross with Christ being whipped by Roman soldiers wearing Wehrmacht helmets.

Later that week Poles in their thousands gathered for an open-air mass by the triple-cross monument at the gates of Gdansk shipyard to commemorate the 1980 agreements that launched the Solidarity movement on the rocky road that had only a month earlier finally turned the trade union into a government. It was not Stalin's arbitration or occupation by Russian troops or Polish communist decree, but Lech Walesa and Solidarity that had made Danzig into Gdansk. But the shrines of Solidarity had no place on the Danzigers' itinerary. Instead they went on picnics, to visit the former East Prussian city of Elbing, now Polish Elblag, or the vast redbrick medieval fortress of the Teutonic knights: Marienburg, now corrupted to Malbork.

It was a difficult experience; for these people, even if Danzig was no longer Germany it was still home. They had not been Nazis, just caught up in the whirlwind of war. But they did not want the world to forget that 'reunification' was a foreigners' myth when it happened, the restoration of East Germany gave back only half of what was lost. They would like, at least, that glasnost's rewriting of history should remember that brutally moving Poland to the West at human cost to both Poles and Germans was not just a historical border correction but another of Stalin's crimes.

The ferry's return trip to Travemünde was notably quieter. For most the experience had been both disturbing and calming. It was like an exorcism, a regretful realization that what was gone was gone. There were others on board too, apart from the Danzigers: old men and women coming back from similar sentimental voyages further east, from Memel, the port that was the north-eastern tip of Hitler's *Grossdeutschland* proper and was now the Lithuanian port of Klaipeda. The Gorbachev revolution in the Soviet Union had at that stage both allowed for a relaxation of visa regulations and given these old people greater confidence to undertake a journey fraught with physical and emotional stress. There were those who had come from Riga, in Latvia, a city built by the Hanseatic League of German cities that controlled Baltic trade and access to Russia. Before the war it had been predominantly

German. Others had been to distant Estonian Tallinn on the Gulf of Finland, a city whose name in the tongue of the natives meant 'Danes' Town' but was, under the name Reval, another outpost of the Hansa, as much part of the German world as Durban or Adelaide were British.

But what was Germany anyway? The greatest difficulty is that only one man this century has had a clear-cut answer: Adolf Hitler. Hitler's magic – which Jenninger in his controversial Bundestag speech touched on – was that he had a vision for Germany equalled only by Churchill's for England. It had been one thing for the Führer to unite all the major contiguous German-speaking areas in a unitary nation-state. This he quickly succeeded in doing, helped by those – notably in Britain – who believed then, as indeed now, that the nation-state was the only stable form of government and hoped to stabilize Germany by allowing him to achieve it. That was why the *Anschluss* with Austria aroused less of a response abroad than even Hitler anticipated; that was why the Germans of the Sudetenland, who had been Austrian citizens up to 1918, were subsequently allowed to be incorporated. There was a moment in 1938 when Hitler had, through expansion, undone all Bismarck's work. He had created a Germany that was no longer a Prussian empire; the imbalance between north and south had been redressed, the eastern frontier rounded off on its southern flank. Hence there had been a sound intellectual background to the attitude that was later denigrated as 'appeasement'.

Unfortunately it was politically flawed in its failure to recognize the true nature of the beast that was Hitler. For it was another thing entirely to try to make the vast, meticulously spun web of Germanic culture that over a millennium had spread throughout, and beyond, Eastern Europe, into the framework of an ironclad empire. Hitler could have had the greatest nation-state in Europe, dominating the continent and a major world force; but he wanted the true trappings of imperial power: subjugation of other races. And he faced another madman: Stalin. The history of our century has been shaped by the clash between these two men who represented systems that were essentially identical in their belief in the triumph of the collective over the individual, and the total subjection of the latter by the former. That is the essence of totalitarianism. The state has all power; the individual has none.

If Germany avoided Russia's long trauma under dictatorship, it has inherited instead a deeper schizophrenia. As if in preparation for the national psychological trial of unification, West Germany had already put itself on the psychiatrist's couch. The fortieth anniversary of the Federal Republic in 1989 had prompted not just ministerial speeches but also much intellectual reflection on the 'German question' that had so long been dormant and was so soon to erupt. In his article in the *Frankfurter Allgemeine Zeitung* referred to earlier, Dr Hartmut Bookmann made a passionate case for an urgent review of German history teaching, which had become a victim of politics. He feared the history of the lost eastern territories would be obliterated through deliberate neglect, a retroactive effect of the postwar frontiers.

In this case, he argued, German liberals – out of their desire to heal wounds and not cause further offence to their neighbours – would in effect be contributing to a rewriting of history as mendacious as anything practised under the communists: 'It would be fatal if the history of the eastern German lands through the pressure of contemporary political realities became part of eastern European history, while German history, bluntly put, ran simply from the Roman provinces on the Rhine and Danube via the Rhine Federation to today's Federal Republic.' Bookmann pointed out that this sort of corruption had already happened under the communist regimes: 'For GDR historians Königsberg or Breslau [today Russian Kaliningrad and Polish Wroclaw] are as off-limits as are Lwow or Vilna for Poles [today Ukrainian Lviv and Lithuanian Vilnius]. . . .'

As the process of unification sped to its conclusion in 1990, there were fears that it might end by putting the German Empire's 'collapsing star' process into reverse. In particular the government in Warsaw was aware that there were many Germans in a country that was now overcrowded who still resented the fact that the border adjustment of 1945 had been dictated rather than negotiated. The treaty of German unification was followed with a bilateral treaty signed with Poland, guaranteeing both the frontier and the linguistic and cultural rights of the German minority who had remained in their ancient *Heimat*. It was a critical political step, recognizing legally the loss of territories that had been considered intrinsically part of Germany, such as Szczecin, the ancient German port of Stettin on the 'wrong', western, side of the Oder, given by Stalin to the Poles out of malicious playfulness to be a future bone of contention between Russia's most troublesome neighbours. There would for a while be those who, like Hans Busch, would speculate: 'I bet that in fifteen years or so there'll be somebody clamouring for a referendum in Silesia and Pomerania just like they did in the Sudeten. Ha, even some of the Poles would vote for Germany, just for the money.'

It was, in fact, a curious side-effect of the unification that a substantial number of inhabitants in Western Silesia who had for years appeared to be Polish, speaking the language and with Polish names, suddenly declared themselves to have been Germans all along. After the war, in order to retain their lands and homes Slavification had seemed the better part of valour. But now the new climate of German–Polish reconciliation had allowed them to come out of the closet, but there were also undoubtedly a few cases of economic opportunism. For Germany, even after the absorption of the anomalous GDR, still retained its moral commitment to the far-flung debris of the nation's complex history. This has been defined, however, as a commitment to people rather than territory. Whatever the hankerings of old people for their lost homelands, there is no support in Germany for reclaiming lands lost to Poland, much less Königsberg/Kaliningrad, which, since Lithuanian independence, remains a sore thumb of Russia, isolated on the edge of Europe like a Gibraltar or, worse still, a Danzig.

Germany *can* be expected, however, to remain committed, at least in principle, to the descendants of its ancient settlers in the East, including the Volga Germans (one-time compatriots of Manne Schulz's grandmother). These settled the steppes for Catherine the Great but were exiled to Siberia, as potential fifth columnists. Germany has not got room for them all, and many of them have little affinity to a homeland even their grandfathers never visited. But there is a moral obligation that is still perceived in Bonn and Berlin.

For most of the new Germans, and many who aspire to such status, the talisman of the new society is not its global status and certainly not military power but the magic phrase *soziale Marktwirtschaft*, the social market economy. Invented by Ludwig Erhard, the political economist who set the guidelines for the postwar construction of the West German state, it was a mixture of welfare state, caring capitalism and enthusiastic industrial and entrepreneurial expansion that made Germany the country with the highest standard of living in Europe. More than any other European state, modern Germany is an artificial construction, a hybrid of older German traditions with overlays of Western European liberal traditions implanted deliberately. Its press, from the downmarket but still newsy *Bild* to the worthy, conservative and intelligent *Frankfurter Allgemeine Zeitung* and the authoritative, investigative *Der Spiegel*, owed much to British and American influence. Nothing in Germany today is a true carbon copy of an alien institution. Rather like a post-phylloxera graft of a new vine on to an old root, it has allowed the development of new, untainted growths that can again be a model for others.

The constitution, which was drafted under watchful Allied eyes, is a model of German law-making, but owes much to Anglo-Saxon concepts of democratic rights and legal accountability. Its greatest fault perhaps it to have instilled in the modern German a certain litigiousness, an over-ready willingness to see everything settled in court. Lawyers do very well. The constitution proved workable and flexible enough in 1990 to achieve within its own terms the goal, only distantly perceived in 1949, of unification through the voluntary, simultaneous accession of the five new, or rather recreated, *Länder* of the former communist state. The men who, under Konrad Adenauer first and foremost, drew up the constitution in 1949, deliberately avoided making the grand social promises contained in the constitution of the Weimar Republic, opting instead for a minimalist approach.

It has served well as tramlines for running an affluent democracy. The electoral legislation barring parties from parliament if they win less than five per cent of the vote has created stability by avoiding fractious splinter parties, and yet still allowed for a voice to be heard when it truly represents a meaningful slice of the public's opinion. The career of the Greens has reflected this in a seemingly irresistible rise to influence for the environmentally concerned lobby that a well-heeled society could afford, and a subsequent decline in the 1990s when unification pressed the electorate's concerns towards other issues. The Greens were initially a political response to a society that some felt had become too hedonistic, too obsessed with the job, the car and the annual holiday in the sunshine.

The external image of the Germans was changed by the *Wirtschaftswunder*, the economic miracle ignited by the Marshall Plan and fuelled by hard work, which pulled West Germany into the forefront of the world economy. The schizophrenia of the world's dual attitude to Germany was neatly captured by the British satirical television programme *Spitting Image*, which depicted a jolly German family, 'the Hitlers', going on holiday through Europe in a tank. The advertisement it parodied was that for Audi cars, which ended with the catchphrase '*Vorsprung durch Technik*', in itself, as the first attempt to sell in the English-speaking world with an untranslated German slogan, a mark of the country's restored self-confidence. The Audi ad was selling its cars as the reason that Germans always got on the beach first. That, by the end of the 1980s, was the biggest complaint against them.

But no longer being the subject of complaint is not always enough. Hans-Jochen Vogel, the mild-mannered, grey-haired doyen of the Social Democrats, voiced Germany's dilemma in January 1991 when he said: 'I wish our friends would make up their minds if they object to us Germans because we have been too warlike or because we are too pacifist.' For Germans the Gulf War was an unpleasant interruption, an aside in the real march of European history, in which their own unification process was a vital link.

There were concrete factors too: one of the provisions of the four-power agreements that cleared the way for German unification was an eventual reduction of the new united German army to three hundred and seventy thousand men, which in 1990 was fewer than the Russians still had on the soil of the five new *Länder*. In other words, a military establishment with a purely defensive capability was written into the treaty that confirmed the statehood of a sovereign Germany for the first time since Hitler's Reich collapsed in ruins. It is unlikely that Gorbachev would have given his critical assent to the new Germany's remaining in NATO when he met Kohl for their remarkable talks in the Caucasus in the summer of 1990, had he envisaged that pressure would be put on the new state to exert its military muscle. Asking Germany to send troops to the Gulf was akin to opening Pandora's box, with unforeseen results for domestic politics and stability in central Europe. It would also set a precedent. No one in Bonn wanted to take that responsibility.

The German army had inevitably posed specific problems since 1945. In the years of partition the Western Allies had to create a defence psychology that would allow West Germans to see East Germans as enemies rather than compatriots. A booklet produced for the Bundeswehr as late as 1987 wisely addressed the problem head-on. Entitled '*Was heisst hier Feindbild?*' ('So what's this talk of enemy image?'), its cover had a picture of an East German poster showing both smiling lads from the National People's Army of the GDR and a group of cheeky, grinning children proclaiming, 'The Party, that's what we'll grow up to be.' It was, in fact, a political and social thumbnail sketch of the East, filled with photographs of queues at food shops, marching monolithic ranks under stale slogans and children being shown how to use automatic weapons 'in the defence of the socialist fatherland'. It was a clever piece of propaganda that treated the conscript soldier as an intelligent human being, pointing out that while NATO was a voluntary alliance, the Warsaw Pact was run on dictatorial lines – 'a system of vassal states' run by a Russian general.

The fact was, however, that West Germany had not been totally free in its military stance. Before unity in 1990 it had in theory, indeed, not had the full rights of a sovereign state. In practice, of course, there had been no problems, because acceptance of NATO was part of the policy of all political parties. In theory, however, though it never happened, a West German government would not have had the international legal right to alter its defence structures unilaterally. The Allies had thought long and hard about how much West Germany was to be remilitarized after 1945. By and large the West Germans had been willing to go along, and wrote into the constitution – to the reassurance of all their neighbour states – the clause that forbade military action outside the NATO area. It was a 'defence only' deal. Thus in 1991 Chancellor Kohl was torn between eagerness to use the sovereignty that Germany then already had, to alter her constitution and abrogate the ability to send troops anywhere, and the worry that if the world really did want a global German policeman, it should make it triply clear first. More than it wanted anything else, Germany wanted to be loved, and not only for its money. Germany had to be worth something to the post-Cold War world.

The great myth of the European Left during the Cold War had been that class differences were more important than national ones. Hence Stalin and his hangers-on created the myth that there had been genuine revolutions in the postwar years that brought the communists to power in Eastern Europe, whereas the real revolutions would be those against the system he imposed. The most insidious myth was that of a socialist German state that was something separate and had its own life.

A separate state in eastern Germany might have had a life of its own, much as Prussia had had or Austria now resumed, but a state based on ideology was a nonsense doomed to failure when the ideology was revealed as false. In the brief months between their gestation and their dissolution the opposition groups in East Germany spent long hours in agonized thought about what would become of their state, yet almost universally failed to carry their thoughts through to their logical conclusion: that it would cease to exist. They relied – as much as their rulers – on assumptions about what Moscow would or would not tolerate. They too had come to see West Germany as a separate state. They wanted what the leaders talked about: peaceful coexistence. But the bulk of the people, the silent majority whom the opposition at first despaired of bringing on to the streets, then succeeded in coaxing, needed the simple solution.

The question of a *Sonderweg* still haunts German political thinking. Is there or is there not a special way for the Germans to go? The answer insisted upon in Bonn is 'No', that Germany is firmly anchored in the West. But the 'West' is no longer firmly anchored in Washington. That was true of the Federal Republic until 1990. Whatever the politicians may say to suit the convenience of the moment, Germany's way can never automatically be that of her Western neighbours; East and West have always met in Germany. To quote President Richard von Weizsäcker, Germany's destiny is to work 'within the framework of the European Community and promote the further cooperation with the former Comecon countries'. Von Weizsäcker would like us to understand that this is not a German special way but the interest of all Europe. But redefining Germany has always – at least since the fall of Charlemagne – meant redefining Europe.

When walls fall, they fall completely. Alex Margan's story is in its way a parable of human adaptability. In the summer of 1990 he and his daughter Alexandra joined my family and me on holiday

in France, already scarcely batting an eyelid at freedoms they
had seized as though never lost. Alexandra was busy planning
a skiing holiday in Czechoslovakia; no longer because it was
this or that side of the fence, but for the best market-economy
reasons: because it was closer and cheaper. In the summer of 1991
they visited London, Alex still revelling in every experience but
Alexandra already working hard to subsume the cataclysm that
had overcome her old way of life into the blasé attitudes of any
teenage girl. It was a survival mechanism.

Barely six months after unification I received by post a calendar
from the government of the newly recreated Free State of Saxony
and an electoral leaflet for the Christian Democrat member of the
state parliament, Ulli Schimpff. It took me a minute to recognize
in the sedate, sober-suited archaeologist and musicologist depicted
on the party hand-out the same bulky, bearded, beret-clad demon-
strator whom I had met on the streets of Leipzig exactly one year
earlier. Punching the air with boyish enthusiasm, he had urged
me to join in the chorus 'Deutschland einig Vaterland'. Enthralled
by his enthusiasm, I joined with him and we hurled the words
like a challenge to history into the frosty night.

History met the challenge; and returned it.